To Tom

Thanks for all;

All best wishes

[signature]

September 3 1998

The Rhodora Letters

THE
RHODORA
LETTERS

Rosemary Seys

Foreword by
Sir John Margetson, KCMG

The Book Guild Ltd.
Sussex, England

The Book Guild Ltd.
25 High Street,
Lewes, Sussex

First published 1993
© Rosemary Seys 1993
Set in Baskerville
Typesetting by Raven Typesetters
Ellesmere Port, South Wirral
Printed in Great Britain by
Antony Rowe Ltd.
Chippenham, Wiltshire.

A catalogue record for this book
is available from the British Library

ISBN 0 86332 846 6

*To Tony, David and all
who lived and worked at
Rhodora*

CONTENTS

LIST OF CENTRE SECTION
PHOTOGRAPHS

FOREWORD

by

Sir John Margetson, KCMG

colonial administrator and diplomat

The White Highlands of Kenya, the last area of the world the British attempted to colonise and settle, have always had a certain romance about them. The natural beauty of the landscape, the colourful Kenyan tribes, the wealth of wild game and the farming potential of the land attracted settlers from 1897. That was the year when the third Lord Delamere, the central figure in the history of the White Highlands, fell in love with the country. Lord Delamere devoted his life to establishing a white dominion on the African equator. It was a dream that failed.

It is not surprising that this short but colourful sixty years of imperial history should have produced some remarkable literature. Nor is it surprising that women, who played a very important role in it, should have written the major works by which the White Highlands are remembered today: Karen Blixen's 'Out of Africa', Elspeth Huxley's 'White Man's Country', and Beryl Markham's 'West with the Night', to name but three.

Rosemary Seys, who now joins this band of authors, makes no literary claim for the Rhodora Letters. It is a book which records in a straightforward way the day-to-day life of Rosemary and her husband, Tony, as they turned 2,800 acres of Kenya into a highly productive farm with the finest Guernsey herd in the country. The book has the feel of Kenya, instantly recognisable; it is the genuine article. Rosemary does

9

not boast; but I and many others who knew Rhodora can vouch for its fame as perhaps the most beautiful and successful private farm in all East Africa.

Capital investment, agricultural know-how and hard work produced the miracle. That is apparent from the book. What is less obvious is the great courage and determination of Rosemary and Tony Seys, typical of so many Kenyan farmers, as they kept going through difficult years. Only those with first-hand experience of Kenya in the 1950's know the strain under which isolated farmers and their families lived during the period of Mau Mau. And only those who have farmed in Africa can appreciate the determination necessary to overcome the difficulties of both nature and man.

I hope that the Rhodora Letters will help to correct the all-too-prevalent image of life in Kenya which derives from the Happy Valley set – a very small group of settlers much given to drink, drugs and sexual promiscuity. Happy Valley did nothing for Kenya except to give it a bad name. The real world of white settlement is to be found elsewhere in the serious farmers portrayed in this book, who formed the backbone of the white community.

The poignancy of the Rhodora Letters lies in the ever-increasing success of the farm set against the threat of extinction by a political process, which in time brought the whole story to an end. Rosemary Seys writes of 'the desolation and disintegration of all we had achieved on our farm.' Characteristically, she shows absolutely no bitterness. On the contrary, what shines through the book is the sheer fun of the adventure and the memory of a remarkable achievement in a beautiful land.

PREFACE

Many of you who read this book may think that the way of life in Kenya during the 1948–62 period – the twilight years before Uhuru (Independence) – was privileged and leisurely. I would like to put on record certain facts to clarify the reality of the situation.

You will see from the Introduction that we visited Kenya in 1947 and Tony fell in love with the beauty and call of the country. Staying with Freddie and Vi Ward, during the evening meal of our first night, Freddie said, 'Rosemary, we are delighted you are considering coming to live here but we are laughing at the idea of your becoming a settler.' I remember thinking, 'What does he mean?' In time I was to find out and, I think, to prove him wrong.

The British Government had encouraged people to settle and to make Kenya their life and home. We found everyone we met firmly believed this. Naturally, we believed it too. Day-to-day life did not just consist of an equable climate, freedom from political worries and comradeship in the white community. It consisted of construction, trying to run things more competently, teaching, showing the way. As far as we were concerned, it was this challenge that fired Tony's imagination into making the decision to be there, which I fully endorsed. I, too, found myself caught up in the fascinating procedure of building up the farm into an efficient worthwhile place, constantly trying to improve the land and the lot of the Africans who worked for us.

To those people who think that life must have been easy, I can assure them it was very hard work, but fun, with no clouds for the first years, though they gathered slowly but surely. Change eventually became inevitable but we had come in good faith and it was a shock to us all, especially to those who had lived there for two or three generations. We could not continue as we had before. The partnership we hoped for was not possible and gradually we realised that the Africans wanted Kenya to belong to them alone.

I hope that these letters which Tony and I wrote *together* will stand as a testament of our love for each other, for Rhodora, and for Kenya itself.

ACKNOWLEDGEMENTS

I wish to thank:

Sir John Margetson for his thoughtful and encouraging Foreword;

Lionel de Rothschild, my nephew, for his willing and untiring, scholarly and meticulous hours of detailed work in helping me complete the manuscript;

Dulcie Fawcett for her endless patience whilst reading with me the 372 letters in the original, initially editing them before typing them up in a presentable form for further editing;

Anne Fairbrace for her constant support and other secretarial help;

and to all my family and friends for their continual encouragement.

INTRODUCTION

Tony and I met in 1939. I was twenty-six years old and married to the younger son of a newspaper magnate. We had two small children, but it was an unhappy marriage. Tony was to be the great love of my life.

The divorce, the agony of conceding custody of my daughters to my ex-husband, marriage to Tony in 1942, and the subsequent war years as a V.A.D. nurse while Tony, as an Army officer, was posted abroad, are still vivid in my memory.

Late in 1945 Tony was demobilised. By the following year he had decided to be a farmer, and with his usual thoroughness took a general agricultural course. We bought a farm in Sussex, where I bred Shetland sheepdogs and took an interest in the Jersey herd, but although our lives were busy and happy enough the farm was not particularly challenging.

Tony, having worked at Conservative Party Central Office before the war, set about pursuing his life's ambition to go into politics, but as a former co-respondent in a divorce, he could not find a constituency to accept him as a candidate. It was 1947; everybody seemed nervous of the future, yet England constantly reminded us of the past. We now had a baby son, and wanted to get away from everything together and build something new. So we looked about for a brighter future in a friendlier climate.

In 1948 we visited Kenya as guests of Freddie and Vi Ward, old friends of my father. Within days of arrival in the country Tony's enthusiasm was apparent, and he was soon hunting for a farm. Early in 1949, on a subsequent visit, he found one.

It was quite near to the Wards' home at Kabazi, and was being sold by Michael Blundell, a well-known settler who had lived in Kenya since he was eighteen. It was a long, low house with outbuildings, set on 2,800 beautiful acres high on the edge of Menengai, the third largest crater in the world. We called it Rhodora, the name of my father's yacht, which was sunk during the war, and a reminder of my father's famous passion for rhododendrons at Exbury.

In the spring of 1949 we moved to Africa and were soon followed by shipments of everything we possessed, including a large amount of antique furniture, the foundations of a Guernsey herd and several pedigree pigs; within a few months of settling at Rhodora, we began to send home a weekly newsletter. We made up to ten copies, which we sent to our very close family. We continued to send the newsletters throughout our time in Kenya, and it is extracts from them which make up this book.

They represent, not a story of pioneer settlement, but a picture of the last stages of life in a colonial territory before the British withdrew. They give a good idea of what farming in the White Highlands of Kenya was really like, and evoke a way of life which has now disappeared and will never come back.

Rosemary Seys
1992

FAMILY AND FRIENDS

The following people received copies of the newsletters as they were written:

Major and Mrs Godfrey Seys	Pops and Mutz, Tony's parents
Wing Commander and Mrs Richard Seys	Richard and Pamela, Tony's brother and sister-in-law
Major and Mrs William Fisher	Charmian and Bill, Tony's sister and brother-in-law
Mrs Lionel de Rothschild	my mother Marie-Louise, affectionately nicknamed Mariloo
Edmund de Rothschild	my brother Eddy
Leopold de Rothschild	my brother Leo
Dr and Mrs Bertrand Goldschmidt	Naomi and Betrand, my sister and brother-in-law
Barbara Berry	my daughter Barbara, or Bar
Susan Berry	my daughter Sue.

Europeans who helped us during most of our stay in Kenya were Lieutenant Commander Varley Everett, who ran the office; Tudor Ace, the stockman; and Tim Mumford, our coffee manager. The reader will also find many references to Freddie and Vi, that is, Major and Mrs F H Ward, who farmed at Kabazi and were old friends of the family.

AUTHOR'S NOTE

The 'first person singular' in the letters is Tony (unless otherwise stated). In fact Tony and I usually drafted the letters jointly, and Tony typed them.

I have written introductions to the chapters, explanatory notes where necessary, and a *Finale*.

1

Tony went to live at Rhodora in March, 1949, and within a few months I had followed him, with David (aged two) and his Swiss nanny, Monique; Beatrice, her friend, who was to help in the house; and the three Shelties – Red, Della and Candy. We were assisted, in the almost-furnished house, by a small group of African servants. On the farm we were helped by a stockman called Clarke, whom we had brought out to Kenya, and about 150 African workers.

We knew few people at first. Freddie and Vi Ward, and their son John (who was shortly to marry Pam Swinton-Home) lived nearby at Kabazi and were our particular friends. Varley Everett, the son of Sir Percy Everett (Baden-Powell's Deputy Chief Scout), and his wife Joyce, lived up the Valley; he was to work at Rhodora, later. In any case we were occupied with getting things straight, and learning about the farm, an endeavour which Tony approached with great earnestness at first (and, as he grew in confidence, with happy flashes of humour):

24th July, 1949

Work on the farm this week has consisted partly in making a start with getting my hands on the stores, and partly in checking through the cattle again. We told you that we have decided to sell a large part of the herd because we have not got enough grazing for the animals. Clarke has examined every cow. At one time he worked for three years with a vet, and his knowledge of veterinary matters is a great help to us. For example, he is able to make pregnancy checks which most herdsmen could not do.

All the details of the animals are entered on a big sheet under

19

various headings, such as teeth, eyes, skin and many other headings which are perhaps a little too agricultural for this letter. With these sheets in front of us, together with the cards which contain details of the breeding and milk records of the cows, we go out into the paddock where the animals are assembled. Here the African herdsmen drive out each cow for us to see as we call its name. With a series of whistles and catcalls they make the cow stand quite still (and some of them are pretty wild) only a few feet in front of us, and it is marvellous to see the way they can produce any cow whose name is called within a few seconds, from a group of, say, 150.

We generally take up our position under some thorn trees, in the shade. Often there is a soft, warm breeze and a strange, delicious smell and somehow, on this farm, in whichever *boma* (field) we are, there is a wonderful view of the distant hills, which change colour all the time – from pale grey, through green, to purple and blue.

In this setting, we two and Clarke make up our minds whether we want to keep or reject each animal, and they then go into the 'in' herd or into the 'out' herd. We have now some lovely cows in our 'in' herd, which would do credit to any herd in England. There are fifty-one milking cows in all. Next week we start choosing the followers (served and empty heifers and calves) to run with this herd. The remaining heifers, of which we have a very large number, are going to run with a bull (needless to say not our Royal Show winner) on our land on the edge of the crater which is a huge tract of nearly 1,000 acres . . .

We are drafting this letter in our bedroom. We have the window open, because David is alone and we are listening for him. Monique, Beatrice, Clarke and Eric (the young man whom Clarke replaces) have gone to the cinema in Nakuru. As the window is open and our temporary curtains are somewhat inadequate, we are being assailed from time to time by revolting African insects. My special horror is a huge malevolent cricket but Rosemary detests most the doo-doo, or monstrous flying ant, bigger than a hornet with a sausage body. Outside, this being Saturday night, one can hear the Africans making whoopee and occasionally beating away at a tom-tom. To add to the general clatter, the bull-frogs have broken into song at night since the rain came and they compete loudly with the insistent note of the crickets; and the wild cat in the roof has given birth to a kitten which is mewing pitifully, and unceasingly, and seems to have been abandoned.

Apart from these little details, there is a deathly hush in the heart of Africa . . .

The other morning I found the fresh spoor of a leopard in the coffee quite near to the house, so we have to be careful with the dogs, to which leopards are very partial. They have the good taste not to be partial to humans under normal circumstances, but they have been known to remove a dog from a verandah at 8.30 in the morning. Dell gives us fits because she will run away and is frightfully nervy but the other three have settled down well.

Here is a sample day which Pops asked for – We are called at 6.30 with tea by Janus, our second boy. Jacob goes and collects my clothes for valeting. By seven o'clock I am out on the farm. You might think Rosemary goes to sleep again, as breakfast is not till eight, but the houseboys see to it that this is quite impossible. They thump about the house to give an impression that they are cleaning it and the pantry *toto* throws water about on the verandah for them to brush down afterwards. Rosemary gets up after breakfast at 8.30 and goes into the kitchen to see Gwara, the cook, and to give out stores. I go into the office to see the Manager. We generally start a specific job at about ten o'clock, and go on until lunch at one o'clock. After lunch sometimes Rosemary comes with me to the farm and some-times she rests. We all have tea together, David, Monique, Beatrice and ourselves on our verandah; and then David comes with us to the cowshed. It is dark by seven and we have a bath and change into dressing-gown and housecoat for dinner – which is an old Kenya custom. We usually go to bed quite early, about nine o'clock, and are glad to be there.

31st July, 1949

Last Sunday we had our first lunch party. It went off very well

21

and we are really beginning to feel more organised now. Some lettuces and small radishes had been sent up from the kitchen garden at the coffee factory. The lettuces made a nice salad but, to our surprise, when the chocolate mousse arrived it was accompanied not by the biscuits which we had intended but by a plate of little red radishes!

There is a man next door called George Manuel who is the local magistrate. He does the cultivations for farmers in the district by contract, if they want it. We think we are going to let him do our cultivations for one year in order to get our land cleaner, and in really good heart. He has much of the latest American equipment and, as we do not possess a tractor, we cannot plough as deeply as we would like. This man is a typical early settler – a rough diamond, brusque of speech and a heart of gold. I spent the whole day on Tuesday walking round every inch of the farm with him and making out my cropping programme for 1950/51. He stayed to lunch and tea.

Charles Long, the local auctioneer, spent the day here on Wednesday and Thursday and we had customers for our cattle. One woman bought thirty-seven at £40 each. Another man, a prince, wasted most of our afternoon and then bought nothing and took the auctioneer fifty miles to see a pony which he also did not buy.

Friday morning is a great day for shopping in Nakuru, and one meets everybody there and hears all the news. People go down with huge native baskets – one for the butcher, one for the vegetables and one for the groceries. These baskets are left at the shop as the order is given. Towards the end of the morning, one sees the Africans walking out of the shops with the laden baskets and putting them into the cars. Rosemary has now got it organised so that she makes a big order once a month, and then only has to collect such things as meat, bread and vegetables on the weekly visit. We have no postal delivery, so whenever anyone goes down to town they call to clear our postbox. We also have no newspapers delivered, and these we get in town. I get the air-mail *Times* which arrives four to five days old. Later we will have a wireless to get the news from London. Incidentally, there is no telegram delivery service so that, if we are sent a cable, it sits in our postbox until we go into town.

Great excitement last night. When I went out at about 9.30 to let out the dogs, I found the *askari* (night-watchman) all worked up. He had just seen two leopards right beside our kitchen window, and whilst I was talking to him, Rosemary heard them cough near our bedroom window. They are after the dogs, of course. We have safety grilles on all the bedroom windows. It does not worry us in the least because they are very elusive creatures and not naturally interested in humans.

David cannot forget the marching of the Guards which he used to see daily from our flat in London. He asks us all the time to play 'soldiers' with him and we have to march up and down like the Guards in front of the Palace.

There is one particularly filthy spot on the way to the cowshed which fascinates both him and the dogs. The latter find a collection of old bones and dead chickens whilst David stands in rapt attention murmuring '*cochons*' as he gazes at the scruffy and disgraceful multicoloured leggy objects which we have here in the guise of Large White pigs.

8th August, 1949

We are starting this sitting on the back seat of the car, which we have put on the ground, at the Dog Show at Nairobi. Benching for the dogs did not arrive out from England on account of the dock strike so the dogs have little cubicles made of bamboo allotted to them. We have a nice spacious cubicle for our Shelties with their baskets. As we write the public are streaming by and great interest is being taken in the dogs, which have never been seen in East Africa before. A man called Dalzell is judging. He is an all-round judge who has been invited out from England by the East Africa Kennel Club. People like smooth-coated animals, such as Bull Terriers and Dachshunds, because they are less likely to pick up ticks and get tick fever. We de-tick ours every night and at first we found a lot of ticks on them and some grass fleas, but now we brush some powder into their coats once a week, which does not smell much and keeps away all visitors.

We arrived in Nairobi yesterday before lunch and spent our time looking at different makes of motor car, because we must have a second car. There is no telephone at home, and we do not like to leave David without a car available in case of emergency. We went up to the Muthaiga Club for lunch and to leave our suitcases. I have just been elected a member of this club, which is the best in Kenya, and very useful because Rosemary can stay there too. We have a large room with bathroom off and the cuisine is superlative. Withal it is much cheaper than a hotel and one meets a lot of quite nice people, who stay there for business or shopping reasons, having come from all parts of the country.

About an hour before dark we found that all the shops were shut, so we motored out four miles to the Game Park. Here we found a pride of six lions and two cubs, and a row of cars watching them, as one watches the ducks on the Serpentine. We edged our way next to a game warden's truck and as it got dark all the other cars went off, so we transferred ourselves into his truck. He took us right in amongst the lions, which are quite accustomed to cars; they walked all round us, and one put its paw up against the window.

This has been Jigger Week at Rhodora. A jigger is a tiny insect which burrows into the toes of the unwary who walk about with bare feet, and lay their eggs. Beatrice was the first to fall victim and she was soundly rebuked by Rosemary for not taking more care. Two days later Rosemary got one herself, although she swears that she always wears stockings, so Beatrice has stopped looking quite so downcast. At any time of the day or night now you will see members of this household anxiously examining their toes . . .

We have, at last, got some pictures hung. The Ziem is in the drawing-room, the Laura Knight and the Munnings in our bedroom and two others in the dressing-room. It has been quite difficult to get some decent pegs to put into the walls.

Since starting this letter we have got back home and it is Monday morning. We found everything looking so quiet and peaceful and orderly. One was able to appreciate just how much ground we have covered towards getting the house the way we want it. It was lovely, too, to get back to smiling faces because not only were the girls and David pleased to see us, but for some unknown reason the houseboys were too, and they ran out to greet us with beaming faces – including Gwara, the cook, who has a quiet and undemonstrative character.

14th August, 1949

Just as David was finishing a belated tea and we were all quite exhausted, the dogs barked and a strange family consisting of mother, father, brother-in-law and two little girls walked straight in on us onto our verandah: they had come to call. Rosemary glared; I swallowed and said how lovely it was to see them. In the end everything worked out all right because, after David had quite finished his tea, the two little girls played games with him and I really think he enjoyed himself more than I have ever seen him enjoy himself before.

People are like that out here. They just walk right in on you. I suppose it is because there are no telephones. As I was beginning to type this letter from the draft (Sunday morning), two different families arrived to call within five minutes of each other and now that I can get back to the typing it is nearly lunch-time and we have John Ward coming to lunch.

On the farm, we drove our last culled cows to Olpunyata station on Thursday. Forty-seven were driven and one had to go in the lorry because it was so weak we did not think it would survive. We also took in fifteen weaner pigs, which were sold because we are dreadfully overcrowded in the pigsties, and cannot start getting law and order until we have culled a lot in this department too . . . A start has been made in the scrubbing out of the cowshed and so-called dairy, and the institution of a cowshed routine. We are also busy tackling the question of improving our pastures. We are putting on about sixty pounds to the acre of fertiliser and then discing and harrowing the land to let the fertiliser in. Now we want rain again to consolidate. I

25

am told no-one in Kenya has ever put anything on their pastures before because they are mostly not interested in intensive farming. It will be interesting to see the results of our experiment.

One evening we went up to see Freddie and Vi with a long list of questions. Among other things, we decided that we shall have to buy a small circular saw because all our water is heated by wood fires, and cutting all the wood is getting beyond the joke. We now find that there are no circular saws to be found in Nakuru, but we are hoping to find one in Nairobi. Our dark brown bath water (which comes to us from the crater stream and which Rosemary considers is the greatest snag to living in Kenya) has also been engaging our attention. It seems that we may be able to get special filters in addition to those we have, and we may be able to have clear water. This is only bath water of course; our drinking water comes from large tanks which collect the rainwater off the roof. This again is boiled, cooled and then filtered each day.

There was tremendous twittering and chattering amongst the boys last night at 6 pm on our return from evening milking. They had discovered two long bright green snakes hanging in the large pepper tree beside the nursery (a pepper tree looks a bit like an evergreen oak but it is much lighter in colour). I went off and borrowed a shotgun from a neighbour and eliminated them quickly. The boys swear they were terribly dangerous snakes but everyone else has told us they were quite harmless.

Jacob, our head boy, whom we told you we did not much like, has solved any problems there might be in the future by giving notice to leave at the end of the month. He says it is too cold here. We shall probably bring Ochieng into the dining-room to work with Janus and we have engaged another nursery boy to come at the end of the month. Our three houseboys will then be of the Luo tribe, who are tall and graceful in their bearing, whilst the kitchen staff, pantry boy and *dhobi* (laundry boy) are all Kikuyu who are considered the most intelligent tribe.

26

21st August, 1949

We did a lot of planning last Sunday whilst John Ward was here. For economic reasons I am afraid it was long-term though a lot depends on getting our coffee crop yielding a regular instead of a bi-annual income.

First we tackled the cowshed and re-designed it double the size with a partition in the middle: one end for our future pedigree herd and one end for the grade herd; the recorder to be in the centre to cope with both herds. Through the central portion of the building one would walk through to a new dairy, which we visualise equipped with a sterilising chest, together with a changing room and washing room for the herd boys. There will be a separate calf house for each herd and separate yards with boxes round them.

We are going to move the native village to one end of the farm, which will isolate the Africans from the cattle, a most necessary measure when you know that every year there is some dreadful outbreak of disease (such as foot-and-mouth or rinderpest) on some farm in this district.

Then a new pig house, with paddocking for the pigs, will be built on the site at present occupied by the native village, about 500 yards from the cowshed. The old pig house will be converted to a food store and a small office for the stockman.

All this involves the re-laying of roads and water piping and the re-setting of many fences. We call it our Five Year Plan, but in her present frame of mind Rosemary will not be able to wait that long before it all has to be done.

Wednesday was the girls' half-day and they set off in the small car to Nakuru to shop and go to the cinema. We also started off, after lunch, to the Bahati Forest to see the Forest Officer about fencing posts. Of course, we took David and the little white dog on wheels which Mutz gave him, together with a picnic tea. It was a beautiful ten-mile drive up to the forest. We passed huge fields of green wheat and maize. The banks along the sides of the road were lush with vegetation and coloured with many wild flowers. Wonderful little birds flew in and out of the flowers.

27

The Forest Officer was out, so we proceeded past his hut and plunged into the forest along a broad red mud road, climbing all the way. It is magnificent – just one's idea of a tropical forest. The trees are enormous and under them is dense and impenetrable vegetation. Every tree seems to have a kind of parasite clinging to it and entwined all over it. This creates a mass of hanging green ropes, which interlock in many places and form a jumbled tracery. Many of the trees lean at funny angles and the huge trunks look gnarled and old. It was dark and sinister amongst the trees but the sun shone on our road and there was something about the general effect which made Rosemary say she was almost back on the New Drive in the woods at Exbury.

We got out of the car and went for a walk. The whole forest seemed to be alive. There was the constant sound of the insects and the vari-coloured birds which fluttered from tree to tree. We heard Colobus monkeys barking all around but unfortunately didn't see them as their noise frightened David – I think because he did not know what monkeys are. We had tea inside the car, because he seemed to prefer the safety of this to being outside, but later he summoned up the courage to walk with us down the road, a tiny figure trailing his little white dog, flanked on each side by the massive trees. There had been a good deal of rain up there and the smell of the trees and the vegetation was delicious.

The next day we had a visit from the Labour Officer whom I'd invited to see us in order to find out more about the management of labour here. I discovered that there are no set hours of work and one can, in theory, work the labour as many hours as one wishes to. But in practice it is a very different matter. They work when one is present but when one leaves the field they sit down! Working them longer hours does not mean more work. The problem is rather one of discipline. Our men now have to work from 7 am to 1 pm six days a week and they think this is very hard. The Labour Officer sent in amongst the men a trusted spy, and he brought back the information that I was considered a *Bwana Mbaya* (bad boss) for making them work like this. But they will get used to it; already there is a great difference in the attitude of the labour on the farm. They are far more respectful and greet you with a '*Jambo*' instead of a sullen face.

As for food, we give our labour two pounds of crushed maize (*posho*) per head per day and a quarter pint of milk. They have half an acre of land of their own to cultivate. As we have about 170 on our books, this means that we have to put aside about seventy-five acres to grow their maize and they also have another seventy-five acres for their own gardens and crops. This cuts into our arable land a lot and we also have to provide a site for the native village. We give them salt but we do not give them meat or beans as yet. They would rather have the maize: it fills their tummies.

The question of African feeding needs more investigation. Different people treat it in differing ways. For instance, at Kabazi they give them one hot meal a day consisting of maize and vegetables but they do not give them milk, and only occasionally meat. Of course, one well-cooked meal is better for them than their own culinary efforts in their huts. One of the reasons why they do not work well is because they are undernourished and their diet is so badly balanced.

In conjunction with this man's visit we went to see a new housing scheme near Nakuru where a native village, rather like ours, was being equipped with various expensive accessories such as a communal kitchen, a communal dining-room, a recreation room, showers and latrines. The main snag to all this – in addition to the heavy cost – is that it needs a European to look after it, for the Africans (though certain tribes will keep their own huts spotless) have not enough sense of community yet to get one of their number to keep any such centre clean. They do not understand these things and might well, for example, use the chairs in the recreation room for firewood. After my visit to the latrines in this place I came away feeling that the present method of manuring our coffee and maize is a better one; it is extremely discreet and one never notices a thing. However, I have promised our Africans here that I will give them decent water facilities (there is no water in the present village) and a better church in their new village.

29

28th August, 1949

We spent last Sunday with Freddie, Vi and John at Kabazi, arriving in time for lunch and, afterwards, going round the cheese factory on their farm where our milk goes. It was spotless and beautifully run. In the store room it was fascinating to see the rows of Cheddar cheeses, some waxed in yellow and some in red. Butter-making also goes on there on quite a scale and we were pleased to see how much yellower was the butter from our Guernsey milk than that from their Ayrshire milk. Their canning factory, next door to the cheese factory, is nearly ready to start up. They have switched the whole of the market garden over from growing produce for shops to producing vegetables suitable for the can. These two factories are something new in the valley and they bear testimony to the vitality and initiative of the Ward family. Freddie gave us a good lecture about our coffee which, he says, is Rhodora's life-blood at present. He wants us to get an expert in as coffee manager when Peter Howard, our present farm manager, leaves, which he must do sooner or later because he has a European Settlement Board farm of his own, to which he will soon have to devote all his time. Freddie says it takes five years to train a coffee man and our 180 acres of coffee need a full-time man. Even if I tried to do it alone, he says that I will know so little about it that I will not be able to carry out properly the suggestions of our visiting coffee agent, Peter McMaster. A difference of only five or six tons of coffee a year will pay the wage of a first class man – whose knowledge should easily make that much difference to the annual crop.

There is always something new to learn about coffee. We had a sack of our own coffee sent up here last week. Gwara roasted it, but evidently not enough because it was bitter and quite undrinkable. Then he over-roasted it and put in some sugar with the beans. Still undrinkable! Now we have shop coffee again, and wait for some expert housewife to tell us where we trip up.

When we find this coffee manager, we await with interest the reaction of our Mr Clarke who has already done his best to

30

displace Peter Howard and seems to be angling for the job of farm manager, a job for which, in our opinion, he is not suited. His family arrive out here in the first week of September. He misses them a lot and we think it will be better when they are here.

After we got back from the Kabazi visit, I was typing the Newsletter on the verandah at about 9.30 pm when a deputation of our houseboys arrived to tell me that the kitchen *toto* had been absent without leave since four o'clock and that he had taken the cook's raincoat, the pantry *toto*'s sweater and fifty-five shillings borrowed all round. All this he had taken to pay his card debts. Our night guard stated that he knew where this 'gambling hell' could be found, so I went off in the car to George Manuel's neighbouring farm together with the guard and Gwara. Then George and I and these Africans set out for the place indicated by the guard.

We went to a group of huts dotted about amongst maize often twice as high as a man. (It was rather like Hampton Court maze, as we threaded our way along the tracks through it.) We spent two hours knocking up huts but we could not find the boy. However, he came back here at 2 am so now he is going to get very little pay for some months until he has paid off his debts. The cook got his raincoat back.

4th September, 1949

We have finally sited the new native village. We still intend to move the existing village house by house, but we shall put better water facilities and a better church in the new village. It is only the Jaluos that we are going to move (they are the majority of the labour); the Kikuyus are already sited in a place where the cattle do not go; the Lumbwas we are going to leave where they are, because they are the tribe which has to do with the cattle.

9th September, 1949

We suspected something queer was going on with David when we saw him bubbling at the mouth one day at tea. Our fears were confirmed the next afternoon, on a walk, when we heard a strange but familiar noise going on – a raucous clearing of the throat followed by a loud spit. It came from His Lordship, who was walking in front of us dragging a stick. Rosemary stopped him and asked him what he was doing, whereupon he repeated the performance – a copy of what our Indian *fundis* (workmen) are doing all day long. Revolting little boy. To cap it all, he started roaring with laughter until he fell over a puddle, stick and all.

One warm evening recently, just as we were thinking about bed, we heard a troubadour strumming a guitar and singing (in perfect English) as he strolled down the road. I rushed out and caught him. He turned out to be our native clerk, Livingstone. All the girls came out onto their verandah in their dressing-gowns, and Livingstone stood on the steps and gave us a little concert singing spirituals, some in English, some in Swahili and some in his native Kavirondo tongue.

18th September, 1949

The vet situation may improve here shortly. The farmers in Solai are getting together to pay the expenses of having one out, just for the Valley. There was a meeting recently and it was quite amusing, because there is a hard core of resistance to the plan from the old settlers who run semi-native cattle anyhow, anywhere, and say that they have managed for twenty years without a vet, and do not see why they should have one now.

One of these old-timers turned up to call at 10.30 on Monday morning. Rosemary was out seeing Mrs Clarke. I had just come down from the roof, where I had been trying to catch a kitten and was covered in cobwebs. Monique was taking a turn at the job so we had an old table, with the steps standing on it, in the middle of the sitting-room, and a gaping hole in the ceiling, through which she ascended into the roof. Upon this scene descended Mrs Baillie in a blue spotted silk dress (obviously her best), a large white felt hat (approximately Ascot, 1910) and white gloves. Her old husband was in tow, having been dressed up in his best grey trousers and sweater. She announced that she had decided not to play Bridge this week but to go calling instead. In her next breath she told us that she had lived in the Valley for thirty-four years; and her husband made me think ruefully of our capital when he said that he originally purchased a block of land of 5,000 acres, in which this farm was included, for the total sum of £35. That was forty years ago. Rosemary arrived back in the middle of this jolly chit-chat and, once she had gathered that it was purely a social visit, became barely civil and kept looking at her watch and answering 'yes' when she should say 'no' and *vice versa*. After a bit the old couple ambled off and, marvelling at the ways of Kenya's early settlers, Rosemary went off to her date with Clarke at the cowshed, where they were examining the senior heifer herd, and I went to my desk.

Yesterday was Monique's birthday, so I arranged that we should all go on a safari to an unknown destination. We set off after an early lunch: David, Beatrice, Monique, Peter Howard, ourselves, both cars, tea and rugs. I had arranged to pick up a guide from the police station ten miles down the Valley, but when we arrived we found that the guide had been sent into the Reserve with a letter for the Chief. However, the policeman himself (very different from the English bobby; more the Army officer type) said that he would show us the road, which was very nice of him and lucky for us.

The Kamasia Reserve is inhabited only by the Kamasia tribe and no white man may live there or enter the Reserve without permission. It is a huge area as big as many British counties together. We plunged in. There are no roads and it was very rough going. It was amazing to see the soil erosion, caused entirely by overstocking with native cattle: there were large bare patches of soil where the land had nearly gone back to desert. Much of it was rocky, and there were wonderful views of hills and mountains near and far. At times we were crossing an open plain or climbing a rocky escarpment or plunging through elephant grass and bush which stood higher than the bonnet of the big car. We saw a little game, such as impala, marabou storks and vultures clustered around a dead cow. We passed a number of very wild-looking men herding the native cattle. They carried spears or bows and arrows and were dressed in skins, and their coiffure consisted of elaborate small pigtails neatly braided and coated with red mud. Instead of skins, some of them wore orange and red cloth sheets, and in the split lobes of their ears were brightly coloured beads with necklaces, bracelets and anklets to match.

We travelled through this country for two hours. It was very hot and we thought we would never reach our destination. David showed signs of feeling car-sick. Suddenly, we were there! We found ourselves at the edge of a cliff from which we looked down 2,000 feet to the glistening blue water of Lake Harington. It was a huge, long, narrow lake fringed in pink by flamingos. The policeman told us that not many Englishmen have seen it. We had a picnic tea at the edge of the cliff, but we were a bit nervous because we had no weapons and it was lion country.

We got back at about 6.30, Rosemary relieved to be safely home because, as she pointed out, safaris are best done on our own, and not with a child of two. But it is certainly interesting to know that such very wild men live only fifteen miles away from us.

We have also had our first experience of safari ants. It has been wet this week, with rain most afternoons, and that is why they were on the move. We found them just at the back of the office, and the column had made a rut in the road because so many had passed by. Yet to our certain knowledge they were still passing fifteen hours later. They present a frightening sight, millions and millions of tiny brown insects which, small as they are, destroy everything in their path. One nasty thing about them is that they all bite to a prearranged signal so that if you got them on you, they would be all over you before you were bitten; and then they would all bite. David's cot stands with each leg in water in case they should ever invade his room at night. They will not cross water.

We have had some lovely letters from you all this week which have given us great pleasure. We love hearing from you and are never bored with anything you tell us. Dad, in his letter, says it is hard for him to imagine our surroundings because the East, as he knows it, is so burnt up. Actually this Valley for nine months of the year is as green as summer in England. It is only for three months that it is burnt to a golden brown but, even then, the trees and bushes stay green. For example, our coffee is always green. Very few trees out here are deciduous. Of course, the crops ripen to a golden yellow, just as in England, and our barley now is just turning from green to yellow and so are some of our oats. The maize is still green and will not go brown until December. The time *not* to see Kenya is in January, February and March, which is what they call their winter. It is hot then, and dusty on the roads. The rains come in April and it becomes almost immediately green again.

Leo, in his letter, asks how we prepare our newsletters. They are entirely a joint affair. We generally start off on Saturday evenings and take it in turns to write the draft, changing over as our wrists begin to ache. Rosemary usually checks the draft and adds little bits and I do the typing and make any other alterations which seem necessary as I go along. So Leo was quite right when he said that sometimes he can hear Rosemary and sometimes me.

25th September, 1949

We were sitting at lunch on Wednesday when Peter Howard asked us what our reactions were to devaluation. This was the first we had heard of it; so we had lived for four days in blissful ignorance of the cosmic disturbance of the descent of the pound sterling. We keep saying that we must get a wireless to keep us in touch with world affairs and we got as far as having one up on appro. but, either because of my great skill in electrical matters, or because the reception is notoriously bad all over Kenya, we sent it back in disgust. The last three times that I have been into Nakuru I tried to get a daily paper but they were sold out. The air-mail *Times* is our only real source of quick news; sometimes it arrives three days and sometimes five days old. However, we have heard this week that we are practically certain to get the telephone within twelve months and maybe much sooner. Being without early news makes life less agitated. Perhaps it is rather like living in the country at the turn of the century in England. Thanks to all your letters, a steady supply of papers and books from England (which arrive about five weeks old) and the air-mail *Times*, we feel we keep more or less up-to-date, but a yearly visit to Europe will be important to shake up our ideas.

Eddy had written that we should be careful of the baboons. He need have no fear, for they never approach far from the edge of the crater and that is half a mile from the house. They do not attack a man unless they are in large numbers and can get him cornered. They are quick to run away when they see the maize guards. I have now managed to find a reliable African and I have borrowed an old twelve-bore shotgun and I have bought some SSG shot. He will get one shilling for every baboon he shoots. We think that this will relieve several of the maize guards for work on the coffee. We have to keep quite a lot of the guards on to protect the maize from the Africans themselves. The curious thing is that the baboons have no fear of women, and will come right up to them, and even take the food they may be preparing for cooking; but they run away from a man or a woman in trousers. My Mannlicher rifle and small automatic pistol have arrived in this country and I hope to have them soon and to reckon with a few of the baboons with the rifle.

2nd October, 1949

On Monday morning we made an early start at 7 am, stopping at the local inn at Naivasha for breakfast, and arriving at Nairobi at 9.30 am. Now that our big car is run-in, we can cover the 108 miles to Nairobi in two hours if we really hurry. It is a straight tarmac road built by the Italian prisoners during the war and there is not much traffic on it. On arrival, our first call was at the office of the Express Transport Company and we were taken round to see our damaged container of furniture. We had to wait while all the things, so beautifully packed in London, were bundled out and parked anywhere on the floor of the bonded warehouse. I am sorry to report that I was so afflicted by waves of uncontrollable anger that Rosemary became ashamed of me and had to wander vaguely around the corner gazing at packing cases which did not concern us and hoping that no one would know that she was anything to do with me. . . .

On Tuesday afternoon the container which was undamaged arrived up here and we all set to immediately to unpack it. David sat on a cushion on the parapet of the verandah with a rapt expression on his face murmuring 'fun' and 'nice' at intervals. Everything came out in perfect order and, in the middle of the load, we found the Van Goyen and the jade. It was quite exciting unpacking them and a great relief to find the picture absolutely perfect and the jade unbroken.

On Thursday afternoon the damaged container arrived. As it approached we saw that one piece of furniture was roped on top, on the outside of the tarpaulin. As it lurched up the drive, the branches of the trees brushed against it. When we unpacked it, we found that it was the wooden cabinet of the grandfather clock, which has a William and Mary front; it was none the worse for wear. The container itself was sitting at such an angle on the lorry that it was a miracle that it had not fallen off and turned the lorry over.

9th October, 1949

The cattle arrived on Monday morning, attended by a charming young man called Edward Latter, who is working his way round the world on the way back to his home in New Zealand, where his family own a sheep farm. The animals were all in good condition. Latter told us that the ship put in for six days at Port Sudan, and the heat was so intense that the cattle lay down with their heads back, gasping. He spent four hours each day hosing them with sea water, and I think this contributed a lot towards getting them here safely. The shippers had provided them with every sort of food that they needed for the journey (except minerals, and Latter got salt from the galley), and the Captain and the crew were most interested in them and made a great fuss of them, especially of the bull, and used to bring them sugar and apples to eat.

They spent two days coming up from Mombasa, and Latter slept in the cattle-truck with them. He groomed them every day and in fact, did his best to look after them properly. I think we told you that the Union Castle line granted him a free passage, in view of the value of the consignment. Valentine, the bull, walked calmly out of the cattle-truck but he did not live up to his reputation for having a quiet and easy temperament when it came to loading him onto our open three-ton lorry. Having been accustomed to nothing but the most deluxe Show cattle vans at Fernhill Park, he found this another blow to his dignity, which, in any case, had been somewhat wounded when he was put in a sling and hauled out of the ship by a crane.

Rosemary met them all at the farm. We got the lorry right up to the pedigree boxes. These are only made of wood at present, but all had been newly whitewashed and disinfected, and clean sawdust was on the floor. We use sawdust because it is tick resistant, and is essential until they have been through their inoculations.

Valentine goes for a walk every day on the farm roads and he, together with the heifers, has been shampooed to get a nice coat after the sea-water. The main problem with the heifers is that some of them are in urgent need of horn-trainers and we cannot get any out here, but we are trying to get copies made of the one pair which we brought out. We are going to try to keep all these pedigrees in show condition because the arrival of these animals, together with our high grade herd, makes us just about the leading Guernsey herd here in Kenya. For one thing Valentine is, so far as we know, the only prize-winning animal (two years running) at the Royal Show which has ever been imported into Kenya and he, the heifers, and the grade herd will probably attract numerous visitors. We are rugging them at night so that they will not grow shaggy coats. The nights are cold here. Clarke's son has been put in charge of the pedigrees under his father and he had two Africans to help him. There are now twenty-six cattle in all, including those which we took over with the farm, and the bulls.

I am sending this week for the first vaccines. There are about seven in all: redwater, anaplasmosis, marginale, anthrax, rinderpest, black quarter and strain 19 (against contagious abortion). All these have to be given at different times, and blood slides taken and sent down to the Government Veterinary Officer. If no reaction is seen on the slides, they have to be done again and thus the whole series may take months.

Mr and Mrs Gaymer came to lunch the following day. She is a dog breeder, while he is a pig inspector for the Pig Board. She has a great personality and Rosemary says she reminds her of Sybil Grant in many ways, especially in her taste in clothes. She wore a bright orange and green dress, an emerald green silk scarf tied round her head gypsy-fashion and embroidered with jade beads which somehow managed to continue on as a necklace, long jade earrings and, to crown the whole ensemble, a pair of bright orange suede shoes in which, in spite of the high heels, she walked smartly round the farm after lunch. She told us that she sleeps out of doors in a wire cage with four Alsatians.

Wednesday was a great picture-hanging morning; with the help of a local builder, and one Indian, we managed to find places for most of the pictures and the Venetian mirrors.

We left at 9 am on Thursday and our first call was at Ngong, some ten miles from Nairobi, where there is a school for training Africans in cattle management and rudimentary veterinary medicine. We made ourselves known to the Principal who turned out to be a most lackadaisical Englishman of about forty with a super-Oxford accent and wearing desert boots, pale blue dungarees and a blue silk handkerchief around his neck. His hair was half-way down his back and must have had most of a bottle of peroxide emptied on it. He sat at his desk gazing at his beautiful fingernails and, after a long pause, said: 'Ai am afraid that mai bays heare, far from being improoved bai our education, tend to become vary cheeky and untrustwarthy.' After pondering on this statement for a while, we decided to try one of his 'bays' for a specific job we have in mind, so we expect that an African speaking the most refined English will turn up here soon and probably upset the whole of our farm labour.

This man showed us round some nice clean whitewashed buildings roofed in thatch and we were very interested to see a Zharwal bull, imported from India, whose recorded dam had given 800 gallons. This is a humped breed (and therefore drought resistant) just as the local native (Zebu) breed is here. The point is that the native breed here yields very little milk and, when crossed with English type bulls, it loses its hump and quickly succumbs to disease if in a native reserve area. It does, of course, yield more milk but this is no good to the natives if it cannot live. So these bulls, from the best stock in India, are being tried experimentally on the native cows, and they have already managed to get a first cross to yield 550 gallons – and it still has a hump.

On Saturday we went out to the Jacaranda Coffee Research Station (passing some ostriches on the road). Here we studied the operation of their coffee factory, experiments which they are making in composting, other experiments in mulching and manuring. . . . Quite apart from devaluation, the world position of coffee is extremely favourable. Brazil has reduced her output from twenty-two million to eight million tons and there is now a world shortage. Even if Brazil tries to come in again, it takes eight years for a coffee tree to come into bearing. All our coffee here could be sold for dollars and the outlook is most heartening.

16th October, 1949

We started the week with a small scare. Karanja, our chauffeur, a delightful and competent fellow, has for some time been negotiating for the purchase of a *bibi* (wife). His

40

prospective father-in-law, who lives at Kabazi, is trying to drive a hard bargain and is demanding an outrageous sum of money and many goats. Last week Karanja asked for one month's leave to try to settle the affair (which is normally a matter for prolonged negotiation), but, before he went, he found us another chauffeur to take his place while he is away.

This second boy we also like very much. On Monday we sent him off to Nairobi in the little Ford Prefect by himself to collect one or two things for us from various shops. He left at 7 am and we expected him back easily by teatime. When nightfall came, he had still not returned, and we began to blame ourselves for trusting him on such a journey when we had known him such a short while. After all, he might have driven the car straight into the Kikuyu Reserve and sold it. Or he might have had an accident and be lying in hospital somewhere with our car being stripped in an Indian garage and no-one bothering to let us know. Or the car might have broken down – and he had very little money, and would not be able to get credit to have it repaired. With all these possibilities, and others, in our minds, Rosemary and I were really worried by the next morning. I went into the kitchen to Gwara, our cook, who in times of trouble with any member of our staff, usually has wise advice. 'Is driver *mzuri* (good) boy or *mbaya* (bad) boy?' I asked. Gwara grinned. '*Mzuri* boy,' he said; 'accident most likely.' When Peter Howard came to work, I told him about it. 'Oh,' he said, 'didn't you know that yesterday was the King's Birthday and a general holiday so all the shops were shut in Nairobi?' The chauffeur duly turned up after lunch, having done all the jobs, with the car looking clean and well-cared-for as usual.

I have at last got down to sorting out all stores and rearranging them, a job held up because we had nowhere to put our hundreds of sacks. Now we have disposed of the sacks in a special store of their own. We have a long row of buildings out at the back of the house. The first partition is the laundry, which we converted and equipped with hot and cold water, wash-tubs, cupboards and ironing table; then comes the general office which is well fitted with desks, cupboards and a built-in safe; next there is room for our trunks and odds and ends of furniture; then a large store for spares such as wire, milk cans, machinery spares, coffee-picking baskets, motor and tractor tyres etc. This is followed by a large shed for consumable stores such as nails and screws, paint, tools and a whole host of other things; then comes a small forge with assorted ironmongery around the walls; lastly, a timber store, where we have got a lot of sawn wood going through the lengthy process of seasoning. The store for petrol and kerosene is quite apart from the other stores as a precaution against fire. Like everything else in this country, all these stores have to be carefully locked up at all times and they have a guard on them at night. The responsibility for the stores will rest with Livingstone, our African clerk, who is quite well educated, speaks English and can type, but neither Peter Howard nor I are temperamentally attuned to him so I do not know how long it will be before he gets replaced. He earns 106 shillings a month, which is more than any other African on the farm.

I have also this week been fixing up my own personal office which we have arranged in a secluded sunny corner of the verandah, away from the main part of the house. It consists of a desk and chair, a cupboard for my files, the large green velvet chair, a row of farming and veterinary reference books and a dog basket, for whichever member of the pack condescends to keep me company.

The gardens out here are really lovely everywhere and one can grow the most exotic things as well as most of the English flowers. This week Rosemary has in the sitting-room a huge vase consisting of red-hot pokers, yellow iris, montbretia, yellow carnations and alstroemeria. They make a wonderful glowing show. On the so-called dining-room table is a flat bowl of alstroemerias, cut short, with montbretias; and on the writing-table is a large vase of deep red and orange-red carnations which she buys from Kabazi for one-and-six a dozen. In our bedroom is a bowl of gigantic roses which Vi gave her. They are all the best English stock and are perfectly wonderful. One can have, for ten shillings, as many flowers as would gratify a film star. Last week, to vary the selection, we had the big vase full of arum lilies and agapanthus, while the dining room table had white freesias and blue anemones and the writing-table had white freesias. The garden outside looks rather bare, the only real colour being the bougainvillea and frangipani, but we hope to tackle the garden soon now.

Today has been David's second birthday. He came to our room after breakfast and unwrapped his parcels himself. We think he was most thrilled with a large red railway engine which the Swiss girls gave him. After lunch we took him out in the car together with the two girls and Mr and Mrs Clarke. We went right round the Solai and Subukia valleys, a distance of sixty-five miles, and had a picnic tea on the way. There was a birthday cake for David with icing and two candles and 'Happy Birthday David' on it, which we had made in Nakuru, because we cannot buy icing sugar out here at present. Rosemary and I felt sad that he will never be two again and we can hardly believe that he has only been in our lives for two years.

23rd October, 1949

On Sunday there was a wild panic. The houseboys cheerfully used up all the water in our tank and then came to tell us that 'Dopey', the boy who comes daily from the farm to pump the water up to the tank, had not turned up. Mad rush by me into the kitchen to have the fire raked out before the boiler burst. Dopey turned up in the afternoon and, so far as I could understand, explained that he had been to visit his deceased aunt's maternal uncle. More likely that he had spent the morning in a horizontal position wrapped in his blanket in the land of dreams.

Then the tractor drivers distinguished themselves. The first day they broke the disc harrows: we could not go on with cleaning the coffee. The second day they broke the baler: we could not go on with baling the barley straw. The third day they broke the mower: we could not go on with mowing hay. As you may imagine I was somewhat annoyed and I made a few disparaging remarks. Repairs are being tackled by Okola, our carpenter and smith, who wears a huge pair of Charlie Chaplin boots and very little else, and by his assistant *toto* who derives his name from the Swahili word '*lala*', meaning 'sleep'. Lala is a wonderful character for he is able to move so slowly that, unless he is chased, he is able to start sweeping out the office in the morning and be still doing it in the evening.

One day when I was going round the work on the farm in the car with Rosemary and the three dogs, we went to see the contractors who are clearing the crater land. It was a lovely summery day (as it nearly always is), with a delicious warm heat. When the bush got so dense that we could not proceed further by car, I left Rosemary behind and set off on foot with Red and Dell (Candy stays behind with her mistress). I was about to cross the crater stream to see the second contractor who is doing that part of the land, when I found four *bibis* (African women) walking in line with an enormous load of firewood suspended on each back by a strap around their foreheads. They did not hear me come so I fell in behind and followed them up a winding track over the hill at the boundary of our farm. In a little while, one of them stopped and, turning round, saw me, and stood glued to the spot with fright, for they came from the neighbouring farm and were stealing wood which is being stocked for our farm village.

I pointed back down the path they had just come up and told them '*Umbwa mbaya sana*' (dogs very bad). Luckily they did not notice that Dell was quite terrified of them and only had the one idea of getting back to the car as soon as possible. They set off back the way they had come, and I fell in behind again with the dogs. In due course we met our *askari*, who has been allowed by the police to have a gun to guard our maize against the baboons. He is a special policeman. He took over from me and took the women up to our native village. Here they were made to hand over the wood to our women. Then the *Wasei* (elders) held a council and fined them each five shillings, total twenty shillings of which ten comes to me and ten to the *Wasei*. They made the women go and fetch the money, and gave them each one with the *kiboko* (stick) before they sent them away. The *askari* gets a shilling above his pay for every baboon he shoots,

44

and now he will get two shillings for every wood thief he can catch in the crater land – though, of course, he will not take his gun down there.

30th October, 1949

On Tuesday night Clarke came to tell us that one of our imported heifers was sick with stomach trouble. After two trips to the telephone box two miles down the road I managed to get hold of the private vet at Rongai, who promised to come along the next morning but prescribed that meanwhile the heifer should be drenched with oatmeal gruel. In this crisis Clarke did not seem to think it necessary to get up in the night, so Roland Williams and I did the job at 2 am and, after we had done it, went round the farm checking up on the maize guards. Clarke is causing us considerable anxiety at present in many ways.

On Thursday we set off at 7 am for Nairobi . . . and after lunch, called at the Coryndon Museum to try to identify the snakes we have had here. On Tuesday a large one was killed by the pedigree sheds, and this we identified as a puff adder. The two green ones which we killed in the pepper tree beside the nursery some time ago were probably mambas. Both these types of snakes are deadly. We had tea at the Norfolk Hotel, hoping to see Deborah Kerr and Stewart Granger, who are staying there during the making of the film *King Solomon's Mines*, but we were unlucky. So we went off to the Game Park, where we wandered on our way for some fifteen miles to the hippo pools. We saw quite a variety of game, such as giraffe, wildebeest, zebra, Thomson's and Grant's gazelles, impala, water-buck, jackal (which slunk across the road just in front of the car), ostriches and, at the hippo pools, the hippos and some small monkeys. We did not see any lions, which was rather a disappointment for Roland.

We saw Roland off at 7.30 this morning. The chauffeur took him to Lake Naivasha, which is half way between here and Nairobi, in the big car. At about 10.30 this morning, as we were walking in the paddocks, we had a fine view of his flying boat passing overhead near the farm on its way to Khartoum and England. He carried with him a little bit of the life-blood of Rhodora for our parents, in the form of a small bag of coffee.

2

Roland Williams had been our first visitor from England. He worked at New Court (N. M. Rothschild & Sons – the family bank) and was on his way to South Africa on business. We suspected that this was a benevolently inquisitive call, to find out how we were managing. As it happened, we were managing rather well. We were settling in, working hard and consolidating the business; we were making our way in the canine world in which I had played such an enthusiastic part in England; we were getting to know our staff; we had imported a prize bull from England with which to build up our pedigree Guernsey herd; and our social life was getting livelier. Chronically allergic as I am, there were times when I coughed my way through the whole day but that was a problem with which we learned to live; there were others, more immediately solvable.

6th November, 1949

After we had seen off Roland Williams and finished last Sunday's letter to you, we had no less than three lots of visitors who came to see our imported cattle. There have been others later in the week and four different people, all concerned with the cattle business, have said that Valentine of Fernhill Park is the best bull they have ever seen in Kenya. . . . On October 17th he was injected with redwater fever vaccine combined with anaplasmosis. On Wednesday evening this week, Clarke came to tell me that his temperature was 107° (the normal temperature of cattle out here is around 101.5°). We injected pirevan, which should bring the temperature down immediately. At this stage we were pleased that he was showing a reaction, because the whole idea of these injections is to give the animal the actual tick-borne disease, under conditions when one can control and watch the illness. Once they have had it they are immune in the future.

However, when we found an hour later that his temperature had risen to 108°, we began to get worried, especially as he was lying down , and refused to get up. At 10 pm I fetched Clarke in the small car and we went up to him again. He was standing up in his box and we were full of hope as we went to take his temperature. We found that it was so high that the mercury had reached the top of the thermometer where it reads 110°. We took it again to confirm it. We shall never know how much his temperature rose above that astounding figure. We gave him another injection of pirevan, keeping carefully by us some adrenalin, for they sometimes have a collapse after this treatment.

It shows the amazing strength of the bull that he expressed his discomfort at such a high temperature by roaring and pawing the ground, throwing the sawdust on which he is bedded up over the rugs on his back. We stayed with him for an hour, standing outside his box in the moonlight, talking quietly; and suddenly, we saw him start to eat a little lucerne. We went in to him, took his temperature again, and found to our intense relief that it had subsided to 103.5°. His breathing was very fast and irregular. We stayed on until he lay down and Clarke himself came back in the early hours of the morning. (I have had a serious talk with Clarke and as a result he has pulled himself together.) He covered him over with sacks and stayed with him a little while, thankful that we had a night guard on the cattle, because he heard many leopards coughing.

After this we had another scare, for we formed the impression that at least half our working oxen did not justify the name of 'ox'. As they are herded in the crater land where our senior heifer herd runs, we set out to examine them. They are the wildest things, and they lash out as soon as touched and even bite. They have enormous horns and humps. With great difficulty, Clarke did examine them all, and we found three which might be capable of ideas above their station in life. These three are destined for the tin, poor dears.

I have been trying to get Rosemary to answer an invitation to lunch for this weekend. She was in the grocer's shop about a fortnight ago when she was pounced upon by a very effusive lady to whom she thought she had previously been introduced. This garrulous person asked her to lunch and Rosemary, not wishing to show that she had no idea who the lady was, said she would see what I was doing and could she write an answer. She was given the lady's Post Office Box number, but in her agitation wrote down our own box number; and so, when she got home, we had no trace of the good lady. Not knowing what to do, Rosemary did nothing, and continued to do nothing for several days, whilst the luncheon date gradually drew nearer. We made enquiries, and reached the conclusion that it must be one of two people; and then, being told that one of them could talk the hind leg off a donkey, we presumed that she was the one. Eventually, in fear and trepidation, Rosemary could not delay writing another single day, so she took up her pen and wrote to thank her for her kind invitation but regretting that we could not accept. When Charles and Mattie Long came to tea on Tuesday we discovered that Rosemary has written to the wrong person. . . .

On Monday, whilst David was entertaining Vi's grand-children to tea and I thought I had a quiet evening to deal with my farm correspondence, a hard-faced business man appeared who extended his hand and announced that his name was Heath. This conveyed nothing to me unless he was related to the murderer which, by his appearance, he might have been. I offered him a chair and a cigarette and we talked about this and that whilst I wondered what he wanted to sell. Rosemary tried to come to my rescue and said brightly that she was just going down to the cowshed with the children and would he like to come and look at the cows? We then discovered that he had called some days before when we were out, and had been all round the stock. Eventually he said he would like some milk, at which I looked down my nose, for I do not like selling small quantities of milk because it upsets the dairy routine. Then I suddenly realised what he meant, and that I was in the presence of the man who has the largest retail milk round in Nakuru. My manner changed perceptibly, I think.

As a result, we are sending all our evening milk (fifty gallons) every day to his dairy. We hope to send our morning milk too later on, because we are shortly going over to a new pig food which will eliminate the necessity for feeding skim.

Unknown to Freddie and Vi, a large number of violet plants arrived down from Kabazi as a gift from the manager of the market garden. I think Rosemary must have mentioned how much she loves violets when she was up there one morning recently. Omadi, our head gardener, grumbled because Rosemary made him prepare three flower-beds before she decided which one to put them in. She promised him and his mate a small piece of soap each, which they love having, if they kept the violets alive. As a result the plants were swamped with water, and many branches were cut off our trees to give them shade. Omadi's last and voluble instructions to Rosemary on Saturday were that she should water them on Sunday, so that they should be alive for him to have his soap on Monday.

I wonder whether I told you a few weeks ago that we had a visit from a chief of the Jaluo tribe. We have something of a Jaluo stronghold on this farm, and with a view to recruiting some more labour for the coffee picking, I made rather a fuss of him. I sent some milk down to Abuaka, the headman, so that he could entertain the Chief properly, and I sent him back to Nakuru in the car when his visit was over. He, for his part, held a *baraza* (meeting) of all the workers of whatever tribe on the farm, and I was rather touched that he came to me afterwards to give me a report on this *baraza*. He said that he had told them that they must all work hard, and that they must not steal anything which did not belong to them. I presented the Chief with a gift. It was rather difficult to find something suitable as he did not drink or smoke, but I managed to find one of those silver coins which were sold at the time of the Jubilee of the King and Queen. I gave him this and showed him the head of the King and Queen on the one side and the picture of the House of Commons on the other. This latter building, I told him, was where they held *barazas* in England when the *Wasei* (elders) held a council.

This week I received a letter from the Chief: 'Dear Sir, I am very glad to inform you about my arrival at home. . . . The medal you presented to me was showed to the District Commissioner and the members of the meeting. Each and every one was very happy and clapped their hands three times for what you did for me. . . . Thank you very much Sir. Hoping for your favourable reply. Sincerely yours.' The letter is signed with a rubber stamp 'Chief Zephaniah Abungu.'

There are a lot of hornets about and we had three nests hanging from the rafters in the boxes of the imported animals. The other evening an African came along with a stirrup pump. After spraying the nests for a moment with water, he took a piece of cloth from his pocket, put it in the palm of his hand, reached up and took the nest with his hand and crushed all the hornets in his palm. Those few which were still crawling around he pinched between his bare thumb and first finger. It was a performance well worth seeing, for these hornets are dangerous insects and can give one a nasty sting.

13th November, 1949

The maize is brown and crisp, but we cannot harvest it because we are busy with the coffee. It must wait its turn and, meanwhile, we have to keep on the guards against the baboons. Setting out to check on these guards one afternoon this week, I found a recumbent form lying out in a field beside the maize. He was sound asleep and covered by a white blanket. Nearby, in a tree, a huge baboon was keeping watch on *him*. *Reductio ad absurdum*. . . .

John Ward and his sister, Sheila, came for the day on Thursday. Unfortunately their visit clashed with the arrival from the station of some forty-five young trees and shrubs which we had ordered for our garden from the nurseries near Nairobi. . . . At lunchtime we heard screams from Monique, who had been to the kitchen about David's lunch, and found a snake with its head peering out from a hole into which it had retired after taking a look at her. I hastily fetched my shotgun and relieved it of its head with one shot. Then I pulled its squirming body out of the hole and found it was nearly two feet long. It was quite a thin snake, which Rosemary identified the next day at the Coryndon Museum as a grass snake, and only mildly venomous. She spent the day in Nairobi sending off food parcels for our Christmas presents to you all and to many others. We hope that they reach you in time.

We went down to the government school late one evening this week to try to arrange about the education of Clarke's second son and, whilst I was talking to the headmaster, Rosemary was engaged in the car in a much more interesting conversation with Karanja, our chauffeur.

'Did you have a good holiday, Karanja?'

'Yes, Memsahib,' said Karanja.

'Did you bring back your new *bibi* with you?'

'No, because I am sharing a room with Maura.' (Maura is the temporary chauffeur we engaged, who is now going to take over driving the lorry.)

Then Rosemary asked which huts were occupied by which houseboys and learned that Gwara (our cook) had at last imported one of his wives, presumably to cook for him. Many giggles from Karanja who said that Gwara's wife was a *Wasei* (elder) and pointed to his teeth to show that she evidently was toothless. Rosemary then asked whether his new wife was also a *Wasei*. More giggles, and she gathered that his wife was short and not tall, and a very young teenager. Then Karanja told Rosemary that Gwara had three wives. Much sighing and he said:

'Ah, three wives no good for any boy, *mbaya, mbaya.*'

'No,' said Rosemary, delighted that he had such an idealistic approach to the subject of marriage. 'I should hate the Bwana to have three wives.'

'Yes,' said Karanja. 'Three wives no good for Bwana or boys. Cost too many shillings.'

So were Rosemary's illusions shattered and the rest of the conversation consisted of Karanja drawing in the dust on the window the figures 1,500 to show the number of shillings he had had to pay for his wife. When I rejoined them Rosemary was agreeing heartily how scandalous and exorbitant the price was (knowing full well that he would shortly ask for a rise in his pay in order to pay off his debts).

We have all been busy with the coffee which is now, at last, ripening up. There are eight separate coffee shambas of different sizes, but each containing some thousands of trees. They cover an area of 180 acres. When a coffee bean starts to turn from green to pink, there are about eight days in which to pick it before it is over-ripe. When large numbers of the trees start turning at the same time, there is a scramble to get round the shambas. This week we have had about sixty of our own men and forty of our own women and some forty women from neighbouring farms picking on an average day. There is still not enough ripe coffee to make for heavy picking, but the amount picked daily is gradually increasing and we picked just over half a ton on the best day.

Later, when the real rush comes, the same number of pickers will pick two or three times as much; and in addition, we shall get more pickers, for they will come from far and near when they hear that picking is easy. Also, to Rosemary's disgust, we shall stop almost all other farm work in order to pick, though really she sees the wisdom of this, now that coffee prices this week have reached the new astronomic world record of over £1,000 per ton at the Nairobi auction.

The picking is picturesque, with the women walking about from tree to tree with baskets on their heads and often with a baby slung on their backs. Each picker has a row allotted to him and one foreman is responsible for twenty-five rows. I walk through them all once or twice. When a picker has filled a basket, he goes to a collecting-point called 'the camp' where our headman presides and measures out their pick, paying them in cents on the spot. A picker earns about a shilling a day if he is picking for cents alone. Our own men have to pick a certain amount on their monthly salary, and they earn cents for any amount above that. The pickers' wages for one ton of coffee come to somewhere around £15.

From the camp the coffee is taken in sacks on the ox-wagon to the factory. Here there is quite complicated machinery for pulping the beans from the 'cherry', or outer skin, and there is a series of washing operations to clean the beans, followed by the fermentation and the drying. The washing and the pulping take at least 20,000 gallons of water each day. Peter goes down in the morning and I go down in the evening to supervise Alalu, our head factory man, and his various minions. Rosemary and David come too and David is fascinated by the whole operation of the machinery and of the water running down the washing channels. He tells us continually in an excited voice such things as 'Wartah!' 'Another Wartah!' 'More Wartah!' 'Look at the coffee!' 'Coffee Wartah' 'Big machine!' 'Look at the machine!' and so on. . . . We think we shall have to curtail this evening visit because twice last week he woke up in the night and told Monique 'Coffee Wartah round and round and round!' so he must have been over-excited. He and Beatrice pick about a quarter of a basket of coffee between 9.30 and 10.30 when he goes for his morning walk.

20th November, 1949

On Friday evening Rosemary and I went to a meeting of the General Committee, and later of the Show Committee, of the forthcoming Championship Dog Show which is to be held in Nakuru in February. Rosemary has been made a Member, and I am Chairman of both committees. Our friend Mrs Gaymer is joint Secretary and she seemed to be the only person who knew the personalities of the dog world in Kenya. We soon discovered that she had many axes to grind and was using our committee of up-country people as pawns to get her own back on the Kennel Club at Nairobi. (She has been expelled from the General Committee of the Kennel Club, though not from the Club itself.) I was having none of this nonsense and, when we came to the appointment of judges, the discussion became quite heated and I had to tell her in no uncertain terms that she was trying to steamroller her ideas across the Committee. After that she sulked, so we were able to conduct the meeting as we wanted. She presented a formidable figure in a large black lace crinoline hat, a green and mauve striped dress, the usual long earrings and a huge Alsatian sitting beside her. Rosemary sat next to the Alsatian which looked at her menacingly each time she argued with Mrs Gaymer. The Alsatian was not co-opted onto the Committee.

We visited an up-country sale:

27th November, 1949

We set off at 6.30 am on Monday morning. Charles Long and Rosemary sat behind while Karanja was in front with me driving. When we got down to the tarmac road which runs from Nairobi to Nakuru (this road is about nine miles from us) we turned right, instead of left towards Nairobi. As soon as we passed through Nakuru the tarmac came to an end, and we proceeded for mile after mile with a huge plume of dust rising in our wake. Whenever we met another car we hastily wound up the windows. It is lovely, driving at that early hour out here. The countryside is bright and sparkling, and it is deliciously cool. The road was a red road, and there was a varying landscape of bright green vegetation stretching on either side interspersed with patches of scrub country and thorn trees or rolling slopes of dried-up grass, or small areas of forest, with pine and gum trees high above us. Continuously, there were wonderful views of distant mountains with their ever-changing colours. We crossed one escarpment at over 9,000 feet.

At 10.30 we had breakfast at a hotel at Eldoret, which is a nice little town, with the streets lined with double scarlet poinsettias. Then on again for two more hours, until we left the so-called main road just before Kitale and turned down real country lanes (tracks out here). Now we were driving straight towards Mount Elgon, which towered in front of us.

Eventually we arrived at the farm at which the dispersal sale was being held. A rostrum and sale ring had been erected, of wattle poles and thatch, with a concrete drinking trough in the middle, and on the floor, maize leaves which looked like rushes. There were a lot of people. We strolled across and looked at the bulls in their loose boxes and we found that Charles was perfectly right when he said that the only one worth buying, as far as we were concerned, was the imported one. He was a beautiful little animal in excellent condition, small and quiet, and had been brought here as a calf from the famous White Ladies Herd and reared for the first six months out here by Charles himself.

As we sat round the ring waiting for him to come in I looked at Rosemary and said with a grin:

'It's been a long, long road for us, from Reading Cattle Market to here.'

The bidding opened at ten guineas, and it soon became apparent that another Guernsey breeder was bidding against us. At forty guineas the crowd were becoming most excited, so in a loud voice I told Charles, who was bidding for us, to go on. However, the other man had had it and, with the drop of a hammer, the little bull joined the Rhodora herd!

On Thursday we went to Nairobi for one night. The main purpose of our visit was to see Angus Lawrie, our accountant. We lunched with him and his wife and daughter, Freddie, Vi and Sheila at the Flamingo, which is one of two excellent restaurants in Nairobi. Later Freddie took us in his car to see Lady McMillan who is also one of the oldest settlers in Kenya and has known Freddie for many years. She is an American, aged eighty-four, and as far back as 1904 she crossed Abyssinia with her husband. She has a lovely rambling house, old-fashioned, and with nice furniture; in front was a charming terraced garden with a lily pond.

In the evening, after dinner at the Muthaiga Club, where we all stayed, Freddie introduced us to many important people. These included Charles Taylor, Chairman of the Coffee Board, and Sir Frederick and Lady Wilson who are the main suppliers of whole milk to Nairobi (and he is Chairman of the Board of Agriculture). When I was introduced to Lady Wilson I did not know who she was, and as we started to talk farming, I asked her whether she had a farm. Later I discovered that she had 20,000 acres and 1,100 cows in milk!

4th December, 1949

This week Rosemary and I began to feel that the coffee was ripening faster than we were likely to get around to picking it. (I told you in a recent letter that after the coffee berry begins to turn pink there are only about eight days before it goes hard and black and becomes unpulpable.) We should be picking up to 700 or 800 *debbies* a day (a *debbie* is a four-gallon paraffin tin; and there are about 550 *debbies* to one ton of our coffee, dry). We were, in fact, picking only about 5–600 *debbies* per day. Of course, every other coffee farmer in the Valley is also picking his flush and there is much competition for outside pickers. People go to all sorts of lengths to attract pickers to their farm, by offering more money, or free cigarettes, or some other bribe. Neighbouring farmers frequently come to harsh words over the matter. I decided that, words or no words, and at the risk of becoming the most unpopular man in the Valley, I would send out our lorry on scavenging expeditions first thing every morning with a specially picked recruiter on board to go to places where we know that there are concentrations of Africans; and I also decided to offer them a special bonus if they pick for six days in the week, and an even more special bonus if they pick for seven. The results have been surprising and gratifying. Our lorry makes two trips each morning and comes back laden to the gunwales with singing and shouting *bibis* who appear to be hanging on by their eyelids all over it, and each one has several children who hang onto their mothers in an equally precarious manner. We collected seventy-three yesterday. Our picking rate for the last two days has been 912 and 860 *debbies*.

Now I am wondering how many local farmers are going to come and visit me with a gun.

11th December, 1949

It is Saturday evening after dinner and we are in the sitting-room, sitting in our dressing-gowns in front of the fire. The dry weather wind is blowing strongly outside. We are both rather smugly pleased that it is Sunday tomorrow. The head boy, Janus, has just removed the coffee with his usual '*Kwa heri*' (good-bye) as he glides out of the room. In a little while I shall let out the dogs, and then take Red around to the 'Swiss Consulate' and check that all doors are locked and that the night guard is on duty, and that water is flowing into our house tank.

Janus's newly-born *toto* has not been at all well the last few days and, although Rosemary cured his *bibi* from various aches and pains after the actual birth, and insisted on regular three-hourly feeds, she felt it too risky to do anything about such a tiny, premature baby without expert advice. She was much relieved when Janus agreed to send it down with its mother in our car to the native hospital on Monday. The boys' huts are at the other side of the lawn, down a little path just outside the garden. This couple keep their hut spotlessly clean, but to see the baby, or do anything for the *bibi*, Rosemary nearly has to lie on the floor herself for Janus sleeps on a camp bed, but his *bibi* and the baby curl up at the foot of the bed in a corner on blankets on the floor.

We also had even newer arrivals, in the form of twins born to our African herdsman's *bibi*. He is terribly worried because it is considered abnormal and unlucky to have twins. They have both died, and we have our suspicions. He wanted to know whether twins are ever born in England.

For some time now we have felt that we did not properly understand the grading certificates which we received from the bacon factory and indeed, that we did not know what good bacon should be like nor how a pig should be fed to produce it, or what was the best breed of pig to produce first quality bacon. So we wrote to the manager of the bacon factory and asked if we could come and see him and visit the factory. He invited us to lunch. . . . The tour of the factory was fascinating. First, we saw the pigs being unloaded from the railway siding at the factory door. From here they were brought up a ramp and rendered unconscious immediately and silently by an electrical device. Then they were slung up on a rail upon which they moved on an endless chain, but always in the same order, throughout all the processes. First their throats were cut and the blood was drained, and this was followed by four different washing processes. Then the pig was divided into two sides and the backbone removed, and blow-lamps put all over the body to remove the hairs. Next the insides were removed and examined by African vets. A European then measured the fat at the shoulder, loin and hams and he weighed the carcass. From there it went forward for examination by a European vet. Then it went into a cooling room for twenty-four hours. On coming out of the cooling room the bacon was examined for firmness, and upon its quality its fate would be decided. The best quality would make York hams for export, while the worst would go for sausage-meat. We watched them making sausages and gelatine and canning luncheon meat, and we saw the huge cold rooms where the bacon matures, and the elaborate system for smoking the bacon. Every piece of the pig is used for something. The whole place was spotlessly clean.

25th December, 1949

Christmas really started for us on Friday this week when we went down to the town to do our shopping. Nakuru was at its gayest with the shops decorated and full of people. It is really amusing shopping there, now that we are beginning to know a lot of people. All the farmers come in from far and wide and one meets all one's friends and hears all the news. First we wanted to contact Vi Ward, so we told Karanja, our chauffeur, to watch and see which shop she went into on arriving in the town. Quite soon he came to the Post Office, where we were, and said that she was in the grocer's; so we crossed over, and there she was. Then Charles Long came out of his office (Chettle & Co., the local auctioneers) with a tiny white

Christmas cake under his arm, which he was taking home. We had a long talk with him and another man who joined us, wanting to buy some heifers. As we stood there, a party consisting of Roy and Nancy Laird (he was Bursar at the London Hospital, but left when they wanted to nationalise him) and Commander and Mrs Everett joined us, all talking at once, one about Christmas presents, another about vets, a third about children's parties (the Lairds have asked David to his first Christmas party on December 28th) and so on. . . . It was lovely bright sunshine but everyone was in a cheery mood and the decorations and the Christmas wrappings round the presents made it all seem as much like Christmas as it would seem at this time in England. We saw many more neighbours during the morning, and ended up at the Rift Valley Club, where we went to talk business with Mrs Stobbs, the new Secretary to the Dog Show Committee.

Saturday, Christmas Eve, was a holiday on the farm. We spent the morning taking a coloured ciné film of the farm for Rosemary to bring back in March for you all to see. After lunch the Headman and the underheadmen came for their presents. We gave them each a sweater, fifty cigarettes, and some money. I think they must have been pleased because later, in the evening, the Headman called on us quite unexpectedly and presented us solemnly with a live chicken as a Christmas present from the Jaluo village. We were rather pleased with this spontaneous gesture. The ordinary run of farm labour received as a gift from us one shilling with which to buy the meat of the ox which was slaughtered for them, a free issue of sugar and one day's holiday (Saturday) with pay. (Holidays, including Sundays, are not normally paid working days out here; a man is only paid if he actually works.)

Christmas morning dawned after a restless night for us all. Actually every night this week has been rather disturbed by the noises the Africans have been making in their village. They seem to think nothing of singing without a pause until three or four in the morning and starting again at six. I think one of the reasons is that we have given them the customary permission to brew some native beer, and two sacks of maize meal with which to do it.

We were called with breakfast at 8.30 and Janus brought in a large bowl containing two dozen eggs, which was a gift to us from Gwara, our cook. Then David and the Swiss girls arrived at 9.15. David had already investigated the contents of the stocking which he found at the end of his bed when he woke up; it had a soft floppy toy monkey sticking out of the top of it. We put everybody's present in a pile beside one of their shoes and David was hugely excited to see his stack of presents. He sat between us in bed and we all worked hard at unpacking. We three were delighted with the lovely presents you sent. David also had several presents from children in the locality. His expression of wonder and amazement had to be seen to be believed. Monique, besides giving him a little toy, had made him the sweetest little red check cotton sun-suit and a beautifully knitted navy-blue and white pants and jersey for when it is cold in the evening. Beatrice gave him a toy and had knitted him two cardigans, one scarlet and one white. We gave him a Kiddicar.

Rosemary had sent a message to the Headman, Obwaka, tactfully saying that we did not wish to be disturbed before 11 am. We had heard that we were liable to have visitors at all hours of the day. Although we heard much noise in the distance it was not until 11 sharp that we heard the sound of many chanting voices approaching us. The first contingent was representative of the boys from the coffee factory, headed by Alalo, decorated with gum tree leaves, bougainvillea and plumbago flowers in their hair and metal discs on their legs. Alalo wore a calf-skin over his shoulders. The effect was rather marred, we thought, by khaki-coloured shirts; but there were also some bright shirts to lend colour to the scene. The dance resembled the Charleston, but with terrific rhythm, helped by the drumming of feet on the ground. The chanting consisted of Alalo singing some words in Jaluo and an answering chorus from the dancers. (The grass is all worn away in a circle on the lawn.) We took some ciné camera shots and after a bit, another band of Jaluos came from the other side and the two parties joined up; there must have been about 100 in all. Obwaka arrived back from Church on his bicycle (he is a Catholic) and we put David on his bicycle in the centre of the dancing ring. Eventually we gave the dancers ten shillings between them, and some cigarettes, and they went off dancing back to the village. Manasseh, our garden boy, stayed behind and (without being asked) cleared the lawn of leaves and bits and pieces and David helped him. We took a film of this too, because Manasseh is very tall and David looked so tiny beside him.

We had lunch at 12.30: turkey, and delicious plum pudding which Monique had made three weeks ago, and which duly came in in flames. At three-thirty the entire Clarke family arrived for tea: we had sandwiches, chocolate cake and a wonderful Christmas cake decorated with a spray of coffee, which, with three red berries, looked very like holly without the prickles. We made the cake from three recipe books – Escoffier, an East African one and one from England – and I must say that the combined recipes made it a pre-war affair and it was really delicious. To finish up we had jelly and cream poured from Mariloo's lovely little silver cow. We are enchanted with this new addition to the Rhodora Herd.

After tea we all walked over to the new house which we are building, and which has now got half its roof on. We think we are going to move the Clarkes up to this house when it is complete, because they will be so much nearer to their work. We showed them all round, and planned out their future garden with them. When we got back, it was time for David to go to bed, and I put on our two ciné films for the benefit of the Clarke children and the houseboys.

Towards the end of the film, the Lumbwa tribe, who work for us mainly as herd boys, arrived silently on the lawn. It was just dusk. They are as fine a collection of men as you could find, mostly over six feet tall; there were about twenty-five of them. Most of them were covered in their tribal decorations, with finely worked coloured beads used as collars, headdresses and over the shoulders. The leader had his face painted white. They stripped to the waist, linked arms in a circle with the leader in the centre, and began to sing in a sort of harmony, in rich deep voices. As they sang, they danced in perfect rhythm. There was quite a variety of dances and songs, in one of which one of them made a mock attack upon another with a spear. We stood on the lawn close to them and we were rather moved by this stimulating and intensely virile performance. They stayed about an hour and then they moved off into the night, under a perfect starlit sky, singing '*Sysirri*' which means 'Good-bye' in Lumbwa.

1st January, 1950

Rosemary and I will always remember David's first party, even if David himself cannot remember it when he is grown up. The Lairds' house is truly delightful. It is built on two floors (which is unusual out here) and plastered white on the outside with a dark red tiled roof. From the verandah on the ground floor and the broad paved terrace flanked with beautiful flowers, or from the balconies on the floor above, one looks down a steeply sloping lawn, scattered with shady trees, to a tiny picturesque lake complete with little boat for canoeing.

The first part of the party consisted of the guests arriving; children, mothers and fathers sat about on the terrace or stood gossiping in groups while I took a colour film of the gathering. David was, as usual, rather shy at first but he soon got over it. Even so, he did not bother to talk to other children much but wandered about, perfectly composed, taking a good look at everything – a funny, sturdy soul, not, apparently, in the least dependent on his parents after the initial shyness had worn off, walking about slowly with his hands behind his back, taking everything in. There were some twenty-five children, and he was amongst the youngest, although the oldest cannot have been much more than five. After tea we all assembled in the hall, and the curtains were drawn, so there was quite a hush when there came a very loud knocking at the door. Some of the older children squeaked 'Come in!' and the door opened and David beheld his first Father Christmas, complete with white pillowcase full of presents.

On Tuesday we went out to tea down the Valley with some farmers called Geoffrey and June Ireland. Like the Lairds they have a charming garden, with a large green lawn sweeping down to a lake complete with diving board, water lilies and so on. The house is not very nice but the farm is truly lovely. We have been there before to see their stock, so this time they showed us first their coffee. We thought it was better than ours. The berries are large and more regular, and the trees were not wilting as ours are. I think the main reason is because they have had eight inches more rain than us (although they only live four miles away) and their crop is not quite so heavy as ours. We often find, too, that other people's farms seem in better shape than ours because they have been working on them for years, whereas we have only been on ours for six months.

From the coffee we went on to see their orange groves. These were fascinating: rows of bushy but tall trees, covered with oranges in different stages of ripening which glowed against the dark green leaves. A golden crop. The trees were in sweeping lines, and the copper-brown earth was neatly raked between each row. The Irelands are a very hard-working couple of about our age, and they are making a great success of their farm.

On Saturday, New Year's Eve, we went to our first dance in Kenya. It was given by Mrs Stobbs at her house outside Njoro about thirty miles away. There were about thirty couples and it was quite pleasant, though none of our actual friends were there. We got home at about 2.15 am.

Next morning we had breakfast at 6.45 am and set off for Nairobi. As we approached the city we stopped to admire a small herd of giraffe, which was grazing on the verge of the main road. We took off from Nairobi West airport soon after 11 am in a nice little American Beechcraft which we had chartered. It is a single-engined affair, but quite as comfortable as a motor car. As we gained height over Nairobi we saw masses of animals below us in the Game Park. We travelled above the cloud, so that it was perfectly smooth, and there was so little noise that we were able to chat and read papers all the way. I sat beside the pilot and was able to renew my acquaintance with the computer, which reminded me of the controller's course which I took at Stanmore during the War.

After two hours in our Beechcraft we touched down on the edge of the sea, right beside the Sinbad Hotel at Malindi. We had lunch and a rest and then started this letter, which I am finishing on Monday sitting on our verandah within a few feet of the sea. We have come 700-odd miles for one week's holiday and rest; it is the only week we can fit in. We are about eighty miles from Mombasa, northwards up the coast. There are quite a few brown-looking people about and we feel very white-skinned at present. The sands are lovely. We walked a long way in the cool of the evening and came back along the beach road. We saw masses of palm trees with clusters of coconuts upon them, and huge mango trees and cotton growing in the fields. . . . We have just had a bathe and it was glorious – so warm. Rosemary was an awful coward and would scarcely come in above her ankles because, as it was a new ocean for her, she had some romantic idea that she might be carried off by a shark, or a giant sting-ray, or something.

8th January, 1950

The inevitable Kenya habit of 6.30 am tea follows us even down here. One awakens to the sound of a voice asking '*Hodi?*' (May I come in?) and one answers sleepily '*Karibu*' (Draw near) and from the balcony the bedroom boy steps in and the day has started. We have brought two Swahili books which we study until breakfast at 8 am, which is brought to us in our room. Then we get up and go for a swim, and walk upon the beach. Returning to the hotel we work on the herd books on the verandah until lunch. From 2 pm until 4 pm everybody goes to sleep. After a quick tea at four o'clock we go out again for a long walk until dark.

The climate here is quite different from the climate up-country. It is extremely hot, and one feels always surrounded by a damp, moist atmosphere. It would be unbearable, were it not that there is always either a stiff in-shore or out-shore breeze blowing. The moon on the sea at night looks very lovely.

The vegetation is also different. The trees are exceptionally fine, and quite the loveliest of them is the Flamboyant. It is a kind of acacia, with bright red and orange flowers, like big orchids, all over it. The flame colour against the blue sky is really breath-taking. Then there are the cashew nut trees, the paw-paw, mango and kapok trees, the coconut palm and the huge baobab trees.

Baobabs are very plentiful in the district. The trunk is far larger than any I have seen before, although the branches are rather small and bare, in little clusters. It is said that when God created the world, he was tired by evening of the sixth day, and he happened to be passing over this part of the world on his way home. He felt in his pocket and found one packet of seed left. Very worried that he should have forgotten this packet, he opened it and threw it over the land. This was the beginning of the baobab tree; but unfortunately, in his hurry, God planted the seed upside down, so that the roots of the tree are in the air and the branches underground. That is exactly what a baobab tree looks like – a giant oak planted upside down. The huge trunks are said to be hollow and the local tribe of natives, the Giriamas, burn a hole in the side and place their dead inside, standing upright, for the ants to dispose of them. For this reason they never cut down or mutilate a baobab, so they are well preserved.

These local Africans are also fine specimens, finer than those up-country, possibly because they have the advantage of fish in their diet. They are a very dark copper brown, not tall, but well built. The women wear grass skirts and are bare above the waist. They are cheery, nice people and they look very primitive.

In the hotel the boys are excellent, willing and well-trained. They are drawn from many different tribes but some of them are Swahili-speaking and we find it much easier to understand them than our boys at home.

Malindi town is very squalid and tumbledown. There are many Arabs living there and one sees their dhows out fishing before the hotel. The town is owned by a sheikh, from whom the British Government leases certain land. He, the sheikh, is the only man who can fly his standard from the ground. The

Union Jack flutters from a flagpole attached to a building.

On Wednesday and again on Friday we called in at Gedi. This city was built in the fifteenth and early sixteenth centuries by Arabs who, for several hundreds of years, had been settled up the coast of East Africa. It was abandoned in the latter part of the sixteenth or early seventeenth century and was re-discovered by an Englishman in 1925.

It was a large city covering an area of some eighty-four acres. Today the scrub has been cleared from most of the area but huge trees remain amongst the deserted ruins, some of them growing out of the very walls themselves. Baboons and snakes now live where once the proud Arab King of Malindi and Mombasa had his summer palace.

Why Gedi was abandoned is not known, but the most likely reason is that the wells dried up. The whole city is built on coral, out of coral blocks, although it is four miles from the sea (the coral reef extends six miles inland). Gedi is one of fifteen ruined and abandoned cities on this coast.

As we were coming away from our second visit we saw a deadly green mamba climbing a column whilst the Africans threw stones at it. I had to point out to them that the column had been there for hundreds of years and it was a pity to spoil it in 1950 just because a snake climbed up it. They pointed out that one of their number had died in less than an hour recently from one of those snakes.

These two trips to the abandoned city were undertaken when we were on our way to the Blue Lagoon. The Lagoon is fringed with palm trees, while the sand stretches, pearly white, around the edge of the water in a big semicircle. The water is translucent and a deep blue, streaked with bright green in places where there are deeper pools. The entrance to the Lagoon from the sea is barred by huge masses of land, and the sea recedes at low tide or advances at high tide through gaps between these land masses.

The hotel has a little snack bar amongst the palms. When we arrived a man who lives in one of the only three houses for miles around kindly sent his boy to shin up a palm tree for us, and he got us each an unripe coconut; he cut the top off it and we drank the milk, which was delicious.

The green of the hinterland, with its graceful palms, contrasting with the white glare of the sands and the blue of the sea made a beautiful picture. We bathed and the water was almost hot; as we walked into it we could see the bottom quite clearly, and it was so buoyant that I could float in a sitting position, with legs drawn up, but without moving my legs or arms. We took a long walk along the beach and picked up many cowrie and other brightly coloured shells to take back to David.

While we were lying on the sand a large Arab dhow with all its sails set passed swiftly across the horizon, and we wondered whether it had come from India or Persia, and where it was going.

On our second visit I was introduced to the sport of goggling. This consists of wearing goggles and special flippers on one's feet for swimming underwater. One has the impression of being at the aquarium. The sea-bed is lit up and clear, the coral is glowing red and white, the seaweed is waving about to the movement of the water, and wonderful fish swim slowly about amongst it all. It is like fairyland.

We are hoping to be able to obtain a new addition to the animal life at Rhodora to take back with us. Think of a word of eight letters, beginning with M, whose favourite dish is snake. They make charming pets and become quite affectionate.

21st January, 1950

On Wednesday we had a wretched day. Directly after lunch we went down to Nakuru where we met Mrs Stobbs, the Honorary Secretary of the Dog Show Committee. We collected the schedules from the printers, and then trailed around the various hotels to see who would take on the catering and bar arrangements for the show. Each one was more disappointing than the last, and at the final attempt we disturbed a pub-keeper in his afternoon nap with his secretary. You can imagine how popular we were.

Then we drove out to Njoro, a distance of some twenty miles, to the Stobbs' house. It was drizzling in Nakuru and windy, but the drizzle was not enough to lay the dust on the appalling road which leads to their home. We were glad to find a cup of tea awaiting us, and then she and her husband, Rosemary and I, all sat round the dining-room table, each with a job. Entry forms had to be folded; entry form put in schedule; schedule into envelope; envelope stuck up; stamp on envelope. We did 360. They have two visiting children who do lessons with their own small girl, and a cousin who is a teacher, to cope; but she does not cope, and the combination of children, cats, dogs, a parrot and a none too tidy or clean room made Rosemary's nose wrinkle in an alarmingly obvious manner. Instead of houseboys they have *bibis* in the house, which is unusual out here. One of these was named Tabitha, and seemed to be called for every five minutes, above the din.

At seven-thirty, the time at which we had said we must leave, we had still not quite finished, so we weakly agreed to stay to supper. This was (according to form) a pale cabbage soup, partially cooked curry and a chocolate mould, of sorts.

Next day in Nairobi we had a busy afternoon, and from four o'clock our peace was shattered because we fetched the little mongoose. If you can imagine a tiny object, about three inches long from the tip of its nose to the beginning of its tail, and then another inch and a half for its tail, you have him in a nutshell. All yesterday the whole household was turned upside down and completely dominated by this little creature. He is full of character and very sweet, almost too young to have been taken from his mother, but full of life and very alert. He makes three noises: one is a squeak when he is a bit lonely and looking for someone to make a fuss of him; the second is a tick-tick noise when he is busy looking for bugs in cracks in the floor and is quite contented; and the third is a purring sound, just like a cat, which he makes if you stroke his tummy. If you hold him in your hand he curls up and goes to sleep. He likes exploring everything, and is a most thorough little busybody, so much so that he decided to climb up inside my trouser-leg and as he neared the top, I hastily had to remove my trousers. Now, if he is about I roll my trousers up to the knee and he climbs up my leg to see if he can get down inside my sock.

When Monique came along after lunch he was asleep in a fold of her dress and he did not fall out, even though she was walking about. He has been so enchanting that no one has been able to do any work, so now he is banished to one of the travelling dog-boxes (with the holes covered with wire gauze) when we are busy. He loves meat but he will not drink milk. Today we gave him an egg, which he loved, but he is still too young to crack it himself. He is naturally house-trained and uses an earth tray at night and the lawn by day. David is not allowed to touch him but is tickled to death with him and goes about saying 'Where is the little mouse?' or 'Where is Wicky?' (We have named the mongoose Ricky.)

David is showing signs of taking after Rosemary's orderly ways. Everything has to be just so. Even if the blanket on his bed is not quite as it should be, he has now taken to making a scene, so Daddy was called in to cope last night. After being terribly severe he nearly spoilt the whole effect by melting when David, in between the most heart-rending sobs, said: 'Poor, poor David is cwying.'

P.S. Since writing this, Ricky climbed up the lavatory, fell in, and drowned. We are all *desolate*.

3

Everywhere was progress, but it was never as fast as we wanted it to be. There were always possibilities, new ways of using this wonderful land. I was concerned with the garden: what would do well here? Just about anything, was the answer to that – so I occasionally had to swallow Freddie's condemnation of a certain flourishing plant or tree as 'ugly', or try to make sense of his advice to make a natural hollow in the land into a lily-pond. (But what if we didn't have the water? What if we did, and we bred mosquitoes? – Freddie crisply advised a lily-pond full of mosquito fish. We installed a lily-pond.) As for more immediately profitable endeavours, we diligently fed our stock on the patent products of Arrow Foods, accepted with delight an official Coffee Research substation on our farm, and generally never stopped making plans for the future. The dogs, obedient to the general spirit of growth and endeavour, produced a litter.

The only cloud on the horizon was Clarke. We suspected that we needed to replace our stockman. We were certain that we needed a coffee manager. In the meantime we had visitors to take our minds off staff problems: our first house guests of the year were Sir John and Lady Mildred Fitzgerald (Jack and Milly).

29th January, 1950

On Sunday John and Janet Byng-Hall came to tea. . . . He has been out here for some years and has worked his way up to the position of General Manager of Lord Delamere's vast estate called Soysambu. Over tea we took the opportunity of asking him whether we might take Jack and Milly to see the flamingos on Lake Elmenteita. The expedition was arranged for the next day, but unfortunately, when Monday dawned, Jack felt very

71

ill with a migraine so Rosemary and Milly planned to go alone whilst I stayed at home to keep Jack company. However, this did not suit Jack, who was determined not to be left behind. Groaning and moaning, he rose from his bed just before we were due to leave and flopped into the back of the car. He would not come in to tea, but stayed firmly with his eyes closed in the back of the car while we tried airily to sort of explain him away to our hostess. . . . After tea we all motored down to the fascinating lake, whilst Jack continued to groan in the back with his eyes shut. Milly said,

'Don't take any notice of him – he always thinks he's dead.'

We took her advice, and will never know how much he enjoyed looking at the flamingos with his eyes tight shut.

As we stepped out of the car on the plain by the lake, we noticed the pungent smell of soda, and underfoot it was crumbly and soft from the dried droppings of the flamingos. We had stopped beside the tracks of a hippopotamus which had recently emerged from the lake and ambled up the stream of a small river which flowed into the lake at that point. We were not lucky enough to see him; perhaps he was busy with someone's crops further up the stream. On the surface of the lake were pink groups of flamingos, whilst round the edge there were numerous dippers of the usual English varieties. There were also many groups of avocets (the birds which have just come to breed again off the Norfolk coast after a break of some eighty years) and those birds were flying up and down all around us. They are said to be quite rare in Kenya but we saw large numbers. On our left, standing on the soda like a group of hunched-up old men, were some marabou storks looking for frogs. We saw small groups of teal swimming about, just as they do on the Round Pond in Kensington Gardens. But our most exciting find was a wood ibis (not the sacred ibis) which arrived whilst we were standing there and settled nearby.

It is an enormous lake (I think about twelve miles long) and John does not allow any shooting there. As we motored away we passed a wonderful fish eagle perched on a bush. John sent his young son, aged about eleven, to wade into the lake with a school friend of his in order to put up the flamingos and try to make them fly over us. They failed to do this, because the flamingos retreated as they advanced, but they did find a dead one, and they brought back some pink feathers for Rosemary.

5th February, 1950

Pigs have been a great source of interest this week. Two of the sixteen gilts which we bought at the Kabazi sale have now farrowed down and each has produced a litter of fourteen. We have a special pig man on duty, hanging over the sty to stop them lying on their many offspring for the first few days. All the gilts are so enormous that they nearly fill up their pens and anyway, being gilts they have no experience as mothers and are likely to be careless.

All the piggeries are now cleaned down daily so that they are spotless and there is a slate up over each pen, showing the details of the occupant. Every bacon pig is ear-numbered and weighed once a week. The whole organisation is backed by a comprehensive herd book which records the full details of the boars and sows showing their litter numbers, the weights of their progeny at three weeks and eight weeks, and the details of their grading after they have been sent to the bacon factory. We expect a baconer to be up to weight (eleven to twelve score) within six months at the most. We have had very good reports back from the bacon factory lately, and we have had top grading price for most of our animals. The reason for the improvement is undoubtedly the new food coupled with better management. In 1950 we expect to send away about 300 baconers.

On Thursday we had a visit from the only Horticultural Officer in Kenya. He confirmed what we had suspected for some time: that we have not got enough water on this farm to irrigate citrus as well as to carry a heavy coffee crop. So we must give up our hopes of growing oranges. He said that the crops which we could grow here without irrigation are peaches, almonds and grapes. The latter is rather an exciting idea. He sees no reason why both table and wine grapes should not grow very well here. Wine grapes would, of course, be difficult, because there is no wine industry in this country. But he sees no reason why there should not be a Kenya wine industry. . . . We want to put every corner of the farm to use in producing something profitable.

12th February, 1950

Sparks have been flying around Rhodora! We have given notice to Clarke, our stockman.

To start at the beginning: some time ago, when a director of Arrow Products (foods) came to visit us he said he thought that our imported heifers were not getting the right mineral mix and were not digesting their food thoroughly. Clarke took offence at these remarks, but we were inclined to agree with the man. As we had earlier proved that Clarke (in the matter of minerals) did not really know *what* he was feeding the animals, we decided to put these heifers onto Arrow Products. After a fortnight of the new diet Clarke said that in his opinion some of the heifers were losing condition; and he blamed Arrow Products. But when we looked into the matter, we saw that instead of giving them as much food as they had been having before their diet was changed, he had actually been giving them only one quarter as much. This was the last straw and there was a monumental row.

Everyone makes mistakes sometimes, and now we must face the expense which this mistake involves. . . . We have offered to pay the return passage for Clarke and all his family, and Clarke has accepted this, because he prefers the atmosphere of the Welfare State, where he does not have to pay for the education of his children, or for medical attention. I am going down to Nairobi tomorrow to find out about getting a passage for him. His son, John, is staying with us for the time being. He will be a good lad, we think, if he can be properly trained.

We have not yet told you about an experiment which we have decided to make, to find out which is likely to be the best type of bacon pig in Kenya, and the best diet for such a pig. We have ordered from England two gilts of approximately eight months old in each of the Tamworth, Large Black and Welsh breeds. The gilts have already been selected from prize-winning herds and will be shipped out by the first available boat. When they arrive we are going to put them each in a different pen and we are getting, locally, two gilts of the Wessex breed and two Large White gilts. One of each breed will be fed on a home-grown mix and the other will be fed on Arrow Products. They will all be mated to our Large White 'Wall Field Marshal' boar, and the progeny will be fed on home food or Arrow Products like the dams. Then we shall see, when the progeny go to the bacon factory, which produces the best carcass and which was the most economical in the production.

19th February, 1950

We went to lunch with Humphrey and Mary Bevan last Sunday. As Mariloo knows, he is a man of about sixty with a wife some ten years younger, and they have a son aged twenty-one. They emigrated here nearly three years ago and bought one of the best farms in the Subukia Valley. Now they have built a charming house there. It is off-white with a shingle roof and a certain amount of wrought-iron, and it overlooks a lovely view. It is furnished with their antique furniture brought from England. They seem to have an even better cook than our Gwara, and the eggs in aspic with mayonnaise sauce, followed by a beefsteak which melted in the mouth, went down very well.

Freddie started us on a wild goose chase after two prospective coffee managers, but when we got down to Nairobi, we found that one was extremely bad-tempered and did not want to come to us anyway, and the other was slowly drinking himself to death.

Tony had been furious with Clarke, and perhaps both sides said things in haste that they might have retracted later. Anyway I was to visit England for a month, and during that time I interviewed and engaged Tudor Ace, a stockman, and Tony found Mumford, a coffee manager from another Kenyan farm. Both were to remain with us for many years.

Ace left for Kenya straight away. His wife and two children followed later with me and Tony's sister Charmian. We left from Heathrow Airport, London.

9th April, 1950

As they walked out to the aircraft Rosemary and Charmian were astonished and delighted to see Mutz, Pops and Leo standing in the enclosure waving a sad goodbye. They must have been frozen and it was very sweet of them to wait like that. The aircraft took off and they peered down to catch the last glimpses of their family and of Heathrow; then they settled down together with books and read and talked the time away. Mrs Ace and her children moved up to the front of the plane so that they should have a table to play games. The journey to Castel Benito was fairly smooth though they landed there looking slightly green and a little ahead of schedule. Rosemary spent an amusing hour smelling Africa again with its aromatic odours (I say Elsans and Camels, but she says I am not aesthetic, and have no sense of smell) and she found a kind of mimosa tree with flowers twice the normal size.

On getting back into the plane they were shown a bad film after dinner; and then, whilst they cruised over the desert, they settled down to sleep, each with a double berth to themselves, as the plane was very empty. Approaching Khartoum the flying became bumpy, and everyone became rather bad-tempered at being turned out of the aircraft at two-thirty in the morning for an hour. Here they were told for the second time that they were ahead of schedule and would arrive at Nairobi at nine-thirty, one and a half hours early. They settled into a fitful sleep until daylight, when it started to be very rough as the plane came over the mountains of Uganda and Kenya . . . and a note was brought round by an officer saying that they had been advised to turn back to Entebbe in Uganda (on Lake

76

Victoria) because the Nairobi runway was flooded with torrential rain.

'But why Entebbe, of all God-forsaken places?' wailed Rosemary, and the officer patiently explained that Skymasters were so big that there were no facilities for such a monstrous craft at any other airport. . . . So the plane bumped them, rabid with rage, for one and a half hours more over to Lake Victoria and they skimmed over the surface of the lake to land on the airfield which is right beside it. There was no proper landing gangway for such a plane and the only way of getting down was by sitting on the floor and dropping, as gracefully as they could manage into a few outstretched arms.

They were taken off to the hotel, which was a surprisingly nice one, very modern and clean, situated at an altitude of about 4,500 feet above sea level. The air was warm and balmy and the countryside green and lush. With great delight Charmian and Rosemary were shown into a comfortable room with bathroom off, and emerged an hour later feeling like two different people, and ready to face the hour and a half ahead of what they know would be the roughest part of the journey. So it was; one non-stop bump; and as they touched down at Nairobi, Charmian (full of dramamine) said 'Five minutes more, and I should have been finished.'

16th April, 1950

We now have seven canines in the house and these represent so many delicious meals to the leopards that they walk round the house, drooling, all night. One night a leopard rattled the grille over the window beside Beatrice's bed, trying to get at Red, who was sleeping in the room – we know it was the leopard, because his pug marks were in the border outside. Monique and Beatrice nearly expired with fright. Another night when the houseboy was coming round the house to turn down our bed, he found a leopard sitting beside our verandah only a few yards from him.

About 250 acres of the crater land is now cleared, and much

of this is already fenced; we shall soon be mowing here too. The coffee is visibly recovering after its heavy crop as the rain sinks in. The two new piggeries, made of wattle poles and *makuti* thatch, are now complete and house some thirty sows and three boars. Our old Danish piggery has become the nursery for our baconers from the time they are weaned at eight weeks. The new cowshed is growing rapidly (Rosemary says it looks like a borstal institution at the moment).

Apart from a baby which fell into some boiling porridge, and got badly burned on one arm, and Gwara, who suddenly developed a serious fever which dispersed within twenty-four hours, there has been no other special excitement this week.

23rd April, 1950

There was a meeting of the Solai Association. This comprises all the local farmers, and they get together about every six weeks to discuss matters of mutual interest. It was the first time that we have been to one of these meetings, which are always held at one of the farmers' houses. This time the house belonged to a Mr and Mrs Milton, a very old couple who have farmed in the district for many years. We all sat on the spacious verandah in comfortable chairs. It was a sparkling, sunny morning after the recent rainy days. Rosemary amused herself by watching the many coloured birds in the large thorn tree on the lawn.

Mr Milton loves hearing himself speak and his wife gazes proudly at him on the frequent occasions when he rises to his feet, beginning 'This question does not concern me personally, but . . .' and as the argument develops, one finds that it concerns him vitally, and he has a strong personal interest in the matter.

Subjects for discussion ranged from water rights, to a request for a licence for a butcher's shop on a farm; from the political situation in Tanganyika, on which Michael Blundell, our member for Legco, ably spoke, to the wages which should be paid to a Kikuyu *bibi*. One felt the rumblings of age-old feuds between farmers who had been in the Valley for years, or heard the open clash of younger and more recent settlers. English was spoken in different ways: by Yorkshiremen and Scotsmen, by South Africans and Germans, by Dutchmen and even by a Frenchman. One felt that all were fundamentally united on the aims and objects of White Settlement.

The Chairman for the year is George Manuel. He made a picturesque figure in his khaki shorts, top boots and broad-brimmed colonial hat, with his thumbs always stuck into his belt. He has no idea how to be a Chairman but nobody seems to mind. There were long pauses during the meeting, with everyone sitting in silence while the Chairman and Secretary (Varley Everett) hastily read up what they should have known all about before they came.

It trailed on and on, and it was 2 pm before we got home for lunch. Charmian had spent a busy morning with the gardeners. We have made her foreman-gardener, and she has begun to get it all nicely in order, ready for the great planting activity which is due this coming week.

On Saturday we went up to Kabazi, stopping at Michael Blundell's on the way. We had heard rumours that his imported bull was the finest that had ever come into the country, and Rosemary was determined to see it, to satisfy our qualms that it might beat Valentine at the show in October. However, now we have seen it we were able to tell him what a nice animal it was with a joy in our hearts, because we do not think it can hold a candle to our Valentine.

We read to David every night before he goes to bed. In the nursery rhyme book there is, of course, the story of 'The Butcher, the Baker and the Candlestick Maker'. These three gentlemen are depicted at sea in a leaky-looking boat. On this particular afternoon I was visited by the representative of a large firm in Nairobi from which we are buying some equipment for the new cowshed. He was a young man with a huge 'handlebar' moustache who told us that his hobby was motor-racing. When I took him in to tea everyone was already seated, so I introduced him all round, saying 'This is Mr Baker'. David's eyes glistened and he began to stare. At the first pause in the conversation he said with awe in his voice 'It's the *Baker*, Daddy'. Almost too good to be true: the character in his storybook had really come to life!

30th April, 1950

On Monday we set off to the field where the herd was grazing, to go through it cow by cow, to decide our breeding policy for each animal. We sat down on the newly-made water trough with our papers, Tudor and his little son and our two selves, together with the head herd boy Kipsang. Just as we were going to start, the tractor arrived to collect some stone beside the water trough.

From this moment our peace of mind and good spirits suffered many setbacks. First of all, the other herd boys had not arrived, and one boy could not possibly collect all the cattle when wanted; so we had to wait for some time before they decided to turn up. Meanwhile the tractor boys were dodging about in a distracting fashion, collecting the stone, and just as they had finished loading and the driver was revving up to leave, there was a loud splutter, and the tractor engine subsided into dead silence. Tudor thought that this was just the moment to display his knowledge of the insides of tractors, so herd books were scattered to the winds and only the back end of Tudor was seen from then on.

At this moment the baboons, which we had disturbed on arriving at the field, were assembled again at a family conference on a nearby knoll, scratching their fleas and making faces at us. This so tantalised me that I returned urgently to the house to get my gun, which I then steadied for a long time on the immobile tractor amidst a crowd of admiring Africans, and scored a direct miss.

We arrived at lunch-time with nothing achieved, except that we had managed to put the cows' yields down for the day by disturbing their morning's grazing.

Wednesday was my birthday, and we planned a picnic lunch and tea with a visit to Cooper's Nursery Garden at Elburgon.

First of all at 9 am I went off to the police court to bear witness against our calf boy, who had tried to steal a bottle of milk. Here I heard some news about the recent incident up at Suk (which was reported on the BBC News) when four European policemen were murdered.

Apparently the Suk are a very backward, savage tribe and this affair arose over a small group of some 300, who were religious fanatics. The Europeans went out with African policemen to recapture an escaped convict who was leader of the group. Whilst they were parleying they were suddenly, and without warning, riddled with spears. The African police opened fire, and killed about twenty of the Suk, including the convict. It is a dreadful business, but it was a purely local affair and does not have repercussions in this district.

In the evening we listened, grandly, to the News from London relayed through Nairobi, on the baby radio which Rosemary has given me for my birthday.

On Thursday I attended a *baraza* which was held by the Labour Officer for all the surrounding farms. There were some hundreds of Africans, including about ninety from this farm, and they all sat around whilst he talked to them. He told them all to be good boys and to work hard, etc. etc. He spoke for an hour and a half and I think he did a lot of good. I brought him back here to lunch with me.

John Ward's wedding to Pam was to be the social event of the year for our circle, and we went down to Nairobi in a mood of delighted celebration, taking the opportunity while we were there to entertain a couple of visitors from France.

21st May, 1950

We arranged to meet again for a quick cup of tea at four o'clock before going out into the Game Park. There, at first we hardly saw a thing, and thought that we were going to be disappointed, until suddenly, against the skyline we spotted a pair of giraffes, and as we came upon them we saw they were males fighting. The method of attack was for one to back into the flank of the other and gradually, step by step, push him across the plain. Then from time to time they would swing their necks and catch each other a resounding *thwack* with their heads, which made a noise that could be heard a long way off. All this took place right beside us, for they were too preoccupied in the fight to take any notice of the car.

We watched for at least an hour, and just as darkness fell, twelve more giraffes quietly and silently arrived on the scene. They stood around and watched curiously for a little while; then they moved off in groups, grazing. We had also a visit from a hyena, which came to review the scene of battle for a moment.

Reluctantly, we left them all when it got too dark to see any more, but still they were fighting, and we longed to know how it would all end. On the way back we found some cars with their headlights on two lionesses. We joined in and stayed watching for a short while. The nearest lioness was about fifteen yards from our car. One of the other cars kept flicking its headlights on and off until its occupants managed to move the lioness away. This is just what the game wardens have been asking the public not to do for weeks in the press, and at the gates of the game park one of them was blocking the exit, as we were there twenty minutes after closing time and it was a very dark night. He was in a furious rage, accusing us of worrying the lions after dark. No excuses were listened to; we were to appear before a magistrate in Nairobi, and could tell him all we wanted to then; finally, he hoped that we would never come into the park again.

Somewhat abashed, we returned to the club and recounted the sad tale to Freddie, with whom we were dining. He and Vi had been down in Nairobi since before the week-end, together with John and Pam and Mrs Swinton-Home. The first three were staying at the Muthaiga Club, but Pam and her mother were staying at Lady McMillan's house called 'Chiromo' where the reception was to be held. The dinner was very gay and consisted of Freddie and Vi, John and Pam, Sir Charles Markham's son and daughter-in-law, Charmian and ourselves.

We went to bed quite late, and the next morning we were up early because Freddie had decided that he and I should go to the office of the Kenya National Parks in order to object to the game warden's rudeness. When we arrived there, bursting with simulated indignation, we told of the treatment we had received at a time when we were entertaining 'important French financial interests' who were now so disgusted that we had great difficulty in persuading them to stay in the country at all. (All this was quite untrue.) These arguments proved so effective that, far from continuing with the threatened prosecutions against us, the Deputy Director apologised to us all the way down the stairs!

On Wednesday morning we set off early to do some more shopping, as we had to be back at the Club by about twelve in order to change for the wedding. The service was charming, with a beautiful choir, the first wedding service to be held in Kenya with choral accompaniment. Pam had to abandon her cream wedding dress, because it was sent off from England by sea mail instead of air mail, but she made a pretty picture with a pinky beige tulle dress embroidered with little gold spangles, and her two tiny pages, and three equally tiny bridesmaids, were in satin suits and dresses of exactly the same colour. The flowers were well arranged and profuse in yellow, gold and bronze colours which blended harmoniously. The reception was at Chiromo, which is a large and spacious house with a series of reception rooms, one leading into another, and from the verandah along the front are steps down to descending terraces, with a winter garden at the far side of the lawn. Massed orange bougainvillea and yellow alamanda interspersed with lovely herbaceous flowers made it all a perfect setting.

4

We were having an exciting few months: Naomi and Bertrand, my sister and brother-in-law, were expected. Dr Bertrand Goldschmidt is a distinguished French atomic scientist and had just been awarded the Legion d'Honneur. *We planned a tour with them which would take us to the Congo. First, we had a less welcome visitor.*

28th May, 1950

Sunday morning was spent dragging a reluctant and uninterested Mr Mark Smith round the farm and stock. Then Mrs Howard (Peter's mother) came to lunch and we showed her the newly-planted garden, which interested her a lot as she is busy making their garden on virgin land a few miles away. Unfortunately, she had to leave early as she has been so ill and 'Uninterest' again settled heavily upon us, following us even to where we have cleared, down in the crater land, where the view of Menengai, coupled with the hum of the myriads of insects, the vivid green of the new thorn-tree shoots and the sweet-smelling wild flowers were all at their loveliest in the warm afternoon sun. On the way back we found the dogs excitedly barking beside a low bush, and on investigation, we found a monstrous, hissing and loudly protesting tortoise. Everyone wanted to bring it home to decorate our lawn, but Rosemary was adamant and said we had quite enough to look after, what with 230 cattle, 150 pigs, seven dogs and one black cat, not to mention Humphrey, the chameleon, and David, the child. Back to a late tea, when Mr Mark Smith eventually announced that he wished to depart, amidst silent cheers and a marked lack of polite protestation.

Having seen him off we all gaily set out to see the end of milking and watch Ace and John busy setting up a high class beauty parlour for the two decrepit cows (pedigree) which were going to be sold the next day at Charles Long's auction ground just outside Nakuru. First, both cows were washed and shampooed from nose to tail; then, horns and hooves were polished and tails crimped and tied into curling rags. Rosemary and Charmian thanked heavens they were not the cows, because Ace has not the gentle hand of Louis or of Elizabeth Arden, and he slapped the soap and polish on unmercifully.

There was quite a crowd at the sale and a certain amount of backchat with the auctioneer. The cattle were mostly Ayrshires, and some were quite nice but some were just awful, straight off the ranch. We took a picnic lunch, and Ace and Mrs Ace, Charmian and ourselves, together with Bill Murray, editor of the Stud Book, got right down to eating it before our cattle came into the ring. At zero hour, our two were led in – which was a great compliment, because all the other animals had been driven in and around. Rosemary and I tried to look as if we had nothing to do with our animals, whilst being secretly smug that they had been turned out to look like aristocrats after their beauty treatment. Somebody in the crowd said 'Ooo, they've washed their tails!' and to our delight, we got £50 and £75.

These two cows were bequeathed to us with the farm. The cheaper one gave us seventy gallons in her lactation and was then relegated to nurse cow in the second lactation; the other one had foot-and-mouth three years ago and took us nine months to get into calf, and also had partial paralysis of the forelegs. Rosemary frightened the life out of me by starting to reveal all our secrets to a complete stranger, whom she termed 'rather attractive', who had bought one of our cows, but who (I happened to know) had a reputation for unsavoury financial practices, besides being a conscientious objector.

4th June, 1950

Last Sunday we set off in the car to Kabazi up the escarpment road, which winds up a steep hill with magnificent views of the Rift Valley on either side. As we approached our destination Charmian was thrilled to see the Sunday native market with all the vivid colours of the dresses, the wares displayed for sale, the chatter, and the bargaining.

We did not stay long at Kabazi, but proceeded to the Charles Longs' house. We sat around talking and patiently awaiting lunch, which was announced at about two-fifteen, by which time we were all three starving. A lovely chicken appeared. It was immediately pounced upon, amidst shouts and screams, by the four pedigree Siamese cats, supported by the Alsatian and prompted by the miniature Dachshund. During the pandemonium the gravy was quietly upset right over Rosemary, from shoulder to toe, by one of the boys, who just gaped in agonised horror and failed to straighten the tray, thus adding bread sauce to the already ruined pleated skirt and pale pink jacket.

After this, it was decided that the skirt must be sponged to get the worst of it out, so off trekked Mattie Long with Rosemary to the bathroom. On seeing the polished floor of the corridor, Rosemary decided that there was only one thing left really to make her hostess happy, so she went sprawling for six, saying to Mattie that a broken leg was what was required to complete the party. . . .

Next day we called at the Post Office in Nakuru and then wound our way up through a bamboo forest, climbing all the time. When we reached the top we felt we were on the lid of the world, and the view for miles was as if we were in the air. After an hour and a half we reached Thomson's Falls. These are five different waterfalls, and the fall of the water is very steep. We sat watching it over an iced orangeade on a bench under a tree and then went in to lunch at the hotel. Our departure was delayed by a garrulous old woman, the owner of the hotel, who told us all about her four sons in England and about people who live at heights of 7,500 feet and over, who, she said, are all quite cracked in the head.

86

From here we went on another eighty miles across a colossal plain, driving straight towards Mount Kenya which was shrouded in clouds. Charles, our new driver, who has replaced Karanja, said that the mountain was unhappy because it had its hat on. We saw buck, baboons and ostriches, some of which were actually on the road. For tea we called at Kenya's latest luxury hotel, called Mawingo (which means 'cloud') at Nanyuki. It is situated on a knoll facing the mountain and was formerly a private house built by a Frenchman named Prudhomme, who had an American wife. It is on two storeys, in the shape of a double L. The top floor has a huge verandah round it which covers a large passage underneath. The house is painted palest grey-blue with soft brown wooden tiles on the roof and pale pink chimney pots. The arms of the double L enclose a quiet, almost monastic, garden with two lily ponds and big flowing creepers and shrubs which climb up onto the verandah, smelling exotically. From the garden one walks on, down through a wrought-iron gate, to a rose-garden, also surrounded by hedges and flowering shrubs of every hue. Inside, the house has been left much as it was when it was sold, which was after its abandonment by the American wife, following the death of her husband when flying during the war. The luxury suites are quite as comfortable as Claridges – in fact even better, because they have a view onto the side of Mount Kenya, which is wonderful.

We went on to the Outspan at Nyeri. We had a quick walk around the garden in the dusk along a border filled with bright red cannas and other flowers, and then back to change for dinner and early to bed. On Tuesday, the White Hunter who was to take us up to Treetops came over to tell us that we were leaving at one-thirty. The party consisted of us three, and a wizened, dried-up little man with his sister-in-law and the White Hunter. At the appointed hour we all got into the cars, the other three in front in a deluxe American car, whilst we followed in the old hotel bone-shaker with an African driver. We were proceeding down the track leading to the disembarkation point when we saw a huge bull elephant with enormous tusks (one broken) beside the track. He did not seem to like us at all. At first he moved hastily out of the way to let the two cars pass; but then he changed his mind and with his trunk held high in the air, started to follow our car which was the rear one. While this was going on our car seemed terribly small and the elephant terribly large. The incident so terrified the White Hunter (a doddery old boy with a shaky hand doing duty in place of Colonel Cochrane, the usual one, who had been mauled by a wounded buffalo the week before) that he bundled us out of the cars and set off with his gun up the forest track almost at a trot. Rosemary and I brought up the rear, panting, as one has to go in single file.

With much relief we all arrived safely at our hotel in the trees and climbed up the long ladder. The outside balcony now has camouflage netting and comfortable long seats, so that one can be outside watching by day as well as by night. Round about 4 pm the animals began to appear, gliding onto the scene from the forest tracks. Beneath the trees there is a large mud pan, about the size of a football field, where salt is put down for the animals. Next to it is a natural pool where they can drink. Our first visitors were bush-buck, water-buck and wart-hogs; then there was a crashing through the undergrowth and out came a rhino, followed a little later by five buffalo cows, each with a calf at heel. As darkness fell, the frogs in the pool started their earsplitting symphony which was punctuated by the weird cries of hammerhead storks, owls and many other birds. All night, the animals came and went and occasionally there was a shriek from the family of bush-babies which lives in the fig-tree itself, right outside the balcony. There were many more rhinos, buffalo, hyenas and giant forest hog, but we were unlucky with the elephants that night, for we saw no more than the isolated bull on the way up.

11th June, 1950

On Monday Peter McMaster came with his wife, who is at least thirty years younger than he is and is kept tightly on a leash (and we think she resents it). That evening we had promised to dine with a couple of old settlers: the wife is short and dumpy; she definitely cuts her own hair, and it hangs dank and straight around her face in a short bob, plus the inevitable slide and kirby grips. Their house is like an old junk-shop, with rhino horns and hooves all around the walls and fireplace. One sits on the sofa and the springs seem to stick into every part of one's body. Black, baleful-looking cockroaches peep at one from the corners of the room. Knowing what we were in for, Rosemary lay on her bed after her bath and refused to get dressed. Eventually, half an hour late for dinner, she was ready to leave the house, armed with knitting, aspirin and indigestion pills, together with a large overcoat. However the hour of dinner did not really seem to matter, for we had to drink Coca-Cola and brandy and soda until 10 pm before we adjourned to the dining room, and did not get away until nearly midnight. In spite of all this we enjoyed the evening, because they are such completely genuine and kind people, free from all pretentiousness or affectation.

18th June, 1950

Immediately after lunch we all set off for a farm at Moiben, passing a few giraffe on the road, a distance of some thirty miles. The Guernsey herd there is owned by a Colonel Wallington whose wife has recently left him and married the son of our corn merchant at Horsham. Our general impression was that Wallington had been somewhat shattered by the breakdown in his marriage and that the herd was suffering accordingly. It was all rather a shambles and the animals looked neglected. The house was sad and gloomy and a wild little boy ran around without shoes.

The next day we went to Kitale and on beyond, through rich arable farming land, up into the foothills of Mount Elgon, to find a man who is a member of the Council of the Guernsey Society. Rosemary excelled herself with a never-to-be-forgotten remark as we approached.

'Oh,' she said, 'Look at those lovely Guernseys!'

We all looked, and it was three donkeys which had coloured themselves in red mud.

This man's house was right on the edge of a wonderful Podo tree forest, and he showed us a fine specimen in the garden which was twenty-three feet around the trunk.

After lunch we called in on another Guernsey breeder, travelling up a long and beautiful avenue of gum trees to a house built in the Italian style, but he was sick in bed. From here we called on yet another, but he was out, though his wife showed us a little of his stock. She appeared in a dressing-gown which did not meet very well, and curling pins, with red-painted toenails – which shook us a bit.

On our return to the Club at Soy there was a telegram awaiting me which I took hastily to Rosemary and Charmian. It informed us that Charles had been picked up dead drunk the previous evening after an accident with another car and that our Ford Prefect was severely damaged. I tried for two hours to get a message through to the Swiss girls but failed. I knew they would be wondering why the car had not come back, and if Rosemary was safe. Then we went out to dinner with the Swinton-Homes who have a lovely house next door. We dined by candlelight off a Dresden dinner service and the dinner was beautifully cooked and served.

In Nairobi, we said a regretful goodbye to Charmian and then –

2nd July, 1950

We went back to the Club for an early dinner and then to the broadcasting station about eight miles out of town. Here I was to give my talk on Guernseys. It was a pouring wet night as we drove up but inside it was warm and friendly. We were greeted by the two announcers, a Mr Forbes and a Mr Bobby, and we sat in an ante-room while a selection of people and gramo-phone records arrived to take their part in 'The Up-Country Programme.' There was Pat Fisher, the beauty specialist in

Nairobi, who came with the gentleman who had recently decorated her new shop and they had a radio discussion on women's faces and new curtains; then there were three gentlemen who were supposed to represent a South American band, and they made queer noises for a quarter of an hour in a corner of the studio; then I came on and talked for about ten minutes. We all made great friends and made faces at each other through the glass whilst we were doing our acts. (At this point our black cat, Rasputin, has arrived on our bed. He says that he misses Charmian a lot but, as he now gets breakfast at the Swiss Consulate, lunch and tea with us and dinner as usual in his bedroom in the office, he is not putting off too much weight.) After the broadcast we went to see *The Blue Lamp*, the film about the British police force, and we thought it was excellent. This was only the third film we have seen since we have been in Kenya and it was a lovely change from cows.

On Thursday I had to call the vet to an eleven-year-old cow which was having a bad calving. The vet stayed for four and a half hours, trying to extract the calf, which had slipped into a completely inaccessible position; by the time he had finished, not only was the calf dead, but the old cow was terribly damaged inside. So I had to have her led into the coffee, which is our animal cemetery, and I shot her. She was a good grade cow which had given us over 900 gallons in her last lactation but, as she was getting on in age, one did not feel the loss so much, though Ace was reduced to tears over it.

Roy and Nancy Laird arrived to have lunch and spend a farming afternoon and evening with us. We like this couple very much and it was an enjoyable day, going round every corner of the place with them.

9th July, 1950

On Monday we spent the whole morning with Mr Sayers, the builder, in our new dairy buildings, planning the water system. The building is coming on well and half of the roof is finished but I doubt if we shall be in before the end of August. It looks derelict just now, stone and wood heaped up everywhere and torn paper from cement bags thrown about, and because we have not had any rain for a little while the dust swirls around. On top of that, much to Rosemary's fury, I am pulling out all the trees along the road there, for they are a type of tree which takes all the moisture from the coffee opposite the bull pens. Next year we shall plant others, of a different type, in an avenue on each side of the road; but just now it adds to the general grimness of the scene, to see large trees torn out by their roots and lying about on all sides. Mrs Cartwright, who is a member of the Council of the Guernsey Society, came to tea and we discussed the details of a tour round herds in Kenya which we are planning for our judge when he comes from England in October. She is in her fifties, husband dead or gone (not sure which) and is one of the Duchess of Gloucester's best friends out here. When the Gloucesters came to stay with her last March she hastily installed indoor sanitation and other improvements in her small house. Now, she told us, Prince Henry had told her he will send out a bull calf from his Guernsey herd at Barnwell.

On Wednesday afternoon, Monique and Beatrice had a half-day off, and we were expecting Mr Eames to tea as he was going to purchase our bull, White Ladies Champion, for whom we paid 450 guineas at Kitale some months ago. David was not in the best or easiest of moods that afternoon. It was hot and sultry, and as Rosemary brought him around, washed and changed for tea, our prospective client arrived. At the same moment I arrived from the opposite direction with a beaming and bouncing Mrs Gaymer and husband in tow. More cups and plates were brought, and Mrs Gaymer flopped down on the sofa talking about dogs and pigs while Rosemary tried to answer her politely, pour out tea and cut up bread and butter for David. Mr Gaymer and Mr Eames, both slightly deaf, shouted at each other across the table. The Alsatian was then fetched to join the tea-party, as he had broken the window of the car trying to reach Mrs Gaymer. She of course insisted on seeing our three dogs and the two puppies, so you can imagine what pandemonium it was.

Naomi and Bertrand arrived from Paris with Naomi's daughter Jocelyne.

23rd July, 1950

On Friday we had Lord Delamere to tea and took him all around the stock. He likes cows of whatever breed (though he is really a Jersey fan) but he wants to know a bit about Guernseys because his stepson, Michael Cunningham Reid, is going in for them on a farm he has just bought not far from here. We had some talk about the locust menace and he told us, just to cheer us on, that he had never had more than 15,000 acres eaten by them at one sitting.

Bertrand and I, with Monique, made an expedition into the crater on Saturday morning. Everyone was terrified of snakes but we never saw a single one. What we did see were a number of hyrax, which are little furry animals, like large otters. The lava underfoot in the crater looked like home-made toffee. We walked for three hours before getting home again. Bertrand has managed to discover a vulcanologist called Monsieur Richard, who lives fairly near us, and this gentleman came to tea; there was much to talk about lava and other scientific matters, and Rosemary has hardly slept since, because he said that the most recent lava in the crater was only 150 years old. She now expects us to be blown up at any minute.

We set off for what was, in those days, the Belgian Congo.

13th August, 1950

We climbed into the deluxe coach of Messrs Overseas Touring Company, and started our journey. First stop Njoro, second Elburgon. Here the bus refused to start, and only after much pushing would it agree to go on. This pantomime was repeated at every stop and soon we were behind schedule. Result: the African driver put his foot down on the accelerator, regardless of steep hills, violent skids through mud, narrow bridges and passing vehicles. Bertrand turned himself back to front and started discussing the Belgian Congo with a neighbour, Naomi and Tony hung onto the sides of their seats and Rosemary decided that the best way to blot out the speeding landscape was to go to sleep. After a time we reached the main, red dust road, along which we catapulted until, with a screech of brakes, we stopped abruptly. A mysterious conversation ensued between the driver and his mate, and we suspected that all our suitcases lay strewn between here and Nakuru. After reversing for half a mile, however, we picked up an empty, flattened, cardboard box.

In Kisumu the following day, we collected our luggage and the little Kisumu Hotel bus took us to the quay. We were immediately pounced on by at least a dozen boys, fighting over who should take our luggage. The cases were nearly torn in half before Tony rescued them and sorted it all out.

The boat is 1,300 tons and has a tall, thin funnel; the Europeans' quarters are on the main deck aft, Africans and cargo forward, and down below were the Asians and the dining saloon. Each couple had a cabin, but on different sides of the ship. These were quite comfortable, with two little beds, two chests of drawers and a wash-basin with continuous hot water.

We settled in, changed into cotton dresses and open-necked shirts, as it was pleasantly warm, and read on deck until lunch. Lake Victoria, which is at about 3,500 feet, is the largest lake in the world and one of the main sources of the Nile. The land looked rather far away, but it was green in the distance with the inevitable blue of African mountains.

Next day, after a restless night, we were awoken at six with shouts and calls as we drew alongside the jetty at Port Bell. After breakfast we went ashore and inspected the miscellaneous merchandise stacked up ready for loading. A most interesting party of coloured dockers, wearing neat khaki shorts, no shirts, and small round khaki caps, were loading 200 lb bags of sugar. They were all tall men with powerful shoulders, and bodies shining with the heat of their work. We reckoned that they had some 1,000 bags to handle before they

94

finished. It was all done to a rhythm. Two gangs were working. Each foreman, with a special shriek or call of his own, started four men lifting each corner of a sack. A fifth man ran underneath and carried it on his shoulder over to another pile, waiting for the winch to descend and pick it up, to hoist it into the hold.

We threaded our way through a crowd of African women and children dressed in the gayest of colours, cornflower blues, canary yellows, poppy reds and every other colour imaginable. Some were sitting on empty boxes and some strolling along with their babies.

We left Port Bell and after lunch and a rest, arrived at Entebbe at about three. A note was brought up to us and we contacted our driver from the Overseas Touring Company, a Mohammedan with a tall red fez, who was standing beside a huge maroon Hudson car. The hotel and grounds were very deluxe, the beds and food excellent. We strolled down to the Botanical Gardens after tea, where wonderful trees of many kinds grow on lawns that sweep down to the lake. On the lake shore we saw a herd of native cattle grazing; a baby calf was born and the herdsman carried it off on his shoulders to safety, followed by its mother.

Leaving Entebbe, we called at Kampala and left in pleasant sunshine at about 10 am. The landscape is very different from Kenya's. On each side of the red, dusty road is high green elephant grass, which obscures the view. In Kenya one can see the far distant mountains that change colour at all hours of the day. Here, there are acres of dense forest, with tall trees and thick undergrowth and areas of native cultivation – small banana plantations, coffee (multiple, as at Rhodora, but not pruned, so that it looks quite different from ours although it bears a heavy crop on its long tall branches), ground nuts and cotton newly planted, looking like little green beans in a vegetable garden. There is also cassava, a small, spidery, sycamore-leafed tree, the roots and fruit of which are eaten by the Africans; sugar canes, resembling maize; rubber trees, and many date palms.

We stopped, at intervals, to examine these products at close

95

quarters, and were also obliged to halt when our luggage rack began to slip off the roof. Halfway, we took our picnic basket and coats and sat under an enormous mango tree just off the road. We remarked that the people of Uganda, generally speaking, have a higher standard of living than those of Kenya. They look better fed and clothed and their houses are less like hovels, and contain a little furniture. A few even grow flowers outside their houses, and it is gay to see an unexpected splash of scarlet cannas or poinsettias or a clump of profusely flowering moon-flowers – a bush with large leaves and huge, cream, pendulant, bell-like flowers.

At the Mountains of the Moon hotel, where we stayed that night, the garden was a mass of colour and there was the largest clump of moon-flowers that we have ever seen. We walked down a track between high elephant grass, with cross-paths leading to native huts, and were followed by a small *toto* with a very 'pregnant' tummy who told us that his home was 'up there'; but when we finally turned back he continued to follow us saying that he now lived 'down there' . . . We wondered if we ought not to take him back to share the half-inch of hot water awaiting us in the hotel, but twenty-five cents sent him joyously skipping in the opposite direction.

Four days after the start of our journey we were on the ferry again, this time with two cars on board, so that the back of our Hudson hung perilously over the edge, and the other car's front wheels were literally only four inches from the water. As we reached the other side we saw a pelican sitting like a small boat on the surface, and two handsome, large eagles, with black and white heads and necks, perched in a tree watching us disembark.

Fifteen miles from this point we turned off the road to the very edge of Lake Edward, and saw a dazzling white sheet of pelicans, the water dotted with the black and pink heads of hippopotami. Some were standing on *terra firma*, but retreated into the lake as soon as they saw our car. They then lay submerged, just offshore, their little eyes watching us, flicking an ear now and then, and occasionally diving or making a curious grunting bark. The smell of pelican droppings and hippopotamus dung was overpowering.

96

By the first of August we were en route from Mutwanga to Butembo via Beni, a distance of about eighty miles. We passed long avenues of palm-oil trees and banana groves and soon reached a small forest which led down to the Semliki river. This we crossed on a raft, which the Africans punted across with poles. On a tree by the bank, hundreds of chattering, singing birds, all black, flew in and out of their nests, which hung like coconuts from the branches of the trees.

At Beni there were shops and neatly tiled houses behind the avenues of palm-oil trees; gay cotton materials hung in the shops. We turned into the Ituri forest, where pygmies live, as well as game such as elephant and the rare okapi. As luck would have it, we came across a group of about thirty pygmies dancing with a reed pipe and skin drum by the side of the road near some huts. These Lilliputians, though they are only about four feet high, have perfectly formed bodies, and the women exceptionally pretty breasts; they all have rather large posteriors. Otherwise, one feels surprised to see people of all ages such perfect miniatures of the ordinary African. The older the woman, the more numerous will be the holes she has in her upper lip. A variety of ornaments are stuck through these perforations: bits of coloured stick, pieces of grass, and even a sort of cross between a safety-pin and a fish-hook. They also have pieces of stick stuck right through both nostrils. They wear very little, a frilly skirt with a bright green bunch of leaves stuck on the back, or a loin-cloth. Their hair is cut like a skull-cap and some of the older men are extremely hairy. The smell was overpowering, and while Rosemary got into the car, Bertrand and Tony took many photographs, and Tony examined their weapons: he saw wooden, pointed arrows, very slender, with poison on the ends – they seem to use a bow and not a blow-pipe. As we left we gave them salt, cigarettes, and a handful of fifty-franc pieces.

One week later we were in Astrida, the bustling little capital of Ruanda-Urundi (a former German province, given to the Belgians after the First World War).

We found the hotel dirty and disappointing. After spinning a coin, Tony and Rosemary got the room with a bathroom (at great expense, 200 francs more than usual) while Naomi and Bertrand were not so lucky. We had a cup of tea and went straight to the rehearsals for the fête in honour of the fiftieth anniversary of the arrival in Ruanda-Urundi of the White Fathers, who are Roman Catholic monks.

A huge stage surmounted by a cross was set on one side of a square, whose other sides were the walls of the seminaries and a very large church, built in soft pink brick with rusty tiled roofs. The actors were 400 Africans, all seminarists, and they were rehearsing a Passion Play, directed by the White Fathers. There was a bevy of loudspeakers and arc lights but we found it difficult to piece it together, although we were interested since there is music and dancing throughout the piece, and these particular people are reputed to be the finest dancers in Africa.

However, we discovered next day that there was soon to be a full dress rehearsal in daylight, for the benefit of the cinematograph companies, so we put off our departure by a day to see it.

When the time came we took up our positions in the stand, which seemed to be reserved for Europeans. Everywhere was a seething mass of African women in their best cotton sarongs; they were mostly Watutsis. The married women had hair brushed up into a cone, so that their heads appeared to be elongated and distorted. The young girls are distinguishable by another hairstyle, the hair being cut in deep ridges, the shape of two half-moons. Some have extremely aristocratic faces, and all are rather beautiful. The other tribe amongst them are the local Bantu, who wear gold bands around their heads and are considered to be on a lower social plane than the Watutsis. Many of them crowded into the stand all around us and blocked the staircase. Behind us were white and black Sisters. The white Sisters wore long white flowing robes, with scarlet cords to their rosaries, and huge white veiled topees; the African Sisters wore dark French grey. They all had wonderfully serene faces. On all sides there were thousands of Africans, and dotted amongst them one saw a few Arabs and the red fezzes worn by Mohammedans.

Suddenly there was silence and little scarlet-cloaked pages appeared on stage, long trumpets in hand, and took up their positions. The three-act pageant began with a fanfare of music.

Act One told the story from the Garden of Eden to the birth of Christ. In the Garden of Eden, tiny half-caste children (who are looked after by nuns), danced out onto the stage with large yellow butterfly wings on their backs; then a real aboriginal Adam and Eve wended their way happily, hand in hand, into the Garden picking fruit as they went, while bird-song and other sounds were relayed in music. They met the serpent, who acted very well, and tempted Eve to pluck the forbidden apple. From then on the Devil and his satellites took charge.

The Devil's part was taken beautifully by a tall, virile black seminarist, dressed in reds of different hue, with excellent elocution (all the spoken words are in the Watutsi language) and he danced superbly, leaping rhythmically and tirelessly about the stage. After the satellites had done their native dance, suffering humanity crowded onto the scene in an endless stream of bowed forms. The Seven Deadly Sins appeared (Idleness was carried in a sedan chair), there was a long portrayal of Idol Worship, and the Seven Deadly Sins scourged the rest of humanity off the stage. With the sacrifice of a small boy to the Idol the scene came to a close.

In Act Two (the Nativity to the Resurrection) Jesus was played by an African, who interpreted the long and difficult part with great dignity; and in Act Three, the Watutsis were seen under Arab rule before the triumph of Good over Evil with the arrival of the White Fathers in 1900. This was when the Ntori, or Royal Dancers, appeared. Their physique is superb. On their heads they were wearing waving headdresses of fur; around the hips, some scarlet and white material; and on their legs, some large bracelets of bells, which rang when they moved.

At the grand finale, twelve Belgian children appeared with their national flag, stood amid the entire African cast of 400, and led them in the Belgian national anthem.

5

Our farming year was settling into a routine, punctuated not only by the usual round of planting and harvesting, but importantly for us, by attendance at shows. In 1950 our cattle did extremely well on their first appearance at the Royal Show at Nakuru; we entered ten animals and were awarded ten prizes. As the years went on we would do even better; but at first there was some resentment at our success.

Livestock suffered from diseases in Kenya which were almost unheard-of in England. We were forever calling out the vet. And human beings were more vulnerable too: I thanked Heaven that I had trained as a nurse during the war, for I had to attend more than one difficult birth among the African women.

The Africans often seemed slightly suspicious of our medicine. Perhaps they had heard strange tales, like the one about Jasper Maskelyne. This famous magician was preparing to settle near Nakuru at about this time. We heard that when he gave a show for the Africans, he got to the point where he sawed a lady's arm off, and the native boy who had got up on stage to help him was sick; and when he began to saw the woman in half, the whole audience got up and left. . . .

When Bertrand and Naomi left we settled down to some hard work, before departing for a short stay at the coast.

27th August, 1950

We have started silage making. The maize is still green, and the cobs are soft. The boys cut a small area with a panga (a native knife) and then the tractor and both ox-carts bring the maize (stalk, leaves and cob) to a huge pit on the edge of the field, where the other tractor is working a cutter-blower machine.

This machine cuts the maize into small pieces, which are more easily digestible for the cattle, and blows it straight into the pit. (David's favourite walk is now up there to watch it.) When the pit is full, the oxen will be walked over it to trample down the silage and then the pit closed with about four feet of earth on top. It should keep for at least two years, and represents a good insurance against locusts.

At the coast. . . .

5th September, 1950

As we write this we are sitting on the broad, airy verandah of the little house which is to be our home for the next three weeks. The house is low, single-storey, and the verandah runs all the way round the double L in which it is shaped. It is distempered white, with a brown *makuti* roof. In the middle is a large sitting-room which nobody uses, as one lives – even for meals – on the verandah. On one side are two bedrooms and a bathroom for David and the Swiss girls, and on the other, a large room and bathroom for us. The bathrooms are sketchy, for one lives in the sea and washes oneself in a tin bath with the brackish water from the well at the back. The house has no windows – just the usual expanded metal grids to stop bats or other animals.

The climate is perfect and I am typing this wearing nothing but a pair of shorts. The house nestles among palm trees, which have a marvellous crop of coconuts; from their branches hang masses of little nests, constantly visited by chattering, multi-coloured weaver birds. The sea is 100 yards away down a wide avenue; the beach is silver-white sand, and the blue water stretches calm and shallow out to the coral reef marked by a line of white breakers.

We brought thirteen pieces of luggage: all the linen and blankets we need here, a sack of *posho* for the five houseboys (who came down on the lorry) and a crate of live chickens and

101

ducks which we brought for our consumption. We have not got Gwara here, but one of the other boys cooks for us. The food is plain and simple, but adequate. One feels very sleepy, having come down from the highlands, and one sleeps well. We bathe and play on the sands with David, or sit on the cool verandah, reading and writing. I am making a determined attack on my Swahili grammar and am well into volume three of Churchill's Memoirs. At the same time, we are discussing together in detail the economy of our farm, having brought with us all the books from the accountant in Nairobi. I work most mornings from breakfast until lunch on these matters.

On Tuesday Rosemary and I went in to Mombasa. The city is situated on an island, and to approach it from here, we have to cross both a ferry and a toll-bridge. The ferry is hand-worked by a chain, and the crew who worked it sang and danced as they pulled us and our car across. The road ran through coconut and banana groves, and occasionally there was a small village of thatched huts, one of which was a settlement for freed slaves, still inhabited by their descendants.

In Mombasa you see Goans, Arabs, Seychellois, Africans and many other races in their national dress. The streets are narrow, many of them impassable by cars, and drainage is extremely rudimentary. Around the back streets by the market there are small Indian shops which sell masses of different cotton materials, baskets, earthenware waterpots, saris. . . . They also sell mixed coconut gratings, ground nuts, betel nuts and betel nut leaves (for chewing), and other spices, of which you could buy a pinch at the open stall as you sauntered by. At one shop the sweetest little Indian girl of about twelve was serving the customers. Nothing would induce her to come down to our price for some baskets which we were buying. Personally, I would have bought the whole shop, because she was so alluring, but Rosemary would not allow it. Itinerant sellers of black coffee, with copper coffee pots after the Persian style, wandered up and down the street, clanking the little metal cups in their hand to draw attention to their presence.

From the Club, where we had lunch, there was a beautiful outlook over an arm of the sea towards English Point, with

102

Arab dhows turning and tacking in the sea in front of us. Small dhows are used for the coastal trade between Mombasa and the ancient city of Lamu; one can see them lying at anchor in the port. Their big masts, instead of springing up straight from the deck, are set forward at an angle of about sixty degrees and look as if they will crash down at any moment.

17th September, 1950

This last week has slipped by imperceptibly, days disappearing one by one, each morning, afternoon and evening much the same as the last, filled with the roar of the sea breaking into a white foam-line on the coral reef, the fluting of the oriole birds calling to each other from the woods, the chattering of yellow weaver birds busily hovering around their little nests. . . . These nests are shaped like an old-fashioned cradle and hang upside down in the waving palm trees flanking the house. Less aesthetic are the sound of my own clacking typewriter, my halting sentences, addressed to a teacher of the Koran who comes daily to teach me conversational Swahili, and the occasional shriek of a bush-baby which punctuates the night.

On Monday we went to the coral reef at low tide, walking across seaweed and splashing through pools, each pool like a showcase in an aquarium with the sun shining through the water and the white sand showing off many-coloured shells, curious seaweed and little fish which slipped in and out of the coral so fast that one could hardly see them. There were bright red starfish nine inches across and smaller editions, in black and white, and enormous sea slugs, a foot long and two inches round, lying motionless in the sand. I met a man who was catching octopi, winkling them out of their holes in the coral with a pointed stick. He had several in his basket, their tentacles up to a foot long. They are considered quite a delicacy, and taste like something between a prawn and a lobster.

The Swiss girls are in the seventh heaven of delight, for on Thursday two charming young Swiss men – sent by our next-door-neighbour – turned up and took them out to dinner. These men work on a large sisal estate just up the road, which is entirely manned by Swiss technical staff and they are all very lonely. Last night they took the girls out dancing in Mombasa and today they are all going out for the afternoon and evening. . . .

Back at Rhodora. . . .

8th October, 1950

We end this week wondering if all the houseboys are about to walk out on us (though somehow we think they won't). It all started on Friday when we had another long morning in Nakuru, where this time I had to attend a meeting of the East Africa Stud Book Committee as the Guernsey Society representative. On our return for a late lunch, we were met by Monique, who announced that the kitchen boy had gone down to Nakuru to see the dentist, leaving chaos behind him. First thing in the morning he had come to Rosemary for medicine, pointing inside his mouth, and she had treated him with cough mixture and aspirin, hoping it would cure his toothache. Quite rightly he had decided that the Memsahib Mkubwa had not given him the correct remedy; and then he disappeared. So Monique told the nursery boy to go to the kitchen to help Gwara, but was met with a flat refusal (such an undignified job for such a superior boy); and the same thing happened when she asked Kitau, the temporary second houseboy. Rosemary, hearing this, went to find the boys and ordered them to do the work. They still refused.

So after a rather cloudy lunch, I ordered a formal court of enquiry in the office and the two boys were on the mat for insubordination. Gwara, asked to give evidence, stated that it was all part of a deep plot in which all the boys were involved (except him, of course) because none of them wanted to do any work at all. In the end we made our two boys agree to do work

104

other than their own in an emergency, and to pay a fine of ten shillings each for having refused to obey an order. Rather to our surprise they both accepted this, and neither has run away so far; one of them is helping quite cheerfully in the kitchen.

Meanwhile, Gwara had raised another point. Neither the kitchen boy nor the pantry boy had cleaned out the grease-trap outside the kitchen for a *whole week*. We therefore called in the pantry boy, as the kitchen boy was in Nakuru. He said that as the kitchen boy had refused to do the Tuesday cleaning, he himself would not do the much-scorned job on Friday.

So we waited until Mwangi, the kitchen boy, returned from a mere twenty-four-hour session with the dentist, and summoned him to the office. Mwangi is tall, very tall and willowy; he sways when he talks, and one does not know quite how much he is looking at one, as he has a faint squint and a habit of rolling his eyes when spoken to. Having first soundly lectured him on (a) departing without leave, and (b) taking all day off in order to have half an hour at the dentist's, we came to the question of the grease-trap.

'Well,' said Mwangi, 'I am not a bad boy and I do not want to leave but, on the way back from Mombasa, I met my father and he told me that my mother, on her deathbed, had made him promise that I should never have anything to do with drains or w.c.'s under any circumstances and so, as it was on her deathbed, I cannot do anything else but refuse to do the work.'

Regrettably, he was sacked. Had he not been, all the boys would have told us that their grandmothers, aunts, mothers and even cousins had forbidden them to do the job – on their deathbeds.

29th October 1950

On Tuesday we started moving the animals down to the show ground in our farm lorry. Ace and I went with the first load, carrying Valentine and a grade cow which was in the milk yield trials. Then he stayed down there and I did the next load, carrying the Butterfat Baby, our little bull Malverley Beauty's Triumph, and the best heifer. After lunch in Nakuru, Rosemary and I had to go to meet the judge, Colonel Brown, so John Clarke saw to the rest of the loading and Ace received the animals at the other end. (Although we entered seventeen animals we took down only ten in the end but it took all day – until after dark – to get them there. When they arrived at the Ground they had to be inspected by a vet, and then they went to the stalls allotted to them.) To return to our meeting the judge – it had been arranged that Colonel Brown would arrive in Kenya on the fifteenth, and stay with a cousin of his wife's called Beauchamp at Naivasha for a night before going on to Kabazi.

Soon after we had passed through Naivasha township Rosemary and I turned off down a ghastly road towards the lake. After thirteen miles we arrived at a house and asked for Mr Beauchamp. His servant said he was not at home, but there was a 'stranger' in the house. Full of hope, we walked in, to find a man in his sixties in stockinged feet, pulling an inadequate dressing-gown around him.

Are you Colonel Brown?' we asked.

'Oh, you must forgive my appearance,' he replied.

'Are you Colonel Brown?' we asked again.

'Do sit down,' he said.

'But *are you Colonel Brown?*'

'I'm afraid Beauchamp is not here,' he answered. The smell of whisky was by this time overpowering, and our hearts sank at the thought of this man being Colonel Brown. Rosemary was frantic, because she thought that under this judge all our animals would be sure to be turned out of the ring, and she refused to say another word until she found out whether this *was* Colonel Brown. After practically assaulting the man, we extracted the information that he was Colonel Hawkins, and Colonel Brown's plane – one of the new Hermes – had been delayed for two days; he had only just arrived in Nairobi and Beauchamp had gone there to meet him.

Rosemary and I returned over the dusty, bumpy road after a fruitless journey, but we did have the satisfaction of watching a magnificent herd of giraffe browsing right on the roadside.

Wednesday was the day before the show, and the day of the Milk Yield trials, in which we had entered a grade cow. We looked around to see what the other exhibits were like, and after a careful search, found a very fine Friesian bull whose owner informed us that the general opinion amongst exhibitors was that either his bull, or Valentine, would win the Supreme Championship. In the afternoon the furniture for the Guernsey Society stall arrived. By this time, the stall had been painted, and a cream-coloured curtain hung as its background. Against this June Ireland, the Honorary Secretary, arranged huge cream pottery bowls of daffodils, freesias and bluebells. The tables were covered with yellow table-cloths and the whole effect was charming.

On Thursday morning we saw that Colonel Brown had safely arrived, which was a great relief; we introduced ourselves formally, while looking over our shoulders nervously to see if anyone was looking who might think we were collaborating, and handed him over to the ring stewards. Then we went to find Ace (who slept throughout the show in an empty bull box between Valentine and the Butterfat Baby) and he was busy putting the final touches to his animals. Valentine was proudly led in, in the Senior Bull Class. The judge was very careful, checking over all the animals in detail, but our hearts sank into our very boots when he pulled out first a huge American bull exhibited by the Artificial Insemination Centre. We had to exercise rigid control because many people were watching who knew Valentine's record in the show-ring in England, and knew that we expected to win. But we were bitterly disappointed, and so was Ace: Valentine was placed second. We have since discovered that this judge is one hundred per cent Maple Lodge (a blood-line which comes from the Island) and does not like the Fernhill type. The other bull covered much more ground, and he found Valentine too short-coupled. One must admit that as an advertisement for the breed, the A.I. bull could not have been bettered; it already had 2,000 daughters!

That night Colonel Brown (the Guernsey judge) went up to

stay with Freddie on neutral ground and we had Mr and Mrs Coxon to stay. He is a pig judge, over from England, and a very famous breeder, and we were asked to put him up as we were not showing pigs. (As a matter of fact we discovered that he had been asked to judge the Supreme Championship of the cattle section, and he told us that he has often done this at shows in England; he himself keeps several breeds of cattle.) We spent a pleasant evening and learned a lot about pigs, and in the morning I took the Coxons around our pigs before we went down to the show ground. Generally, he gave them a very good chit, saying he liked the way we kept them, and our system of recording. He also made several useful suggestions. What really shook me was that when he saw our main stock boar, Kabazi Majestic King the Ninth, he said he would have given it the Championship had we shown it! He has told other people since that he thinks we do not realise what wonderful pig stock we have here.

Judging day. . . .

Then came the great moment at three in the afternoon when Rosemary and I went to the main stand while the champions and reserve champions of all the breeds were led in for Mr Coxon to judge. The arena was large and well laid out and thousands of members of the public were watching. There was the vast Friesian bull whose owner was so confident, and huge Ayrshires, Shorthorns, Red Polls and Jerseys. . . . Our Butterfat Baby looked tiny among them, for he is only eighteen months old. The beautiful animals circled round the judge and Chief Steward for some time and then the judge sent out about eight of them. We were still there, and so was the Friesian. There were now four left, all breed champions: the little Jersey cow, the white Shorthorn bull , the old Ayrshire bull and the Butterfat Baby. The judge took a lot of trouble with them. He walked them up and down, examined their teat placings, felt them all over, and finally brought them all into line. We

108

thought he was sending Ace out of the ring, and we were going to get up to leave. At that moment there was a shout of 'Well done!' from our friends in the stand, and only then did we realise that we had won the most coveted honour in the show. Our little bull walked slowly right around the arena while the huge Ayrshire, which was second, lumbered after it. Rosemary and I nearly swooned!

We hear that there is a lot of heartburn that such new settlers should win the trophy. It was later broadcast over the loudspeaker that the judge said it was the finest Guernsey bull he had ever seen anywhere (which honestly is not true; Valentine is far better!).

I believe the whole show has been written up for *Sport and Country*, so keep your eyes open for it! Later there was a champagne celebration at the Guernsey stall and we had to go to an official cocktail party given by the Royal Agricultural Society of Kenya for the overseas visitors. Tired but happy we came home with Colonel Brown, the Guernsey judge. He is seventy-four and after his rotten journey had been feeling none too well. He is most charming and knowledgeable about the breed. He is very keen also on polo ponies and polo, and has spent many days at Laversine (Paris) with Rosemary's Uncle Robert and Aunt Nelly. He remembered a younger sister there, and was enchanted when he heard it was Rosemary's mother.

A hundred people came to our open day on Monday. In the morning, Mr Coxon gave a lecture on pig breeding and management. (We had built a ring in the yard of our new cowshed building, and we arranged tiered seating around it.) He managed to slip in some very nice remarks about our stock, which he used to illustrate his points. When he had finished Mrs Coxon gave a talk on Young Farmers in Britain. Then there was a buffet lunch in our new, unused, pedigree cowshed, at which Mrs Mumford, Mrs Ace and Monique assisted, and Mumford dispensed the drinks. The menu was chicken and ham mousse, sausage rolls, salad, jellies and trifles, cheese and bridge rolls. After lunch Colonel Brown gave a long talk about Guernseys; then there was tea, and people toured around looking at our stock, both pigs and cows.

19th November, 1950

Last week we were separated: I decided to stay here while Ace was in bed with flu, while Rosemary left with Colonel Brown for Nairobi. They stayed in Lady McMillan's house. (She is a very alert, keen breeder of Guernseys, aged eighty-four. The house, Chiromo, is large, and set in a beautiful garden on the outskirts of the city.) Nairobi was at her loveliest: the little rains have come in large quantities there and the jacaranda trees are a mass of blue-mauve blossom with emerald grass below them. Rosemary and Colonel Brown visited Lady McMillan's farm on Sunday; on Monday they went to the Veterinary Research Laboratory and the Artificial Insemination Centre, and in the evening they went to the Game Park and saw lions; on Tuesday they went to the Coffee Research Station, where Guernseys are kept, and thence to lunch to see the herd of a nearby coffee farmer. I joined them on Tuesday evening in time for our joint broadcast.

On Wednesday we had a day's shopping, and Lady McMillan had a big dinner party with fifteen guests in the evening. She had invited the Governor, but he could not come. However, the Commander-in-Chief East Africa (General Sir Frederick Dowler) came, and the High Commissioner for South Africa, and the Governor of Somaliland, among others. Life at Chiromo is delightfully pre-war. Each bedroom has its sitting-room, dressing room and bathroom, and we slept in a four-poster bed. One changed into a dinner jacket every night, and there were never fewer than six or eight guests invited, besides ourselves. Dinner normally consisted of seven courses with excellent wines.

Rosemary was absolutely delighted to see me when at last I arrived, for she said that Lady McMillan refused to recognise her as a person, but only as a poor substitute for her husband, and would accept no excuses for my not having turned up. I also discovered that Rosemary had unconsciously aroused acute jealousy, for Lady McMillan complained that Rosemary had Colonel Brown – aged seventy-four – 'like a puppet on a string' and said that whereas he had developed a soft spot for

110

Rosemary, she herself was of a *much* more suitable age.

The three days before I joined them were spent in wild activity, for I suddenly made up my mind, in view of the threatened locust invasion, to drive a road down through our crater land into the Menengai crater itself, where there is a large area of hay which no human being has ever been able to touch. This will involve a tricky bit of road-building on our land, and the construction of a sort of escarpment road over a small cliff into the hay-land. I have not yet received permission from the Government (which owns the crater) to take the hay, but I have seen the Provincial Commissioner, and am full of hope.

I rang Major Kent and got him to come and stay for an indefinite period, and he has a gang of ten boys. He takes a picnic lunch and spends all day down at the new road, planning and supervising the building. He says we shall be able to have machinery in the hay-field this week, and we are hoping to get about 100 tons of hay this year and much more next year.

3rd December, 1950

Last Sunday we all climbed into the big car with a picnic lunch and set off for the crater. The road we have built has been named in sections. You start off on Seys Avenue; then Quarry Bypass; then Howard Bridge, because Peter Howard built it when he was manager here; then, Seys Avenue Extension; then First Escarpment; then Swamp Road; finally, Kent Escarpment Road, and you are in the crater! It is two and a half miles from our house to the top of Kent Escarpment. Here we met Major Kent, who, although it was a Sunday, had been supervising the mowing of the hay since 7 am. Rosemary and David had never before seen either the swamp or the crater land.

We decided that it was too hot to lunch amongst the hay, so we moved down to a shady part of the Kent Escarpment Road, overlooking the green swamp. This was not a great success, for the new road was covered in black lava dust, and David had to

111

eat his lunch out of a drinking mug. Towards the end the vet joined us; he had been delayed on a case. In his rather cautious Scottish manner he is busy courting 'our Beatrice', but we do not know whether he is making much progress.

On Wednesday we de-horned twenty-five grade heifers and a cow. The vet gave them all a local anaesthetic in each horn first, and then snipped the horn off with a wonderful gadget which left a ghastly hole in the animal's head. They all bled terribly. However, we have been dressing them every day and they are recovering fast.

10th December, 1950

Come with us for our usual evening walk with David.

David is trailing his favourite stick in the dust; all three dogs are chasing birds, people, leaves or anything else they happen to see. We start walking down a long avenue of markhamia trees, tall, with shiny large leaves and a yellow flower. It is cool, for the trees almost meet overhead and the green coffee extends on either side. Turning left at the end, we walk a little further and enter one of the two *makuti*-roofed piggeries where the breeding sows live. We walk slowly down, checking each pen and the details on the slate above. We ask Menue, '*Habari?*' (What news?) and he tells us if Champion Queen has eaten (she has been sick) or if Princess the Tenth has farrowed, and so on. Menue is in charge. He is round-eyed and in tatters, a dismal character who takes life very seriously. We recently had to take away one of his helpers because Menue complained that his life had been threatened – we could not discover why. Feeding is finished and the sows are lying down peacefully: some are waiting to farrow, some have tiny little pink piglets skipping around them, and some have families of larger piglets which are approaching the sad time of eight weeks when they will be taken away from their mothers and sent down to the bacon house. Menue is very efficient in spite of his appearance, and is a most important part of the two maternity wards.

David takes a great interest in it all and demands to be lifted

112

up to have a good view of the occupants of the pens. He has been made to leave his stick at the entrance and quickly runs for it as we go on to our next port of call.

We walk now to the bull pens where we are greeted with a cheery *Jambo* from Arap Juma, the head bull boy, who stands about three feet high. He is looking very smart in the special uniform we have issued to all the boys who work in the cowsheds. As we approach he is busy brushing Valentine. On the parapet around Valentine's pen sits a little bunch of red bottle-brush and blue jacaranda flowers. We have not yet discovered who it is who places those bouquets at frequent intervals on his pen, and Rosemary quickly removes it, for fear it will either poison Valentine, or make a cissy of him. . . . David says 'What a shame' as the flowers scatter on the concrete. Valentine huffs and blows and rolls his eyes, pretending to be very fierce, but he knows Rosemary's voice, and when she speaks to him and pats him he becomes quiet.

Next door the other bull boy is grooming Kali Charlie (Kali means bad-tempered; his real name is Rose's Robert's Lad the Second of Fernhill Park). Each bull is groomed morning and evening (there are five bulls) and it is the responsibility of these boys to feed and water them, and to take them for an hour's walk daily.

Having satisfied ourselves that all is well here, we turn in through the archway into the main pedigree yard. The dogs are put in the office, from which they keep up an incessant whining protest, and we cross to the pedigree milking shed. The head boy in this department, Moustachio, is a dapper little man with a moustache like a sergeant-major. He is busy grooming each of the seventeen animals in turn. On one side of the shed stand two older milking cows, which we took over with the farm, the three recently-calved heifers, and some which are due to calve in the next few months; on the other side are the younger heifers and those lately served and not due to calve down for some months. Each animal is fed differently, according to a chart pinned up on the food-room door, and this chart is changed weekly according to the amount of milk the animal gives or the closeness to the date of calving.

113

Two tall milkers sit themselves on minute stools and start milking. Rosemary and David stay and watch and Rosemary stands beside the heifers to keep them quiet, for they are a bit restless. Whilst the milking is going on Tudor Ace looks in with his cheery face. He is very busy on a multitude of jobs but he stops to exchange the latest information.

When the milking is over we walk through the dairy to see the milk being weighed. The head dairy boy is busy with the cooler and in the corner, his dairy *toto* is turning the handle of the huge separator, which is taller than he is. It is emitting its characteristic hum and clanging its bell from time to time. The *toto* has a wall eye and a charming smile, and as the handle comes round with each turn, his feet nearly leave the ground.

From the peace and quiet of the pedigree shed, where the animals are all well-groomed with shiny coats, and silence and spotless cleanliness are the order, we pass into another world. In the grade milking shed, some eight boys are rapidly milking seventy-seven grade cows and heifers in relays. There is noise and bustle, with cows milling about, and Arap Karimbi, the fat sleepy recorder, is calling out from his list (when he remembers) the amount of food for each cow as the head boy moves down the feeding passage with the bucket. The first batch of thirty-six have been milked and the second lot come into the shed. There is much banging, heaving, pulling and clanking of chains. The boys whistle to the cows to keep them quiet. David gets mixed up with them all and somewhat frightened, and Rosemary rescues him. He is showered with '*Jambo* David!' by the boys; to be called by his Christian name, and not Bwana, by them, is complimentary, and shows his popularity. David mutters '*Jambo*' back and occasionally gives a beaming smile to his special friends.

We walk on to the trough outside where the forty-three grade heifers are being fed their concentrates by a delightful old man who herds them by day in the crater land, and his tiny little boy, who does all the running about for him. . . . We cross from here to the grade calf pens. Rosy-faced Mrs Ace is busy preparing the *ooji* (linseed gruel) for the older calves and the milk for the younger ones. There are forty more of these, so she has quite a big job, and is assisted by one African and another *toto*. The former is rather a trial; he smiles sweetly, says 'Yes', and does nothing. Linda is here, helping her mother, and soon she and David are discovered sliding down the stone ramp outside the calf-pens with shrieks of delight and much damage to their clothing.

Our next stop is the bacon house, where unearthly grunts and squeals proclaim that feeding is in full swing, supervised by John Clarke. We check all the pens again, and Monique turns up with her knitting to take David slowly back to the house and to bed. The dogs go with her for their meals and for de-ticking. Rosemary wanders back, inevitably, to her precious pedigrees and pedigree calves, and I go to button up anything I may have noticed and help Ace where necessary. Eventually Rosemary walks back to the house in the dusk to read David a bedtime story and tuck him up.

17th December, 1950

The crater fascinates everyone who sees it for the first time, so much so that we are a little nervous that strings of cars may start arriving from Nakuru with trippers. In the morning, just as we were getting up, Lord Waterpark, with his fiancée, his mother Lady Kenmare, and another man, arrived in a land rover and asked if they could visit our crater. Harry Kent made a point of telling them there were no snakes. The land rover duly trundled off down the new road, but suddenly they saw a large puff-adder in the middle of it. Naturally, Lord Waterpark alighted and shot it! They came back to tell us the story and we were dreadfully embarrassed that they had met such a dangerous snake when we had told them there weren't any. Harry Kent then doubled up with laughing, for he remembered that the old man who herds the heifers had killed a large puff-adder the day before and left it in the middle of the road, and he knew that Lord Waterpark had shot a very deceased object.

115

6

The account of our second Christmas in Kenya includes a (highly oblique)
reference to Legco, the Legislative Council, which was to play such a large
part in all our futures. But at this time we were preoccupied with other
things. Monique had become engaged to a young Swiss man, and was
shortly to leave us; the cattle were still suffering from intermittent bouts of
sickness, and we had no confidence in our vet; and of course, we were
anxious to do our best at the shows. We travelled 140 miles up-country to
the Eldoret Show (where we met Nellie Grant, the mother of Elspeth
Huxley the authoress, for the first time) and 100 miles down to Nairobi for
the East Africa Kennel Club Show.

31st December, 1950

Christmas Eve was exceptionally warm and oppressive. A few
of the senior boys from the farm wandered up for their presents:
gaily coloured pullovers done up in Christmas paper and
labelled with a Swahili greeting 'From the Bwana and the
Memsahib.' We went up to Kabazi for a mixed gathering of the
staffs of Rhodora and Kabazi with their children and a few
friends of Vi and Freddie. Tea was laid on trestle tables with
benches on the terraced lawn under a large thorn-tree.
Chocolate cakes and strawberries and cream provided the
highlights of the feast, and Vi poured about sixty cups of tea
from the large silver urns we had lent her. When tea was over
and balloons and paper blowers had provided sufficient
amusement, games were organised, and David was introduced
to 'Nuts in May'. The game was enthusiastically led by
Freddie's burly, rather dour, Scottish head market-gardener.

116

Suddenly we heard hooting and Father Christmas drove up in a huge car. (Gasps of dismay from Pam and John, who had spent the entire morning decorating a Jeep with white sheeting, Christmas trees, cotton-wool snow and silver bells; however, as Father Christmas on other days is a busy Legislative Councillor known as the Honourable Michael Blundell, he no doubt failed to see it because he was thinking of high politics.)

The children surged up the steps onto the top terrace and into the house after Father Christmas. The tree was in the dining-room, and he distributed the presents there. He was very genial, but failed to modify his voice, so that his four-year-old daughter announced loudly:

'That's Daddy.'

Towards the end of the party a series of Vi's washtubs were pushed down a long steep bank with excited children inside – as good as any Cresta run! David loved that, and many people remarked on his pluck.

7th January, 1951

We have been saving an amusing incident which happened on a hot, sultry afternoon before Christmas. Lord Waterpark visited us, with his attractive French fiancée and two other beauties, a blonde and a brunette. These last two announced that they had come to buy for their hostess, a Mrs Newall in Subukia Valley, a Christmas present: an in-calf Guernsey heifer. Rosemary and I looked at each other, swallowed hard, and said that we had really no heifers for sale but – as this was such a special request, would they like to stay to tea? For by the time it was over, the senior grade heifers would be up at the cowshed for the evening checking and feeding. . . . This they accepted with alacrity. Lord Waterpark and his fiancée disappeared in their car to Bruce McKenzie's farm nearby, where they were going to deliver a miniature tractor for Bruce's son and heir (Lord W. was a pupil there for over a year before moving to his own farm). Rosemary took the two Lovelies round the pigs, which seemed to interest them a lot, to her surprise, and after a tour of the cowsheds they returned to tea. The brunette was doing up her face at the dressing-table when Rosemary came into the bedroom to see if they had everything they wanted, and she was asked,

'Is this a photograph of your mother?'

'Yes,' said Rosemary, 'why?'

'Well,' said the brunette, 'I was at Exbury in August playing in a tennis tournament, with your brother Eddy as my partner. I'd been brought over by Edward Montagu.'

This decided Rosemary to let them have one of her precious heifers, so after tea we went to see the animals. Their requirements were for one with 'a sweet face, large eyelashes and soft eyes' and we managed to find one answering to all this but which also had a black nose, so we should have culled it sooner or later anyway. It must be admitted, however, that she was in calf to the Butterfat Baby, so we should normally have waited until after she had calved before selling her. When the party had left we looked up Leo's letter of last August describing the tennis tournament. Here is an extract:

'Edward's girlfriend, who was partnered with Eddy, was so glamorous that I am surprised Eddy had time to look at the ball. She wore a pink, very open-necked shirt and the shortest green shorts I have ever seen . . .'

Next day they all turned up dressed like Land Girls in the back of Lord Waterpark's new lorry, and very professionally loaded up the heifer, which we had bathed and clipped for them. The loading was accompanied by many 'Sweetie pies' 'Darlings' and 'Treasures' (alluding to the heifer, not me). They drove away with much hand-waving and we heard later that the Christmas presentation was a great success: the animal was handed over to her new owner with a wreath of flowers round her neck and a large satin bow. How they got her to walk respectably, I do not know, as she had never been led in her life, and had certainly never had anything to do with anyone more glamorous than the wizened old man who herds the grade heifers all day in the crater.

14th January, 1951

Sunday was almost entirely occupied with Tip's Joan of Flemish Farm, the heifer which is seriously ill. John, the vet, called in the morning and decided to get a second opinion from Brian Sherriff, his senior partner.

At seven on Monday morning John called and Rosemary and I went up to the cowshed to await the arrival of Brian Sherriff. Brian is a much more decisive and energetic character than John, with more experience; he quickly decided that the heifer had acute peritonitis and pneumonia. He told us to take the heifer out from the new buildings, up a paddock, to the old wooden buildings, which have an earth floor. There we were to build a ramp so that her forelegs would be at least a foot higher than her rear legs, and she was not to be allowed to lie down for a week to ten days. (We had to treat a cow like this at Elliotts, and we saved it.) He prescribed digitalis for her heart, four quarts of liquid paraffin and eggs, brandy and milk every four hours, all to be poured into her down a rubber tube, for she would not take anything but a little water herself.

The heifer was too weak to take a single step of her own volition, so we all had to push and heave; eventually we hitched her to the back of John's land rover and drew her forward step by step. In the middle of the paddock she had to cross, she collapsed. We agreed, feeling the break-neck speed of her pulse, that she would die if we took her a step further, so we got her up and put her forelegs on a hillock. Then we brought bales of hay and built a windbreak around her. She stayed there all night, with a guard and the flickering light of a hurricane lamp.

The next day we built a canvas roof over her against the sun. She seemed to maintain her strength through the day and at about tea-time Ace asked Rosemary for permission to move the heifer on a stretcher up to the proper ramp at the top of the paddock. Accordingly, after milking a padded gate was brought and with all hands, the heifer was slowly lifted on to it. At the moment of lifting, a tremendous gust of wind enveloped them all in a dust-storm so that they could hardly see what they were doing; when the dust cleared, they saw that Tip's Joan had quietly died. Her heart had given way.

It was dusk, and Ace went off to fetch John to do a post-mortem. Meanwhile we got the lorry out and moved Tip's Joan to a corner of the coffee shamba. When John arrived it was quite dark, and we operated in the lights of his car. We found a small piece of wire in the second stomach, but the real trouble was acute inflammation in the fourth stomach; this has been sent down to the vet-lab. We are all very sad, for the heifer put up a game fight for five days for her life. I examined the three-month-old foetus at the post-mortem. It was a heifer.

28th January, 1951

David understands everything you say to him in French but he will not utter. On the other hand, he is also learning Swahili fast, and in this language he sometimes comes out with some surprising remarks. Last week we went through the archway into the pedigree yard and Anniefur, a grade cow, was waiting for her pedigree bull foster-child. Rosemary pulled David away and hid behind the gates, explaining to David that this was a very bad-tempered cow.

'*Ndio*,' said David, nodding his head until it nearly fell off, '*kali kabisa*' (Yes, completely fierce).

It was the perfect expression, intoned exactly as the Africans would have done. His progress in Swahili comes from his watering of the garden. In this he has long sessions with Manasseh, our charming garden boy, and he simply loves it. He has learned to turn taps on and off, and Rosemary finds him rearranging the position of her garden 'swizzler', while up at the cowshed it is not uncommon to find that the water-bowls suddenly do not fill, nowadays. Anything to do with water fascinates him.

4th February, 1951

On Thursday we went to Nairobi, taking the Aces with us. Our first stop was Army Disposals, where we found a mixed crowd of rapacious-looking Indians and tough-looking Africans waiting at the gates to claim as much as they could of the one and three-quarter million shirts and shorts and so on which the Army was selling off cheap. We inspected the samples of the garments, joined the queue, and bought four bales of shirts, long trousers and shorts – 100 in each bale – made of good khaki drill and working out at an average of about three shillings per garment.

We left Ace to pay the cheque and went on to the vet-lab next door to see Dr Shirlaw, the scientist who is tackling the 'Rhodora plague'. From the calf we took down there last week, he has isolated a bug which he showed us under the microscope, but he refused to commit himself as to whether this was the source of the trouble and said he wanted more cases. We said 'Heaven forbid!' but he said if the bug was to blame, he knew how to cure it. The little calf itself is doing well, and he is giving it Bemax to eat in case the problem is vitamin B deficiency.

11th February, 1951

On Monday a niece of the headmistress of Rosemary's day school in London arrived with her husband, brother and sister-in-law. To her astonishment, Rosemary recognised her quite easily, although it was twenty-four years since they had last met. We took them down to see the crater – a never-failing source of entertainment for visitors – and when they saw the so-called swamp, which is now nearly all cleared ready for ploughing, they said they would try to see if there was any water there, as two of them are water-diviners. Sure enough, they could find water all over the place, though they could not tell in what quantity, or at what depth. I asked them if they would show me how to do it, and I found that the stick reacted with me as much as with them and in the same spots; it would not react for Rosemary.

On Tuesday by a strange coincidence, a little man turned up, whom Rosemary described as an Adonis, from the hydrographic department of the Government. He took scientific tests down in the same area and reported that our chances of getting a bore-hole anywhere on this farm were remote, owing to the volcanic nature of the ground, which contains immense fissures on and below the surface. However, he did think that it would be worth digging a well in the swamp, although he said that if after 120 feet we had not struck water it would not be worth going on. He blazed a tree at the best point to start digging. Now we have to find someone who will take on the job. Our Adonis showed no enthusiasm for water diviners.

On Friday Dr Shirlaw turned up. We nearly expired with delight when he said he had come for ten days, if necessary, to study on the spot the peculiar calf disease we have here. He is staying in a hotel in Nakuru, and we think he has in tow a rather nice-looking middle-aged widow whom he brought here yesterday afternoon. (This may account for his prolonged visit, as she also has to be in Nakuru for ten days.) Our office looks like a laboratory, with microscopes, and slides, and strangely coloured fluids. We collect the most revolting samples for him and he spends many happy hours looking at them. He thinks he is on the track of something, but will not commit himself yet.

11th March, 1951

I went to the vet-lab in Nairobi on Monday morning. I was warmly greeted by Dr Shirlaw, who had the usual microscope, retorts, Bunsen burner and other paraphernalia around him, and a number of boxes. As I came in he was waving a slide about. He explained to me, indicating an open box, that one of his colleagues was ill and he was trying to discover what type of amoebic dysentery he was suffering from. Then, indicating an identical box, he offered me a stick of Edinburgh Rock. I accepted, in order not to appear fussy. An angular girl in

122

trousers came to the door and was sent off to prepare the two calves, which Rosemary had left there the week before, for their journey. Dr Shirlaw and I strolled down to the paddock and the calves were safely installed in the Ford Pilot in the place where the back seat should have been, with Brown Eyes, the second head Lumbwa, sitting on the floor beside them. When Dr Shirlaw heard that I was going to call at Nakuru on the way back, his face lit up, and he asked me if I would take a parcel to the hotel for his lady friend, Mrs Green, who is still sorting out the accounts there. We went back into his laboratory and he produced a new box of Edinburgh Rock out of the cupboard where he keeps all his specimens. Wrapping it up in an atrocious piece of brown paper, he handed it to me. I carried it safely back to Mrs Green in Nakuru and she seemed delighted to receive it.

We had decided to sell a couple of heifers to a Mrs Daly, who arrived late one night after an overland journey of 750 miles from her farm in Tanganyika.

I got up at dawn and went out to make sure that the heifers which we had put aside for Mrs Daly to choose from were looking their best, and after breakfast, while Rosemary took her up to see them, Captain Webb and I went down to the Veterinary Officer in Nakuru for a permit to move the cattle. Captain Webb is sixty-five and is the vet Mrs Daly had brought with her. We were confronted by a straitlaced junior who told us that there could be no variation from the rule (which we did not know about) that the animals could not be moved without agreement from the authorities in Tanganyika. This would take at least three days to obtain.

Mrs Daly is the sort of person who is not pleased if she does not get her own way, and Captain Webb, who is terrified of her, warned me that she would go up in smoke. Back at the house I confronted her. She was irate, and announced that she was prepared to forge a letter from the Tanganyika authorities. I

123

began to realise what a difficult woman I was dealing with. She is about forty-two, powerfully built, with an immensely strong character; she is Irish, with an accent and a loud voice; she was for many years Master of the Galway Blazers (one of the most famous packs of Irish foxhounds); she has had three husbands, and the latest is a charming and very correct man, who has been in the Blues and was a previous Master of the Galway Blazers.

I said that I would not be a party to any forgery, since the good name of this farm *vis-à-vis* the Tanganyikan veterinary authorities was more important than the deal we were doing with her. She threatened to take the cattle away without a permit, and I said that I would not help her to load, or provide fodder, or condone her action in any way. Finally she threatened to go without the cattle.

At one stage I went down to a solicitor in Nakuru for advice! But in the end we triumphed, and she agreed to give in and wait for the permit to come through. I was very pleased, for we sold her six in-calf grade heifers for £75 each (which is a very good price for grades) and this represented possibly the first export for Guernseys from Kenya to Tanganyika. In the evening, she borrowed our car and driver and went off to Nakuru. She came back feeling better, for she had found a friend who was going to phone the Tanganyika veterinary authorities at Mpwapwa to hurry things on.

While all this hullabaloo was going on, Rosemary was still coping with the builders, with Mrs Daly's equipment which she had turned out from the lorry and which lay strewn all up the garden path, and with General Hawkins, who arrived by appointment at 10 am, picking his way over the litter, to select some animals which we had offered him for sale. He was very methodical, critical and businesslike, and having pretended he knew nothing about Guernseys, he picked the six best and earmarked four more.

25th March, 1951

On Friday Lady Claud Hamilton prinked onto the lawn. She

had come to lunch, but her husband had boils so he was left behind. After refusing potatoes, we presume on account of her figure, she managed to consume two large helpings of strawberry fool so the lunch, at least, was a success. We talked a bit about 'our' Lord Claud, David's godfather. She told us that when she first married 'her' Lord Claud, the other Lady Claud was not too pleased because 'She kept receiving my bills and I got all her party invitations.' After she left, we decided that she only came to see one thing: our bulls. She wanted to form an opinion about whether her Shorthorn or our newly-imported Guernsey bull would win Supreme Champion at the show in October. After showing her the bulls, we tried to interest her in the other stock, but she could not contain her impatience, and unaccountably had another engagement, to which she rushed off.

Returning from a stay in England:

17th June, 1951

We had a good journey to Rome where we were amused to see a letter on the notice-board at the airport addressed to Roland Williams, whose plane from Tokyo was due in the next evening. We scribbled something to him on the back of the envelope. Lydda was reached late in the evening and we climbed into the booked sleeper which had been prepared, but Rosemary was suffocated and could not breathe, so she sat in a chair most of the night while I dozed fitfully. On the whole we think it better not to have a bunk; it is too hot and stuffy.

After breakfast in the morning Rosemary went forward with the Captain to look out for Rhodora. We landed only twenty minutes late, and as we stepped out onto Nairobi Airport into soft sunshine and exotic, flower-scented air, we took a deep breath and said,

'Oh, how lovely to be back in Africa!'

Customs caused us no trouble at all. Although Air Freight

was closed because it was Sunday, by asking our Indian friends in the ordinary Customs section to help us out, we were able to clear the four suitcases which we had sent by Passengers' Luggage in Advance. Both cars were waiting, with the lorry driver and the chauffeur (now well after the dreadful burns he received when the electric light engine caught fire just before I left) grinning from ear to ear and coming forward to shake hands with a cordial '*Jambo*.' Soon we were flashing along the main tarmac road to Nakuru, the country looking beautiful and green so that it was a joy to get to the top of the escarpment about three quarters of an hour outside Nairobi, where you have a view that seems to extend half across Africa. We turned into Rhodora at 12.30 pm our time and what a change greeted us! The house, now painted white with black roof and paintwork, is flanked by the office block and implement sheds and garages all painted the same. Grass such as we have never seen waves emerald green and lush all round, and everything sparkles and smells warm and fresh.

The rest of the week has been spent quietly getting on top of everything again in the office. One morning David, Rosemary and I drove down Seys Avenue to the crater. Here some five acres have been fenced and cultivated. The land lies in a natural basin surrounded by cliffs and a large gang was there that morning, planting lucerne. Within a few years we hope to have paddocks all the way down to this area. The earth is nothing but topsoil, rich and black, and should grow anything one wants.

Many of the boys have come from their various farm jobs to greet us and ask news of England, but the second headman really excelled himself for, after shaking me earnestly by the hand, he said,

'Thank you for coming back to us!'

I felt somewhat overwhelmed and wondered vaguely if he was about to ask for a rise, and where he thought we would go to, if we had not come back to Rhodora.

I presented Kipsang, the head herd boy, with a thirty-shilling Ingersoll watch from England. He is immensely pleased. The next day Beatrice and David, on their usual morning safari round the farm, met him at the dip. He came forward and asked,

'What time is it?'

'About 9.30,' said Beatrice, puzzled. Kipsang, with a flourish, produced a large flannel rag, unwound his watch out of it, and told her that the correct time was 9.35.

1st July, 1951

Rosemary went up to a farm in Subukia, miles past the Wards, to a dispersal sale. She went to see a young Rhodora bull re-sold; Ace also went in his little van with Mrs Ace and their daughter Linda, to buy a fridge.

The auctioneer was not Charles Long, but a rival firm. He excelled himself by merely saying of the bull,

'Er . . . er . . . I have . . . er . . . er . . . seen Mrs Seys this morning and she tells me that she hopes the bull's dam will do better this lactation.'

Effectively damned, the bull sold for a song – 110 guineas! Then a man came up to Rosemary and asked,

'Are you Mrs Seys? I have been wanting to meet you for some time, and I hope to come and see your Guernseys.'

'Yes,' says Rosemary, meekly.

Then, turning to Ace, who was sitting next to her, he said,

'And are you Seys? I am so glad to meet you.'

Rosemary must have looked stunned, because Ace came to the rescue with a quick reply:

'No. I am the stockman who looks after Mr and Mrs Seys' animals.'

John Robertson, the vet, has not been a success out here, either with our Beatrice, or with his clients. Rosemary and Sheila Reynard took a sick dog belonging to John and Pam to him and after examining the dog he asked his classic question.

'And what do *you* think is wrong?'

Sheila suggested M&B and he, of course, agreed. The latest story about his skill is that he went to a neighbouring farmer to do a Caesarean on a cow, and as he was cutting her open, the farmer remarked that he thought he had cut her intestine. However, the vet proceeded with the operation and after a long search, announced that he could not find the calf, so he sewed the poor cow up again. Shortly afterwards the animal calved naturally and two days later, died of peritonitis. John Robertson is said to have told a friend that he had never actually done a Caesarean before, but he had seen it done. Now there is one more farm added to a long list which he won't be asked to visit again.

Brian Sherriff, his partner, is a very different person – brisk and efficient.

We have already taken the hay in the crater land; now we are cutting a lot on our pastures, using one of George Manuel's machines to do the cutting while we do the raking and baling. We had no idea that grass could grow the way it does on our farm, and we are cashing in on it, especially in view of the locust threat, by taking every bit of hay we can. Working two teams, we go on from dawn until dusk. Our crops of oats and maize are also infinitely better than we have seen before. This is partly due to the better rains, and partly to the extra fertiliser we put on. It is really thrilling to go round the farm and see these crops and makes us realise that we have a farm with first quality land. We killed a pig and gave George a leg; he killed a sheep and gave us some mutton in exchange.

I am finishing the typing of this late on Sunday evening by lamplight in the office, while Rosemary is starting her bath. During a pause from the sound of the typewriter I heard a sound which is familiar just now, the talk of the huge flocks of geese which pass overhead at night. In the moonlight one can see them, high in the sky, in perfect formation.

15th July, 1951

Having watched the seed planting on the farm and having assisted at the planting of his own garden, David is beginning to grasp the principles of crop growing. One night this week as he was being put to bed, Rosemary remarked how tall he was becoming and she said that soon he would be as tall as Daddy. 'And then are you going to have a moustache like Daddy?' she asked. 'No,' said David. After questioning, he pointed, giggling, to his upper lip and said, 'No seeds to grow!'

22nd July, 1951

I asked a disgruntled gentleman named Molony to come to tea, with his wife, to discuss the appalling fact that the Guernsey Society has increased its annual subscription from twenty shillings to forty shillings. This move had already provoked Mr Molony into a series of letters and arguments that owners of only a grade bull should not be subject to the increase.

Tea-time arrived, and with it Mr and Mrs Molony, but by some unfortunate mistake we had put it down on the wrong day, so Rosemary started off well by asking him who they were and what they wanted. After an extremely sticky tea, we migrated with our visitors to the cowshed, where they melted, and became quite human, and discussed each animal intelligently and knowledgeably. We are always amused at the variety of things good and bad which impress different people who visit Rhodora. Mr Molony's deepest impression was when he gasped to his wife, as he walked down the rows of grade cows being milked:

'Not one of these animals' legs are tied! Think of that – not one!'

Typical old Kenya settlers milk their grade cows in tumble-down shacks, and usually tie their legs because they are so wild – never being handled, except at milking time. Molony nervously picked his way across the dispersal yard, through the quiet cattle, and was amazed that many of them took no notice of him at all, even continuing to lie down chewing the cud. We patted them and pushed them aside to make room for him to get across to the heifer pens. They left us at dusk, full of enthusiasm. And no more mention, for the time being, of increased subscriptions.

29th July, 1951

I was busy typing in the office when up drove a car, and out of it stepped Freddie Ward, unexpectedly, with Mr and Mrs Cavendish-Bentinck. He is known throughout the colony as C-B, and is the Member for Agriculture (the equivalent of Minister of Agriculture in England). He recently married an attractive lady of strong character who is half his age.

We set off for the farm buildings with them, and Rosemary followed soon after. We saw the pedigree females, grazing in a paddock alongside the sheds, and I found John Clarke and Kipsang to bring out the bulls. Tudor Ace was on his way to Nakuru with a load of cattle for sale.

I sent John to lead out Malverley Beauty's Triumph, the eighteenth-month old bull, while the party was looking at another bull. Hearing an ominous noise, I rushed around to his pen and when I looked over the door of the box I saw John taking refuge on top of the ironwork of his yoke. I called Kipsang and we got hold of the bull's ring and tried to get his head up. Unfortunately, before we had achieved this, the door of the box flew open and he charged out into the yard, with all three of us hanging onto his ring with one finger. He pinned John to the wall with Kipsang and me on the edge of his horns. A desperate struggle ensued, but we could not get his head up, and poor John was as white as a sheet. The door of the yard was, of course, closed, and C-B looked silently on while Freddie, Mrs C-B and Rosemary leant over the wall shouting advice.

We did not know what to do next, for we did not dare let go of the ring. Having been waltzed around a bit, and being very frightened, we made the only possible plan and all suddenly let go at the same moment and made a mad rush to leap over the wall. This manoeuvre was successfully accomplished, and the only reminder of the incident was John's badly bruised and grazed rib. It was not until we had collected our wits again that we noticed a little heifer, due to go to the sale, which Tudor Ace had washed and put to dry off in a pen next to the bull pen. Unfortunately, Malverley's Beauty's Triumph happens to have a habit of seeing red whenever any of his prospective wives are nearby.

7

There was now so much to inspect and supervise at Rhodora that it seemed a good idea to buy horses on which to ride around the farm. I was responsible for finding suitable animals, and greatly enjoyed the task: by the end of 1951 we had acquired three horses and later, David would have a pony of his own.

Beatrice was soon to return to Europe. John Clarke went home too, and was briefly replaced by a young man called Walter. After this we relied on Africans to do the jobs previously undertaken by Monique, Beatrice and John. Tudor Ace cleverly slipped a disc in the same week that his wife gave birth to a baby son, so they both ended up in hospital at once!

Miss Goodwin, who had been governess to my brother Leo, arrived to superintend David's education; he adored her. Leo himself arrived, strung about with photographic equipment, and enthusiastically snapped everything in sight when we three went on safari. There was a great deal of travel and our social life seems to have been undertaken on a rather grander scale than before in Kenya and South Africa: we stayed, briefly, in Johannesburg with Sir Ernest Oppenheimer.

Tony had by now become a Director of certain copper mines in Central Africa, which meant regular trips to the Copper Belt of what was then Northern Rhodesia.

19th August, 1951

The trip to Rhodesia started very early in the morning from the deserted airstrip at Nakuru. The aircraft was a tiny single-engined Beechcraft Bonanza. It was 1,050 miles to Nkana and we made two stops on the way. The arrangements the other end were most comfortable and the directors, who all came by

132

air, were put up in a guest house managed by an efficient Scottish housekeeper named Mrs English.

I left again very early the next morning, and for half an hour we cruised around, keeping the mine in sight because the compass would not work properly. Eventually we got on course and in due time arrived at Tabora, in Tanganyika, for lunch. After this the self-starter would not start, and I was getting rather bored. Suddenly the engine fired and, to my consternation, the aircraft began to move rapidly forward – there were no chocks under the wheels. The pilot made a leap to get onto the wing and back into the cockpit, but he missed, and fell on his face on the runway. My mind and body were at first paralysed, but as we gathered speed I began to realise that I must do something. Fortunately I knew where the throttle was – but at first I pushed it the wrong way and we went faster than ever. In the end I managed to bring the aircraft to a stop within a yard of a deep ditch.

I was not awfully pleased with the pilot for this incident.

The last part of our journey took us for about an hour over a very high and bleak area called the Mau. We encountered some nasty storms, which we had to skirt around, not daring to go through them. We finally crossed the Mau with our altimeter showing 10,000 feet and dense cloud above and below us. It was a relief to see Rhodora. We flew over at about milking time, and they waved and sent down a car for me. Fortunately, I shall be able to go to the next meeting in November by the regular Central Airways route.

We are very busy, because Mumford is away on holiday; the rain is good and the coffee is ripening well. Rosemary is plagued by minor clinical troubles among the farm boys. Whilst engaged on this work she was chatting to the clerk about his children, whom he has just brought from the Reserve. He was telling her about the two young ones.

'What about the third one?' Rosemary asked, referring to a little girl of about seven.

'That is not my child,' he replied, in all seriousness. 'That is my *ayah* (children's nurse).'

133

I have been tackling wage problems in the office. One tiny little boy came to the window wanting an increase in pay.

'What work do you do?' I asked.

'I hoe in the coffee,' he replied.

I called the second headman, Odera, who supervises that type of work.

'Do you know this boy, and is he a good worker?' I asked.

'Bwana,' he said, 'This boy is a superlative worker. He does the work of a full-grown man and he is never late.'

'That is curious,' I said, 'For I have not noticed him before. Tell me – has he any relatives on this farm?'

'Yes,' said Odera, looking down his nose. 'He is my son.'

We prevailed upon Leo to record his impressions of our safari:

30th September, 1951

The next morning we set out in Colonel Gethin's lorry. This is not entirely a satisfactory vehicle, being a smallish Ford pick-up with open sides. We took up the positions that we were to keep throughout the trip – ladies in front with Colonel Gethin, and men behind, with our view to the front partially obscured by the driving cab; and so we jolted over forty-odd miles to the site. With a certain amount of leaning and scrambling, one was able to see quite well. The chief difficulty lay in conversing with the driver, the only way of asking him to stop for some particularly exciting or photogenic beast being to thump hard on the sides of the lorry. This generally annoyed the driver and frightened the animal away, and was not popular.

At every turn there was something new: a brilliant flash of wings as some exotic and jewel-like bird sped by, a swirl of dust as herds of zebra and wildebeest plodded across the dusty plain, the stir of a leafy tree as a giraffe's head appeared, ludicrously, over the top – and so on, with rarely a dull moment. Game such as zebra, the tiny, bambi-like Thomson's gazelle, the larger Grant's gazelle, giraffe in herds or families, baboons and Sykes monkeys scrambling about in the under-growth – these were always to be seen, and while looking for rarer animals they always held the interest as they strolled, trotted, galloped, munched, or just stared at intruders. It is a strange fact that one is able to get very much nearer to a wild animal in a car than on foot and, in this way, we had first-class views of nearly everything that we spotted.

The Rhino Camp itself consists of several thatched reed huts in a forest clearing. Camp beds, a couple of tables, no flooring and a mosquito net are featured in the bedrooms, although there is a tin bath with running hot water. On the whole, the middle of the jungle seems quite a civilized place, except for the evening when Rosemary and I thought we saw a mouse scampering towards us along the ground, bent to look at it, and found it was a tarantula – of the more deadly variety. Colonel Gethin quickly trod on it and passed over the incident lightly, but we were rather shaken, and in no way comforted later when hyenas began howling quite close to the camp.

We were woken next morning at 5.30 in time to see an amazing equatorial dawn, which started with an orange glow in a gauze-like sky, turned a bright yellow and then gradually faded until, quite suddenly, the sun shot up and the icing-sugar top of Kilimanjaro glowed a tempting shade of pink. By sunrise we were already on the move, watching huge herds of wildebeest storming across open space and admiring a pelican roosting on top of a tree. There were many different varieties of eagle, including the gaudy Bateleur who ruffled his wings beautifully for the special benefit of my camera, less attractive vultures by the score, and a carrion marabou stork, looking like a wise and hideous old man. At one point we saw a hyena enjoying a good meal and went closer to see what it was eating. The two African boys, whose wonderful eyesight led us to most of the big game, and Colonel Gethin had got out of the lorry, when suddenly one of them cried out, very excited: we all looked up (of course, I was just in the middle of changing a film) and there in a tree, about six feet away, was a leopard devouring a newly-killed impala. No sooner had we looked than he streaked down and off into the forest.

Two more highlights remain from an interesting morning's expedition: chasing, and running parallel to, an ostrich at about thirty-five miles an hour, its ludicrous toe-pointing stride an admirable parody of a middle-aged ballerina; and then our first good view of a rhino. He was standing alone in a clearing and showed no inclination to charge.

We returned to an enormous breakfast and after a wash and tidy-up, went to see a nearby Masai village. The Masai are the local tribe. Some of their more engaging habits include the killing of a lion by every male before he can be considered a man, turning old people over a certain age out into the jungle with one day's supply of food, and the employment of dried cow-dung in the construction of their long, low, igloo-like huts. As a result they are perpetually surrounded by swarms of flies, everywhere. We were received with great respect and hospitality. One little girl, fascinated by Rosemary's lipstick, pointed at her mouth and in a piping voice shrilled out, 'It's painted, it's PAINTED!'

In spite of the flies they seemed a healthy, good-looking people. We took a lot of photographs, for which we handed over the regal sum of five shillings.

Back at Rhodora, Tony took up his pen again.

7th October, 1951

Rosemary spent Monday dealing with the still fluid horse situation. She went up to Kabazi to ride Nyota, and has become resigned to the fact that the mare will always be a temperamental lady who looks at tractors and bicycles with distaste. At least she does not attempt to run away, or kick, or buck. She and Rosemary suit each other very well, and the more Rosemary rides her, the more confidence they get in each other.

In the afternoon Rosemary went over to Elburgon to see a horse which might possibly do for either of us. There has been much rain and the roads are terrible. She took the old road by mistake, and the car had to be pushed up most of the hills by gangs of boys who were waiting for just such an eventuality so that they might earn a few cents. We now have a Lumbwa driver who drives beautifully and is very brave. Thanks to his calmness, they extricated themselves from what might have been a nasty situation and arrived at a tumbledown Kenyan dwelling which housed the prospective horse.

After one look at it, Rosemary decided that its mother must have been a mule and, with many apologies for bothering its owner, she faded away to find another, and better, road home.

13th October, 1951

On Sunday the entire Blundell family came for the day: Michael, Gerry, their daughter Susan, and the Danish nurse. After an excellent lunch, produced by our young kitchen boy who is still doing duty in the absence of Gwara, we took Michael and Gerry round the farm. As Rhodora was bought from Michael he naturally has a special interest in it. After tea, leaving David and Susan quarrelling happily by the pond, we paraded all fifteen of our show animals for Michael to inspect, criticise, and judge whether he has something of his own that will beat us. (In the general enthusiasm all outside competitors were overlooked.)

On Thursday we went to tea with them, and the rôles were reversed: we were the eager spectators at a private showing of Michael's show animals. Comments at the time:

'Now we really *are* depressed. . . . I can't keep my eyes off that *magnificent* bull. . . . What a lovely heifer, our Beauty will have a tough time to hold her own against *her*. . . .' and so on.

Comments in the car afterwards:

'Did you *see* that bull's back legs. . . . My goodness, *weren't* they in bad condition. . . . Not really a *patch* on our own animals . . .'

Long may our illusions last! Nevertheless, Rosemary could not resist looking anxiously at the Butterfat Baby and Beauty the moment we got back, even though it was so dark that we practically had to feel our way over the animals.

Leo wrote the following account of the Royal Show at Nairobi. (We would never *have noticed 'shiny new cars' when there was livestock to look at.)*

21st October, 1951

The main arena (a vast affair, described somewhat over-enthusiastically in the handbook when referring to the children's musical ride as 'the plains of the wide arena') was kept busy from morning till night with horse-jumping of one sort or another, while all manner of horses were judged in numerous adjacent rings. The trade stalls were numerous and often ingenious in their efforts to catch the eye. Air France sported a sort of film-set replica of a French provincial town. Motor firms paraded shiny new cars and tractors which looked well to the frustrated English eye and the inevitable clatter of agricultural implements whirred and rotated and clipped and jiggered before an open-mouthed and motley audience of Indians, Africans and 'visitors'. I cannot stress too strongly the feeling of efficiency and confidence that permeated the show. A young community was putting on a jolly good performance, and knew it.

The real excitement for Rhodora came on Thursday when we sat by a small ring, sandwiched between the Jerseys and Friesians, and watched Rhodora sweep the board with their aristocratic beasts. Rosemary and Ace had made sure that every animal looked its best: beautifully trained and polished horns; sleek, shining coats; healthy condition; clean bodies; gleaming hooves. Rhodora animals stood out in the ring and it was not surprising to find, at the end of the morning's judging, that they had won every class, except one, in which they had competed. I could hardly hold the battery of still and ciné cameras with which I was determined to record the event for posterity.

5th November, 1951

Yesterday evening we all went to a Charity Dance in Subukia. As we were leaving, Leo remarked on how suitable our attire was for a night's expedition into the jungle: dinner jackets and gumboots. After the ten-mile journey up to the Wards our Peugeot gave out on their front drive and Leo and the driver had to push the remaining 100 yards. On the way up we had passed a car stuck in the mud at the foot of the drive, and John had to take the land rover down to pull them out. We also saw several cars in the tow of a tractor; the mud was indescribable.

We managed to arrive without too much of Africa on our evening clothes. At the foot of the steps leading up to the house a shoe-shine boy had been stationed, and proved much in demand. The dance was in the best of Western traditions, with a good band and cabaret. In the buffet tent an invasion of safari ants caused consternation for a short time. We slithered home down the steep escarpment road at 2.30.

All this week our lawn has been graced with the visit of a pair of African hoopoes. These little birds, with splendid orange and black crests, disproportionately long curved beaks, orange bodies and black and white wings, are described in the bird book as 'veldt birds, widely distributed but nowhere common.' They make a charming sight as they hop about, poking their long bills into the grass in search of grubs and worms, the male bird often flying over to his mate with a particularly tasty morsel, which he places gently in her mouth. When other birds approach he takes off, and petulantly beating his wings, scares the intruders away. We think the cause of this tender behaviour must be a nest, but it seems strange to see one fully-grown bird being fed by another.

18th November, 1951

The head calf boy went sick this week. He is highly thought of by all the others and they put him in the hut used by our syces near the cowshed, where we could get at him easily. Rosemary and I went in to see him on Thursday night. He was lying patiently on a wooden bed. The hut, spotlessly clean though very dark, was crowded with other herd boys. One was playing a primitive musical instrument rather like a lyre, while another was preparing some posho (maize pudding); others were sitting talking quietly. Rosemary felt his pulse, which was running into the hundred-and-forties and his breathing was difficult. We decided to move him into hospital in the morning when she and Leo left for Nairobi (Leo for a safari to Tanganyika and Rosemary for a meeting of the Kennel Club). They left at 7.30 am on the Saturday and the Matron of the hospital thought the boy might have typhoid fever.

In between the rainy evenings, David has been riding his tricycle on our evening rounds of the stock. Armed with a mackintosh and a jersey in his handlebar basket he presents a sturdy little figure in royal blue trousers on the pillarbox red tricycle, and he guides it expertly round puddles and ruts and enjoys it enormously. We have some rather nice film of him, taken by Leo, which we tried out on Friday night. Leo's films of the animals at Amboseli have not come out well. We think it is something to do with the telescopic lens.

2nd December, 1951

Sometimes we have been playing simple card games with David and he has become quite good at them now. This led to a misunderstanding when Miss Goodwin was telling him about a church service she had just attended. She mentioned that they had prayed for the King and Queen: 'Did you pray for the Jack too?' said David.

9th December, 1951

We feel inundated not only with rain, but also with work. Ace is still on his back in hospital. The wet weather brings a spate of minor complaints in the cowshed – bad legs and eyes and so on,

140

all of which have to be treated night and morning. A sow has gone sick and refuses to feed her four-day-old babies. The two newly-imported animals are reacting to their last inoculation. In the grade calf pens, which are chock-a-block with calves just now, the youngest ones are still suffering from the mysterious Rhodora scours which the best brains in the vet-lab cannot yet put right for us; we struggle with countless different treatments in order to save their lives, and for experimental purposes.

Outside the rain is making it most difficult to dry our coffee just at its peak. Some of it began to smell this week, and we have had to spread some out on Mumford's verandah. No sooner do we put it out to dry than a shower comes and we have to bring it in again. The fields are choked with weeds, and the maize is sprouting and we might lose a large proportion of the £2,000 crop. Coughs and colds are everywhere amongst the Africans and Rosemary is exhausted from washing out cups of cough mixture. What a contrast with the past two dry years.

After this good moan, let us tell you that the three horses in the isolated loose-boxes, round the corner of the cowshed, give us no cause for worry; Arap Genich and Arap Marisim carry out their duties with devotion and thoroughness.

We saw in the New Year at the Stragglers' Club Dance, where we noted that 'the girls picked their way over a soaking wet lawn to get to the house. . . .' On New Year's Day we held a 'sundowner' at Rhodora, and sent home this account of it:

6th January, 1952

Most of the morning and afternoon were spent in and out of Nakuru collecting things: huge bunches of yellow alstroemeria with which Rosemary decorated the place, last minute cocktail pastries from Spekes, bread and sausages for Gwara to make other toasties from. Time flew by to zero hour, six o'clock, when the first guests arrived. The champagne cocktails went with a swing although the glasses we were able to hire were

141

smaller than real champagne glasses, and everyone's drinks had to be replaced by circulating the boys quickly amongst the guests and arranging an efficient system of glass-washing. There were about fifty-five people and John and Robin, Liza and Pam took charge of the bar for us. We only had trouble with one man, who insisted on coming up to the trestle table at frequent intervals and tipping a brandy bottle liberally into a tumbler. John got hold of a bottle of brandy, added plenty of water and left it in a prominent position. After one or two more visits to the table, the man began to smell a rat, and looked around for a real bottle of brandy, but John and Pam had the real stuff all tucked away under the table, and our hard-drinking visitor was disappointed.

On Saturday we were asked to a barbecue party on a neighbour's farm. We had been asked to go as shipwrecked mariners, and we managed to find two navy blue sweaters, and got the local Indian tailor to put H.M.S RHODORA across the front. We put these sweaters over white silk shirts and navy blue ties. Rosemary had a pair of navy blue slacks, and I had another old pair of hers which she had long since given to Beatrice. We each rounded off our nautical dress with one of David's little round white hats on our heads – exactly like American sailors' hats.

At the party we found Roy Laird was Captain of the Ship, with his Captain's hat and duffle coat. He hailed us with glee as two of his crew. One lady had her bath-hat on (she said she had been in the bath when the shipwreck happened). A young man came in a stiff shirt and black bow-tie, but no trousers; he preserved the decencies by wearing two pairs of pants, one pair in reverse. The party was in the garden and it was a perfect, moonlit night. We all sat around a huge log fire and roasted our own food (bacon, lamb and sausage impaled on a stick). Someone had a banjo and we sang songs until about eleven at night, when Rosemary and I came home.

24th February, 1952

We are afflicted by a virus disease known as Rift Valley Fever. This disease is well-known in South Africa but has not been seen in Kenya for twenty years, and then it only affected sheep, and was unknown in cattle. It is undoubtedly associated with the enormous numbers of mosquitoes which are a legacy of last year's exceptional rains, and which are still breeding in millions in the grass.

The cattle get a very high temperature and their milk drops to zero. If the cow is pregnant, abortion often follows. On several farms there have been thirty or more abortions; fatalities amongst mature animals are rare.

So far we have had twelve cases, seven in the pedigrees and five in the grades. We have lost one pedigree first-calf heifer, three pedigree calves and a pair of aborted grade twins. This adds up to about £1,000. Our champion Guernsey female, Beauty, has had it and got over it; we now wait to see if she will abort.

The vet-lab had in stock some vaccine from South Africa when the disease first made its appearance, but the stock was out of date and South Africa could not spare them any more. They have now managed to make up some of their own, but we are not advised to use it until they have tested it. Meanwhile we watch and pray and wonder which of our precious animals will be hit next. One curious feature of the disease is that it does not seem to affect bulls, only females. We spray our stock against mosquitoes every evening now.

There is also evidence that the disease can be carried to humans who are involved in a post-mortem. We suspect it may also be transmitted through the milk of infected animals, before they lose their milk completely. We have had no less than fourteen herd boys ill at one time, and many of them are still away from work; for them it is like a very bad flu, and for about four days they feel very ill, with pains in the back and the back of the head. It takes about three days after this for them to recover the strength to work again.

These cases among the herd boys have made it most difficult

143

to carry on the daily work, and now Ace has developed it and is in hospital. They are treating him with aureomycin and he is rather pleased, because they have told him he is making history for they know so little about Rift Valley Fever in Kenya. When we sent an African into the native hospital, they treated him with quinine, as if he had malaria – even though the slides were negative for malaria. When he got back here the poor boy had a severe relapse and is still away. Now I treat our boys myself, giving them aspirin and M&B. In many ways I think it would be better just to leave them to sweat it out without any medicines at all. They say there is only one known case of its being fatal to humans.

Rosemary went down to the hospital and had a long talk with the senior Medical Officer for Health for Kenya. He merely confirmed how little they all know about it, and in any case, both the medical and the veterinary people have other preoccupations, because there is bubonic plague at Rongai (about twenty-five miles away) and foot-and-mouth (which has already caused the cancellation of the Eldoret Show) is sweeping the country. We have long since instituted certain precautions here against foot-and-mouth. At the moment it is not on any farm nearer to us than twenty miles away.

We are sending you an account of the Queen's visit to Treetops, written by the man who owns the Outspan Hotel, who was in charge of the party. That afternoon a water-buck suffered its death throes in the pool outside Treetops before crawling away to shore, leaving a trail of blood. There is a story going round that when a herd of elephant came onto the scene after the dying buck had limped away, they smelt its blood and were frightened. They let out the peculiar high-pitched trumpeting of a frightened elephant and the African bearers in the party turned to each other and said 'That sound means that a Chief has died.' Of course, it was the night the King died.

* * *

ROYAL VISIT TO TREETOPS

The following is a letter from Mr Sherbrooke Walker, owner of

Treetops, to Sir Philip Mitchell, Governor of Kenya, describing what Her Majesty The Queen and The Duke of Edinburgh saw at Treetops on the night of February, 5th.

Dear Sir Philip,

You may like to have a report on Treetops.

At 1.30 pm I came down from the tree to meet Their Royal Highnesses at the car halt. My wife was to come to the foot of the tree to meet them, and I asked her if any dangerous game came into sight to hang a white towel out of the kitchen window.

As the royal party arrived at the car halt, a runner from my wife came along to say there were both elephant and rhino under the tree.

Their Royal Highnesses, Lady Pamela Mountbatten, Commander Parker and Mr Windley duly arrived; Windley had a rifle, and I gave one to the Duke, and of course had one myself.

Halfway along the path to Treetops elephant could be heard trumpeting so to reduce the size of the party Lady Pamela and Commander Parker were left each at the foot of a ladder and the remaining four of us went on. When we got near Treetops, the white towel was to be seen hanging out of the window. Mr Hayward (of National Parks) with a rifle was watching the herd of elephant, and Col. Cowie, also with a rifle, was hiding unseen in the bush.

I asked the Duke to remain at the foot of one of the ladders with Hayward, so as to concentrate on getting the Princess up the tree as soon as possible. Windley and I went forward with her; she walked quietly towards the ladder, and directly towards a very large cow elephant standing some thirty yards away in the shade of the tree, with a low bush between us. With the greatest coolness and courage the Princess continued going forward, and quietly climbed the ladder without any suspicion of hurry.

(Next day I measured the distance of the imprint of the elephant's front feet to the ladder, and it was eleven yards).

Then the Duke came up and we collected Lady Pamela and Commander Parker who had wisely climbed their ladders when they heard the trumpeting close by. So they all got safely into the tree, and the privileged few who were there know they have a very brave little lady to be their Queen. They got some photographs of the herd of forty elephants before they moved off. Then baboons appeared, and put up their usual clownish show. The Duke was on the crow's nest on the roof when a water-buck came dashing up pursued by another. The leading one had a great bleeding wound on its back-side, and the other one had its horn tipped with blood. It dashed into the centre of the pool and gasped and panted, while the victor stood over it for half an hour, gazing at what appeared to be its dying struggles. We thought it was going to drown, but after an hour or so it staggered to shore leaving behind a trail of blood.

At 5.30 pm a herd of elephant arrived (including two babies a few days old). They stayed milling about under the tree for an hour or more, while Their Royal Highnesses took photographs.

About 8 pm the rhino came, and remained snorting and blowing until 8 am next morning, sometimes eight at a time being in sight. The flood lighting, fixed up by the National Parks, showed the animals up very well all night.

Their Royal Highnesses, who did not retire until 12.30 am got up four times during the night, and finally came out just before dawn, to watch two bull rhinos having a fight, and stayed on the verandah until breakfast.

As they were getting into their car, I could not help saying 'If you have the same courage, Ma'am, in facing whatever the future sends you, as you have in facing an elephant at ten yards, we are going to be very fortunate.' She smiled, the Duke laughed, they stepped into their car and drove to the Lodge to receive the tragic news of His Majesty's death.

Very many thanks for allowing me the great privilege of showing the animals to such delightful and appreciative guests; they had royal luck for in the twenty years' existence of Treetops, I do not think there has ever been such a congregation of elephant and rhino.

Yours sincerely,
Eric Sherbrooke Walker.
Nairobi,
12th February, 1952.

8

Even the sadness we all felt at Princess Elizabeth's bereavement did not dim our enthusiasm for the future. Both the coffee and our herds were making marvellous progress; we had every hope that we might be able to solve the farm's water problems by finding a new source on the land; and we felt proud to be here, making this exciting country grow, yet so closely linked with Britain. (On Battle of Britain day in September the African population and others were somewhat amazed when four Vampire jets flew low over the town and stayed around for ten minutes, flying in perfect formation at all angles. They were followed by a Canberra jet bomber.)

Yet we were all aware of the first rumblings of Mau Mau unrest, like the sound of distant thunder growing closer.

Tony continued his regular trips to the Copper Belt; I judged at the Nakuru Show, and made a successful expedition to a sale in Tanganyika. And Rikki arrived.

2nd March, 1952

We made an early start for Nairobi on Tuesday and found the city so hot that we could hardly move to do the little bits of shopping we had to do. . . . At 5.15 we sank with relief into the seats of a cool, dark cinema and saw *An American in Paris*. Then we returned to bathe and change and dine at the Club. At 8.45 we set off for the airport. It is a fascinating place at night. The Hermes we had come to meet came taxi-ing in at the speed of a walking man, a huge giant, lit up from stem to stern. We stood at the freight shed watching as it came to a halt in exactly the right spot.

It was a balmy night, warm with a slight breeze, the sky

perfectly clear, so that one could see all the stars, and the heavy scent of Africa was in the air. We waited about half an hour, idly talking to the Indian customs clerk, whilst they lifted freight from the monster. Eventually a box appeared which we thought might contain our treasure. It was tipped on its side as they brought it down. However, it was brought right to our shed and into the light and, with mounting excitement, we opened it and extracted Champion Riverhill Rikki, straight from his triumph at Cruft's. He was looking fine; the straw in his box was as clean as when he left, and I was at once struck by his enormous coat and perfect ears. He looked every inch a champion as he stood and blinked at us in the lights of the Customs shed.

23rd March, 1952

On Monday Peter McMaster paid a routine visit to see the coffee. We wished particularly to consult him about the pruning. He was staggered by the size of the crop we have on the trees, estimating it at 150 tons, or nearly double the large crop we had three years ago. It is only possible for the trees to carry this because, in the intervening years, we have followed his advice and pruned the trees so that they have much more bearing wood. They are much bigger trees than they used to be. However, he says that if we leave so much crop on, we shall seriously damage them, and we have decided to take his advice and prune a lot off. This will also improve the quality. A great deal depends on this year's rains, which have not yet broken.

Incidentally, I also had a meeting of the Coffee Marketing Board this week. The price outlook is again favourable: this past year, we shall get about £320 a ton, and we have picked twenty-four tons. For the coming year, I do not think we shall get less than £350 per ton and we estimate a minimum of fifty tons. Peter McMaster has said from the beginning that when we get into our stride, under his pruning methods, we should get a regular crop of forty or fifty tons every year.

30th March, 1952

We met Nancy and Roy Laird at five o'clock at one of the cinemas, where we saw *Cry, The Beloved Country*. This is a grim film, without a smile anywhere, but it is a fascinating study of the racial problem in South Africa. We came back to the Club for a bath and a change and all re-united for a really good dinner. Later we joined John and Margaret Monck, who were with Sir Charles and Lady Mortimer (he is Member for Health in the government). John beguiled us with his talk about ranching and dairying in Canada and the USA and about growing pineapples in Hawaii and Kilifi until 1.30 am. He is a wonderful talker and we were all much amused.

On Tuesday we came home, arriving in Nakuru in time for lunch. The general effect of the week has been to rivet our attention on social and housing problems relating to the Africans. The first stirrings came when Rosemary came to collect me from tennis on Sunday. She had been to see a *bibi* who was ill, and had been appalled once again by the conditions under which this woman was living. Then the Governor, in his speech, said that the one thing which would ruin this country would be if the Bwana were off playing polo while his labourers lived in squalor (I cannot see myself playing polo, but still. . . .). Then there was the film, which reduced us to jelly and, finally, a visit to the Labour Officer in Nakuru, which finished us off: he said that with inflation as it is, employers should reconsider the usual wage rates and scales of rations. Then there would be no shortage of labour, and the labourers would be happy. As a result some long-thought-of plans for the betterment of African conditions on this farm are being put into effect forthwith. We have started by increasing all their pay and the free rations, and various housing plans are afoot.

6th April, 1952

The draft of this is being written on Saturday night. Rosemary has just arrived back from Nairobi, and we are expecting Joanna, the driver, to give in his notice. Rosemary left the Mansion House in the centre of Nairobi at 4.15, after a meeting of the General Committee of the Kennel Club, and arrived back here at 6.15: 110 miles in two hours! Joanna spent the entire drive shaking his head and saying 'Never again!'

On the down trip (accomplished at a more sober speed) he nursed one of Rosa's pups, which went to its new owner, a Mrs Holmes, who is a hotel-keeper. Inchmery Apple Blossom cost the hotel twelve guineas, and Rosemary says it is sheer robbery to sell her at such a price, for she has ears which are pricked and look like a bat's and are as big as her whole little, snipey, papillon face. She is not one of the Inchmery Kennels' best efforts. Mrs Holmes seemed pretty fed up anyway, as her husband had let his hotel for some years and then had to take it over again in appalling condition.

Incidentally, for those of you who do not already know, the dogs here are run under the prefix Inchmery, and not Rhodora, because Rosemary had already so well established the Inchmery name for dogs in England before we came out that we thought it best to carry on. The cattle and pigs, of course, carry the prefix Rhodora. The coffee is still known by the initials of the first owner of the farm. We have not changed this, for the mark is still well known to coffee brokers in England. Our best coffee is marked AJP and our second grade, AJP/Solai.

The pedigree cowshed yard is now finished, a glorious expanse of well-swept concrete with green grass squares at each end, complete with pigeon-cotes. Foot-and-mouth has broken out only eight miles away and we have imposed strict precautions. Everyone who visits us has to drive over sacks soaked in disinfectant and the wheels of the cars are sprayed. There are foot-baths everywhere, and a barrier on the road beside the office reading NO CARS BEYOND THIS POINT, PLEASE. The bulls are no longer allowed out for their morning walk. Instead they parade around the new yard, doing twenty circuits each morning. Rosemary says it reminds her of watching, from her bedroom window as a child, the hunters being exercised around the stable yard at Ascott (her grandmother's house in Buckinghamshire). The milking herd and the heifers are all in the centre fields of the farm, and there are no less than nine guards on our perimeter fencing to prevent visits from strangers from other farms.

13th April, 1952

All those of you who have written this week have referred to our remarks about African welfare. We are glad you approve of our plans to try to do something more for our Africans. In addition to their ration of maize meal (*posho*) (which on this farm is two pounds daily instead of the usual pound and a half), milk daily, vegetables weekly and salt monthly, which we give them, we have introduced – since we last wrote – a free issue of half a pound of sugar a week. This week, when we at last receive our annual accounts from the auditors, we hope to be able to afford to give them 1 lb of meat each per week (instead of the monthly biltong ration they get now) as well as some beans, potatoes, and fat. If we can afford all this they will have a balanced diet as a free issue. We consider this their first requirement. Next in importance is their level of wages: these we have already increased by two shillings a month for every man, at an extra cost of £180 a year to the farm. It brings the lowest-paid worker's wage to twenty-one shillings a month, plus a free house and the rations outlined above. If we feel we can well afford all this (which we are determined to be able to do) we hope to make a further arbitrary increase in the wages. We also want to introduce a bonus system for all workers based on a certain sum for every bag of coffee which leaves the farm. Our wage rates are already slightly above the average for the district, and there is no general farmer in the area, to my knowledge, who gives the full scale of rations. In all these calculations, you must remember that we have to have 150 Africans to run this farm, and we would like 200, if we could get them. The output per man-hour of the African worker is nothing like as great as that of a European. There are many reasons for this, and we certainly cannot hope to overcome all the factors which prevent an African from working hard. However, two of them are undernourishment and lack of incentive, and both these we can do something about.

Our labour is well-housed by normal standards. Most of them have large stone huts (a single room) with thatched roofs, instead of mud and wattle huts. We are about to build four superior houses for our head houseboy, cook, personal boy and old laundry man. We think we should start with them because they have seen how we live, and have a higher standard in their minds. These houses will have a living-room as well as a bedroom, and two other small rooms for a washroom and kitchen. We shall put in ceilings, and give them proper windows and a little furniture. Our clerk already has a house on these lines. Later we shall build one for the Headman, and perhaps for the junior headmen, but before we do this, we want to try and build a general recreation room in the village for all the workers.

Of course none of this building is done by contractors, which would make the cost prohibitive. We employ our own African stonemason and carpenter, and design the buildings ourselves. The stone is cut in our own quarries, but the cement and the wood for the roofs (we are putting shingles on the roofs) are obtained outside and are very expensive.

4th May, 1952

On Wednesday at 8 am we set off for Sotik. Normally this would be merely a long drive (260 miles return) but in view of the copious rain and terrible roads, it turned into an expedition. We took not only raincoats and gumboots, but a handgrip, filled with emergency kit in case we should get stuck en route.

The purpose of our journey was to visit some people who bravely bear the name of Bastard, and inspect their Guernsey grade cattle for the National Grading-up Scheme. At Molo we collected a man named Upton; he, Rosemary and Geoffrey

Ireland are the three Inspectors for the Register, and they make it a rule never to visit a farm alone, for obvious reasons – they always work in pairs.

The tea companies have built a narrow tarmac road for fifty miles from Lumbwa, through Kericho, to Sotik; however, the rivers were raging torrents, and more than one bridge was threatened. Arriving at Sotik, a desolate little village, at 12.30, we telephoned the farm and were told by Mrs Bastard that her husband had come in to meet us with his land rover. We duly contacted him, left our car in the village in the care of our driver, and climbed into the land rover for a ten-mile trip to his farm. It was swamp nearly all the way, without any proper road – terribly rough going. We were plagued by vicious horse-flies, and it was hot and sultry.

Mrs Bastard, a vivacious red-haired woman of about our age, came out to welcome us and took us in to lunch. We were in a tearing hurry to get the job done and start for home again, for we knew it was bound to rain on the way back, but our host and hostess, who, we imagine, seldom have a chance to see other human beings, were determined to make the best of us, and we dawdled over the meal. Eventually we managed to drag them to the cows, where we found that none of those we were to inspect had been separated from the herd. They tried to make us wade through grass knee-deep to see them, but Rosemary and Upton were having none of that, and Rosemary said she would stand by the gate and see each one driven up to her, inspected, and passed through the gate into the cowshed for the earmarking. After much delay we got them sorted, and six out of seven were passed. As we walked to the cowshed, we were suddenly surrounded by three fully-grown bulls, shaking their heads at us. The Bastards had had them let out of their paddock so that we could see them better! Rosemary nervously said that the first one she saw was marvellous, and that seemed to satisfy them, and the bulls were driven away. Inside the cowshed was more chaos: the ears of the animals had not, of course, been prepared, and they were filthy with matted hair. Ear numbers were dropped about on a floor heavy with dung.

It was raining when we got to Kericho, and there were some

bad patches on our way back to Molo. Several times we were not sure whether we would get up a hill or not, and once we had to ford a river which had broken over the bridge. We felt no confidence that the bridge would last much longer. But we finally got home, in darkness, at 8.30 pm.

18th May, 1952

We have already started picking coffee: only a small amount each day, but I doubt if any coffee has ever before been ripe in May on this farm. It has big, bold berries too. I expect we shall be picking, off and on, right through until the end of January. The early crop and the size of the beans are due to the wonderful rains last year, and the excellent rain so far this year. Peter McMaster thinks we have now pruned the crop down to a certain seventy tons. . . . The prices of wool, sisal and cotton have receded sharply, but coffee has shown no signs of weakening yet. You poor people in England have just had the price of coffee put up, presumably to meet the higher price we are going to get next year if the proposed contract offered by the Ministry of Food goes through. However, we feel we must have a really strong second string to our bow on this farm, and we are building up the grade Guernsey herd as fast as we can, refusing all demands (which we constantly get) to sell animals.

25th May, 1952

We have been gay and dined out twice this week. Once we went to Kabazi to see a film. They get one about once a month complete with sound-track from Nairobi, and they are generally quite good. This one was by Somerset Maugham, called *Trio*. Robin and Liza Long were there, and the following evening we went up after tea to their place, looking at their racehorses and yearlings and dining afterwards.

One teatime David was scribbling on the floor of the sitting-room. 'I'm wery busy,' he said. 'I'm wery busy writing lots of

155

letters and just now I'm writing to that one what's had the operation.'

The next day he was examining the flush mechanism in his lavatory when the heavy porcelain lid slipped off, fell on the seat, and shattered the lavatory pan. Cost of repair about £10 and mess everywhere. Shortly afterwards he came round to see me:

'Daddy, I've broken the lavatory; I was looking to see where the water went to. I will pay for it with my own money.' (He gets sixpence a week pocket money.)

I was busy reading *The Times*, so did not take much notice. After a long pause, David added,

'You know, Daddy, I haven't got wery *much* money.'

31st August, 1952

Some of you may have read in the papers about unrest in Kenya amongst the Africans. It is not as bad as it is reported to be. There is an underground organisation known as Mau Mau, which is openly anti-European, and this the police are belatedly taking strong measures to combat. In some ways, the Mau Mau is a nationalist movement of the Kikuyu tribe. We are not very concerned about it here, because we have few Kikuyu on the farm and if we ever did have trouble, I would call in our Kipsigis, who hate them and would quickly make mincemeat of them. Do not allow these newspaper reports to cause you anxiety. There is no situation out here even approaching that of the planters in Malaya or the gangsters who break into your houses in England.

The garden is really quite lovely just now. Huge pink, yellow and ruby red cannas flank the pond, mixed with blue salvias and Michaelmas daisies. Behind the pond, in the large border, three different mauve bougainvilleas are growing, one of them a large deep purple avalanche, a cascade of flowers which almost hurts one's eyes. Near it is a paler, lilac mauve, a deeper lilac mauve, and a magenta. White bauhinnea trees stand behind them all, and many other flowering bushes and trees of all colours are a mass of blossom.

156

14th September, 1952

On Friday there was a collective auction sale of pedigree and grade Guernseys in Nakuru. We entered two yearling bulls sired by Valentine, and four in-calf grade heifers which we could not stand the sight of any more. The man who brought the heifers lived 200 miles away, and he told me that he came expressly to buy them on the reputation of Rhodora alone. When he saw them, he said he felt confirmed in his decision. (When we saw them, we felt confirmed in our decision to sell them.) The two young bulls got by far the highest prices in the sale and our heifers were the highest-priced females, with one exception. We entered these animals in the sale primarily to keep our name before the public. We now have 210 Guernseys on the farm. So long as coffee prices stay up, we can go on ploughing profits back into the farm by building up these herds and developing the land to feed the increase. This also builds up our milk income. I believe this farm could carry over 500 milking cows.

We are delighted with the news that an oil refinery will be built at Mombasa. It is encouraging that the British Government and the Shell Company take such a good view of this country's future that they are willing to make a new, huge investment here. We are also pleased with the vigour with which the Government has tackled the Mau Mau unrest among the Kikuyu; it gives one great confidence that the Government, and not only the settlers, intend that Europeans shall stay in this country, to lead it and develop it and show the Africans the way to a higher standard of living in which all communities can take part. Michael Blundell has been mentioned frequently in *The Times* of late, and he has been the main person concerned in galvanising the Government into firm and energetic action. This man is maturing fast and well and you will hear a lot of him in the future.

21st September, 1952

On Sunday we set off with David in the car to visit a farm where there was a very 'quiet' pony for sale, which Rosemary thought would be nice for her. This farm was near Ol Kalou, where we had never been before; it is very high, undulating country at eight and a half thousand feet.

A ghastly track that threatened to disembowel the car was the approach to the place. The house was a wooden shack. A woman appeared, with seven mongrels, and warned us not to let the driver, or the *syce* (groom), whom we had brought with us, get out of the car, or they would be eaten by the dogs. She agreed that she had received our two telegrams saying that we were coming, but her son had gone out, and she did not know which horse was for sale. There were sixteen horses, and the one and only groom had run away.

Eventually a lazy-looking boy found the pony in a rickety shed. Outside the shed was its foal, a year old, and taller than its mother. As soon as the pony was led out the foal tried to suckle it. With great difficulty, the foal and the mare were separated, and an old settler's mildewing saddle produced, and a bit with only the curb rein intact. The pony was a nice chestnut but terribly neglected; it seemed quiet. I kept watch on the dogs while Arap Genich mounted the pony. At once, its placid eye assumed a baleful look and it tried to buck him off. He took the protesting pony up the road, and then, shaking his head, murmured to us that it had a very hard mouth and certainly would not do for the memsahib.

The woman knew nothing about it – not even its name.

5th October, 1952

Once a quarter Mr Mayhew, the vicar from Nakuru, holds a service on one of the farms. There is no church in this district, and various local people offer their houses for the ceremony. Mrs Mumford has had it twice before in her house here but we have been away; this time, we decided to take David down there, because he has not yet been to a service. There were about twenty people and a harmonium. Menengai, blue shadowed, watched us across the stretch of green coffee

158

through the open window. David could scarcely believe his ears when all the grown-ups burst into song, and could not help staring at Mrs Howard, nearby, who trilled and quavered on the high notes, having learned singing (as all well-brought-up girls did) in England some seventy years ago.

On Monday evening David came along with me to shoot some baboons. He marched sturdily behind me in his gum-boots and mackintosh right through the big dripping maize field (for it had been raining heavily) above the top piggery. The maize is dense and eight to ten feet high just now. Then we went through long grass up to his waist. He urged me on with loud remarks, meant to be *sotto voce*, such as,

'I'm sure we're getting nearer now, Daddy.'

When I fired down into the crater he stood beside the rifle and was unafraid; in fact he was rather fascinated, as the echo of the explosion rumbled down below.

19th October, 1952

Tomorrow Rosemary and I go to Nairobi for the night, and the following morning, early, I fly off to Rhodesia and Rosemary sets off on her great adventure to the show in Tanganyika. She takes the lorry, the car, three grade Guernseys, three dogs, some parchment coffee, Ace, Bill Murray (editor of the East African Stud Book), Ochieng the personal boy, two drivers, and the dog boy. Miss Goodwin and David will be alone here, but by night they will be guarded by Kipsang, our head herd boy, who stands about six foot four and has a figure to match. It is not only his physique, but his character we admire, so he might well be named Umslopogaas. David and Miss Goodwin will be all right in his hands, and I doubt if any Kikuyu will attempt even to come near the place knowing he is here; if they did, they would feel his spear pretty quickly.

Moustachio, head boy of the pedigree section of the cow-shed, is going to sleep on the Aces' verandah guarding Mrs Ace and Linda and their baby Peter, though Walter, the junior stockman, is near them, so we need not worry too much.

We are taking these special precautions on this occasion because of the present Mau Mau difficulties in the colony, but we think these difficulties are a passing phase, and that the Government is soon going to adopt very stern measures to put an end to the trouble. As you know, by day there are always a lot of people around, both Europeans and natives of many tribes, whilst for protection by night we have grilles on our windows and keep our doors locked. I personally always have a small automatic pistol by our bed (and have had, ever since we have been here) and lately I have taken to carrying it with us in the car when we are out at night.

Apart from the special guards, we have taken no measures which might indicate to the Africans that we are at all apprehensive, and we do not propose to do so. There are some farmers' wives who will not stay alone on the farm, and it is a great nuisance, both for them and their husbands.

26th October, 1952

Thank you so much for all your nice letters and thoughts. Please do not worry about us. It is all very peaceful and quiet here. Every European man in the district (myself, Mumford and Ace included) is enrolled into the police reserve, and we all do a duty patrol in pairs, on a roster system. It works out at two or three patrols per week per man, each patrol being of three or four hours' duration. All the farms are visited at intervals, day and night, and no one need feel lonely or neglected.

During the two nights when David and Miss Goodwin were alone, Mumford came round continually, and no fewer than three Kipsigis, including Kipsang, guarded the house. But all is quiet in this neighbourhood and the police have told me that they soon intend to relax the patrols. The Kikuyus with whom we come in contact seem bewildered and astonished by all that has happened. One feels that most of the leaders of the Mau Mau movement, including the dangerous Jomo Kenyatta, are now behind bars. All the other tribes are right out of it and, if anything, are rather more friendly and helpful than usual; but of course, one does not want to stir up inter-tribal bad feeling.

We are convinced that the Government have acted correctly in taking firm action to stamp out the fire before it can become a conflagration. It will take them time to complete the job but they have got away to a good start, and our personal risk in this district is not great; it does not compare with the risks taken by civilians in England during the war. Once the present lawlessness and unrest amongst the Kikuyu has been suppressed, then the best way to combat future outbreaks is for all us Europeans to feed, house and pay our labour properly, and to make them feel that in time they may aspire to the same standard of living as Europeans. We must build schools on our farms and introduce such social institutions as the St John Ambulance Brigade, Boy Scouts and general welfare work. We must try to get into closer contact with them and work with them. As you know, we have already made quite a good start in these things on this farm; we shall go ahead with our plans and in no way be put off by these events. Incidentally, these remarks only apply to the Africans who are working in the settled areas. The vast mass who live in the Reserves must be catered for by the Government, and they will need all their statesmanship if, after these dreadful events, a chasm between the Kikuyu and the white man is not to open up before us.

One thing is clear, and that is that a great deal of damage has been done to race relations in this country by people from outside it. I do not refer only to Communist influences but also (and especially) to people such as Fenner Brockway and Dugdale and some other Socialist MPs. They come out here for a very short visit, their minds entirely set on taking the part of the black man, and unable to find any good whatever in their fellow white man. Even they cannot realise what terrible damage they do in a short time. I quote from a leading article in one of our papers:

> . . . *None can doubt that part of the responsibility for this tragic State of Emergency rests with the remote doctrinaires and the demagogues who have so recklessly and so unrealistically intervened in the Colony's affairs and policies. . .*

2nd November, 1952

On the farm this past week serious coffee picking has begun, but a new problem is connected with it, for under the State of Emergency regulations Africans are not allowed to move about on the roads. In previous years we have always sent up our lorry to the native market to get extra pickers, and these extra pickers have always been Kikuyu. The position is complicated by the fact that some of the farmers in the vicinity of the market have objected, because they said we drew away their own labour; those very farmers are now in the Special Police, and in a position to stop my lorry under the Emergency regulations.

So I went to see the two gentlemen who are most difficult. The first shouted at me for an hour, in an amicable way, and I agreed with him whenever I could get a word in; the second *offered me a cup of tea*, and I felt I had to be more wary. Meanwhile I checked up on the legal position and got a special permit from a higher authority, so when the lorry was stopped by one of the farmer-policemen on patrol, the permit quelled him at once. The net result is that we are getting our Kikuyu pickers, and the coffee is coming off. This week we have averaged about half a ton a day, so it is not a frantic rush yet, just nice steady picking. It is fine to see the red tinge over the whole coffee shamba.

On Tuesday we had a Committee meeting of the proposed Dog Show. Various worthy lady dog breeders attended. Everyone suddenly became hopelessly undependable. They would all love to help, but. . . . One had to man the telephone because her house had become a local police post; another could not leave her sick husband; and so on. By the next day, I had decided it was no good going on, and advised the Kennel Club that I was not prepared to do so.

We think it quite deplorable that Hale and Fenner Brockway (both Socialist MPs) should have been allowed to come here at this time. (The former arrived wearing no hat, tie or socks.) These two men are at this moment in the Kikuyu Reserve, staying at the house of Chief Koinange, who is one of the chiefs at present in prison, accused of the murder of Senior Chief

Waruhiu. In other words they are staying in the house of one of the Mau Mau leaders! Our Africans knew they had arrived before we did: 'The Bwana Mau Mau has come,' they said.

9

Our attitudes were already, subtly, shifting. When the Mau Mau threat seemed distant in every way, we expressed a degree of sympathy for the social unrest among Africans, perhaps rightly perceiving it as partly caused by poor conditions of life and few prospects.

We thought their living conditions and education should gradually be brought up to European standard and then the unrest would cease.

However, Mau Mau were in a hurry. They decided that they would never get economic or political freedom unless they got their land back. Since the land they wanted included Rhodora, and since the Mau Mau were notoriously violent, our minds became wonderfully concentrated on protecting everything we had built up.

As usual, we took positive action. We imported a couple of Alsatians (called Ajax and Diana) to guard us, became active in the St John Ambulance movement, and stepped up the guard on the property – and carried on with our everyday life.

At the root of our anger was a sense of betrayal. At first it was directed against Her Majesty's Opposition, and later against the British Government itself. Much later, we never really came to trust Kenyatta. But at this stage we were simply bewildered, and fully backed Michael Blundell and Legco's attempts to defend us.

30th November, 1952

The Annual General Meeting of the Solai (local farmers) Association was held at Kabazi. People who did not belong to Solai flocked to the meeting to hear Michael Blundell make an excellent speech. He said that the policy of trying to rally the moderates amongst the Kikuyu has not been a great success,

The unloading of our furniture from England, 1949

The arrival of Valentine of Fernhill Park and the first
imported cattle, 1949

Primrose's Robert of Fernhill Park, our Butterfat
Baby, 1950

Valentine of Fernhill Park, Supreme Male Champion
of Breed, 1951

The Long and the Short of it (Tony and David) on an
evening round of inspection before the yard was
concreted, 1951

Kipsang, our head African herdsman

The staff who helped to win the cups, 1951

Rhodora Beauty's Valentine, Breed Champion, Royal
Show, 1953

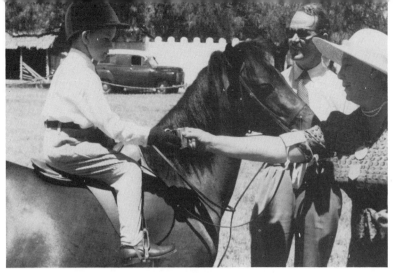

Nakuru Horse Show, 9th January, 1953: David is placed first in the Leading Rein Class and presented with a red rosette and cup

Tony and two members of our Rhodora Defence Force, 1953

Whately with some of his friends, enjoying
refreshment after a night in the crater chasing Mau
Mau terrorists, 1955

David with Ajax and Diana

A heavy coffee crop,
1956

Tony and Rosemary and some of their Guernseys,
1958

Coed Coch Prydus, 1960

Horse of the Year Show, 1961: David and Reeves
Porcelain

nor have the police been entirely successful in rounding up all the ring-leaders. The great majority of Kikuyu are still too frightened of Mau Mau to come forward and help the government forces. Therefore, the policy is being changed, and where there is trouble there will be mass reprisals in that area. For example, near Thomson's Falls, where there have been some unpleasant incidents, a district has been cordoned off, all native stock and moveables, such as bicycles, impounded and all the Kikuyu in the area (some 3,500) taken back to the Reserve. By these means it is hoped to make them respect the authority of the Government, rather than that of Mau Mau. Michael, in his speech – and later in the week on the wireless – asked the settlers to follow the lead given by their elected members (of whom, as you know, he is the leader) and not, under any circumstances, take the law into their own hands in independent action, however much they are provoked. In some parts of the country, the settlers have been sorely tried by repeated and brutal outrages and people are beginning to voice the opinion that all Kikuyu should be moved out of the settled areas back into the Reserve. We think that it is too soon for this to be necessary and, if it were done, the economy of the country, the post, telephone, railways and so on, would be brought to a standstill for a time. In recent speeches Lord Stansgate and other Labour politicians in England seem to make out that the Kikuyu are responsible world citizens; they ignore the present outrages, which show that fifty years of civilization have not changed their savage hearts. At the moment people in this country are not so concerned with the welfare of the Kikuyu as with the safety of all law-abiding people, black and white.

We really are in as good a position as we possibly could be, under the circumstances, with only twenty Kikuyu on our farm against ninety Jaluo and thirty-eight Kipsigis. We are not near the Forest or the Reserve, and there are four European men, including myself, living on the farm. Most of our friends are in more dangerous areas than we are. For instance, on Thursday Rosemary was with Gerry Blundell, who the night before had been up the whole night because twenty-six Kikuyu were caught in the middle of a Mau Mau ceremony on their farm.

165

Gerry is alone a great deal in their house with Susan, her little daughter, and the governess. Her brother-in-law runs the farm when Michael is in Nairobi, and there is a Dutch stockman who comes up to the house from time to time. The Mau Mau meeting was being held to plan an attack on Michael, who had already received a threatening letter. One of the boys at the ceremony who did not want to take the oath was strung up by his neck, whilst a knife was brandished before his naked belly. Under this duress he took the oath but soon after contrived to escape and ran to the night watchman and asked him to get Michael's brother-in-law. He came down, rang the police, and caught the whole lot. All the same it was not very nice for Gerry.

The Government has now insisted that Michael has an armed escort wherever he goes, though it is made as un-obtrusive as possible. Both Michael and Gerry are superb examples of how to behave in danger and Michael is becoming a first-class leader. Freddie and Vi too are next door to Michael's farm, and on the edge of the Bahati Forest. They are surrounded by Kikuyu, and even have entirely Kikuyu servants. They keep a loaded gun always handy (as we do) but they are perfectly calm about it.

7th December, 1952

The Rhodora Defence Force was formed yesterday! It consists of eight of our most trusted Kipsigis braves, led by Kipsang, our Umslopogaas. We did our first night exercises on Thursday night, when I visited all the Kikuyu huts. The total haul was one stranger and one old man, whom we put inside for brewing native beer, and Gwara, our cook, in bed but completely sozzled.

I carefully told the braves to go ahead of me, and surround each group of huts silently before I started to examine them, in order to catch anyone who tried to flee (it was a very dark night). As I approached the first group of huts, instead of silence, I heard a noise fit to wake the dead. I hurried forward with some anxiety, fearing that the Force might have got out of control and attacked the Kikuyu. All I found was a very old Kikuyu bellowing with fright, for they had stolen upon him silently when he was sitting under a tree with his trousers down.

I have equipped the force with black armlets, inscribed with RDF in white, and they are all armed with sharp knives except Kipsang, who carries a spear. They are at instant readiness day and night in case of emergency and two of them will guard David and Rosemary and the house at night while I am away in Rhodesia this week. Later I am planning to have them reviewed by the local magistrate, and I will try to send you all a photograph of them, which might amuse you.

21st December, 1952

On a farm four miles from us there has been a case of arson, where a store has been set alight and the farm lorry and a tractor destroyed. In addition the Headman on the farm has disappeared, and no one will say what has happened to him; foul play is suspected. There is also evidence that Mau Mau meetings have been held there. This week, owing to the lack of co-operation on the part of the Kikuyu on the place, the police removed all their stock. I think this has created some impression amongst them.

The humanitarians in the Opposition party in Parliament should really come and live within four miles of Mau Mau meetings before they start saying that collective punishment is immoral. We are beginning to think that it is the one form of punishment which really touches the Kikuyu, as they are mercenary by nature. We have all been warned to be careful over Christmas and I am going to have members of the Rhodora Defence Force on special duty.

28th December, 1952

I have heard no reports of any Mau Mau trouble in the

European areas over Christmas but we have all been taking special precautions and we have tried to prevent Africans moving on the roads during this period. In the Reserve, some eleven Kikuyu have been murdered by their fellows. We have all been involved in extra patrol work and last Monday I went on a rather longer one than usual, run in conjunction with the army. We started out at 4.30 am and we combed an area near here. The 'bag' at the end seemed to be quite a large number of Africans but they were quietly and efficiently screened by the police and only a few were taken off. The job of our local people was to guide the army personnel and I also took along our lorry as they were short of transport. I got home about 9.00 am for a late breakfast. I took with me two members of our Defence Force to give them an outing!

4th January, 1953

Calling at the cowshed on the way back, we found a heifer which was having trouble calving. It proved extremely difficult. I had a frantic search for a vet, and at last we got the calf out (dead) at 1 am. I think the heifer will survive. I got to bed at 2 am and was up again at 4.30 to go on another large-scale raid with the police over a tract of country about seven miles from here, where there have been a number of cases of arson, caused by Mau Mau adherents. Our job was to collect up all the Kikuyu sheep and goats, because they have refused to co-operate with the authorities (not the sheep and goats, but the Kikuyu!). We assembled over 500 animals and they were driven off to a holding ground.

It had been a bad week for Mau Mau, with a number of murders and attempted murders. The settlers are considerably disturbed. It is felt that owing to political considerations in England, the Government of Kenya is afraid to take sufficiently stern measures. The Kikuyu are undoubtedly fighting a war against us; why can we do no more than take police action against them? If their dogs give warning of our approach to the huts, we are not even allowed to shoot them, in case the

168

newspapers in England should headline the news that the wicked settlers are slaughtering the poor Africans' dogs. It is a pity that many newspapers and politicians (and, presumably, numbers of the public too) in Britain are so anti-British and pro-African. In particular, the Labour Party have obviously no interest in the welfare of Kenya, but only seek to use the present troubles out here as a means of embarrassing the Conservative Government. When lives are being lost in Kenya and when – with every day that this Emergency continues – the economy of the country is being grievously damaged, that is a truly wicked thing to do.

Here is an extract from the *Daily Mirror*, printed in the form of an open letter to Sir Evelyn Baring when he arrived in Britain last month. The *Daily Mirror* has a circulation of about four and a half million, and this despicable letter, which has been widely publicised out here, has caused deep resentment.

> *You have to contend with a revolting pagan organisation trying to undermine you on one side, and a trigger-happy white minority on the other already howling for Kikuyu blood, and who will, no doubt, soon be howling for yours. . . .if you go back with a constructive and liberal policy to replace the vindictive and hopeless measures now in force. Let the settlers howl: we shall be for you, and there are more of us than there are of them. But before you go you have a few momentous days in which to do your duty by your high office and the liberal traditions of your Service, and tell Mr Oliver Lyttelton the truth . . . that his present policy will poison the future in Kenya for generations.*

In answer to a leading article in the *Kenya Weekly News* which we sent to Eddy and Leo, Leo has written that surely it would be folly for this country to think of trying to break away from Britain and turn its eyes south, as the article suggests. He does not appreciate the strong feeling out here (amongst people who, generally, feel that they are part of Britain itself) that British policy in Africa is vacillating and weak, and that a large section of the British people are not so concerned for the safety

169

of their own people and for respect for the law, as for the opportunity to use African problems as a football in the political arena. The result is that the Colonial Office officials who rule this country not only failed to see the trouble coming, but now seem unable to bring it to an end. On the other hand, one feels that if it were the South African Government which was tackling the problem, law and order in this country would long since have been restored. In Southern Rhodesia (which has also broken away from the Colonial Office) the Africans seem to be more contented than anywhere else, and one feels that the Southern Rhodesian Government has a clear-cut policy and knows how to carry it out. Is it not high time that, in the face of inept interference in African affairs by powers outside the African continent, there should be some closer association of all the peoples of European descent living in the countries of Africa? There are great practical difficulties in the idea of a Federation of the countries of Eastern and Central Africa, but if enough people start thinking about it, the plan might one day take shape. Meanwhile, some people feel that far from being alone if we began to look south, we might find friends with more sympathy and understanding.

We went up to see Michael yesterday and he dropped in here to see us at tea-time on Friday. It still comes as something of a shock to see him followed around all the time, wherever he goes or whatever he does, by a charming, quiet young man with a huge revolver at instant readiness. Michael is, of course, in grave personal danger. But it gives one an uncanny feeling that this way of living is now accepted by all. What must his little girl think it all means? And what did David think when he saw the revolver lying on the sofa during tea, while the young bodyguard ate his food, carefully keeping one hand free?

Life went on nonetheless. Alain and Mary de Rothschild visited from Europe; and we set off with our usual vigour for the Nakuru Horse Show:

11th January, 1953

On the Friday Rosemary, with Miss Leftwich who was to ride Gold Lace, arrived early at the show ground to get the horses ready, while I came at eleven with David and Miss Goodwin. David was suitably clad for the occasion. He had his jodhpur boots and trousers on, a white silk shirt with the little silver Chinese coin cuff-links which Pops once gave me, the tie which Charmian gave him for Christmas with the horses on, a brown velvet riding hat and brown gloves. Jenny Wren, under Rosemary's influence, had been polished and brushed, plaited and combed until she looked a real picture. The saddlery, too, had come in for a lot of spit and polish. We mounted David and I led Jenny with a white leading rein. With about twenty other ponies and riders we entered the judging ring and walked round and round. The judges whispered together. Some of the other children were older and some younger than David. Some were eliminated; and at last, David and I were brought in first, and the others were left strung out in a line beside us. The judge gave David his red rosette and a sweet little cup, and we did a last tour of the ring with David holding the rosette between his teeth just like a grown-up show rider!

Back at Rhodora at tea-time, David, very quiet, suddenly announced between mouthfuls of bread and butter,

'*I* won the leading rein class.'

Immediately, in unison, we said,

'*You* did not win it. Jenny Wren did.'

David relapsed into silence again.

18th January, 1953

On Monday night, just as I was about to turn off the lights after a busy day, one of our Kipsigis came onto the verandah and told me that he had seen one of our men in the company of two strange Kikuyu and a native goat, proceeding down a track towards the crater. With visions of Mau Mau ceremonies, I leapt out of bed, summoned the Rhodora Defence Force, and

171

collected Mumford. After much walking, we collected one stranger but no goat; and after handing our prisoner over to the police, I got to bed again at 1.30.

On Thursday night there was a huge fire in the crater, although fortunately the wind blew steadily away from our farm all night. On Saturday at seven in the morning I set off for the crater with the police. The crater fire appeared to have been started on our land. It was very hot down there, and one got very dirty with the ashes from the fire. There were numerous tracks of Africans' movements and the tracks of a large python.

When I got back I was trying to clean myself when the following conversation took place between Rosemary and Ochieng, her personal boy:

Rosemary: 'I do hate dirt.'

Ochieng: 'White people are never dirty.'

Rosemary: 'Oh yes, they are. Some are very dirty.'

Ochieng: 'But white people with lots of shillings are never dirty!'

1st February, 1953

At present the Mau Mau troubles are not improving in this district. Earlier in the week a farmer lower down the Solai Valley (about ten miles from here) had thirty-four calves burnt to death in a shed. They have caught the men who did it.

Up at Kabazi (nine miles from here in a different direction) the Labour Officer and other officials went to register all the Kikuyu for a new type of registration card, which is now going to apply to all members of the Kikuyu tribe working outside their Reserve in the White Highlands. For this new card, they have to have their photograph, just as in our passports. All but ten refused to be registered. A magistrate was brought up, and those who refused were given fines and terms of imprisonment of up to six months. Some 180 of them went off to prison, singing and cheering; but we do not think there will be so much cheering in the prison itself, which is meant to hold 600, and now houses 1,500. Every houseboy and nearly all their garden boys went, nearly all the cattle boys, all the pig boys but one, and so on. Kabazi are in the midst of their harvesting and asparagus picking. Freddie and Vi were in Nairobi when this happened, and Pam is still in hospital with her baby. Their son John coped splendidly. Freddie and Vi have now arrived back with two cooks (of a different tribe, of course), one for each household, and two or three other boys. We have lent them a garden boy, just to keep the watering going and help feed the hens. We could hardly believe the news when we heard it, for we know there were several boys, especially houseboys, who had been with them for fifteen to twenty years, but it appears they were all terrorised by an agitator.

15th February, 1953

All this Mau Mau business does not make for interesting newsletters, for it is not very convenient to leave the farm, and one day of busy routine follows another. I have had rather more than my share of patrols lately, and though no doubt it is a good way of keeping fit, I do not find so much physical effort enjoyable.

In any case, the patrols have now become much more dangerous, not because the enemy is more in evidence, but because we have now been declared a Special Area, which means that the police may shoot at anyone who fails to stop. (The danger from our own side far exceeds the danger from the Kikuyu.)

I do not think the position has yet improved in this area; I think that it is worse than it was. However, there are signs of improvement in the really troubled areas where the Government are concentrating their forces, and no doubt later on we will get more attention. We did have the first case on this farm of a man who had taken the Mau Mau oath and, I am sure, might have done us some harm. It arose out of the incident I related when a man came to our verandah one night and said that one of our men and a strange Kikuyu were passing through the farm with a goat. Later, the man who brought us

173

that news unaccountably left our service. Then another man, his friend, came to us and said their lives had been threatened by one of our Kikuyu because they had given information to us. Not only had the Kikuyu threatened his life directly, but he had repeated the threat before others, saying that I was a bad Bwana and no one should stay on this farm.

On hearing this, I collected the witnesses and the Kikuyu and took him along to the police station, and I hope we shall not see him again. The two Ireland brothers, who have farms on each side of us, about four miles away, have been unlucky. One has had his Headman murdered, and the other has been informed of a Mau Mau meeting on his farm at which they discussed how to murder him. The wretched thing about all these cases is that the most trusted boys are always amongst the villains.

22nd February, 1953

We celebrated our eleventh wedding anniversary, and it was another of many happy days we have spent together. Alain and Mary de Rothschild had wired us that they would be in Nairobi and were leaving for the Belgian Congo the following day, Thursday, so we went down to the Norfolk Hotel and Rosemary spent the morning with them wandering about the Indian bazaar whilst I went to see about the new shooting-brake model Peugeot which we were exchanging for our family model. We all had lunch at the Norfolk and Alain asked for a bottle of champagne on account of our celebration, which we thought very sweet of him. Their American friends, the Phipps, were with them. These people have a farm in Florida employing an entirely coloured staff and they told us how much it resembles Kenya.

We crawled back home, running in the new car, and found a letter from Hamadi Madi, our Comorien head houseboy, who is on leave for a month in Zanzibar. He announced that he would be back at the end of this month with a Comorien cook. So at last it looks as if poor Rosemary is going to be forced to

174

make the change, which she has put off so long. We have been several times advised that it is dangerous to have a Kikuyu cook, but Gwara has been with us ever since we came out here, and he knows the routine so well that it will be hard to change. We think we will send him on six months' leave and see how the new man turns out before we make a definite break. But Gwara, in any case, has often said lately that he is getting old and tired and would never work for another memsahib.

15th March, 1953

The Mau Mau situation in this district is quiet, marked by an exodus of Kikuyu back to their Reserve. Strings of them are on the road to the station every day, with great loads on their backs. It looks as though there are going to be very few left, and as this movement is also afoot in other areas, it is sure to have an effect on the economy of the country. We are wondering where we are going to draw the outside labour to pick our next coffee crop, and what is going to be the effect on our workforce (of other tribes) of the increased competition for the labour which is left in the Highlands. Wages are going up rapidly.

One other aspect of the exodus is a shortage of vegetables, because the Kikuyu where the main producers of vegetables on their small plots all over the place.

The rains have not yet broken. The dry weather wind is still blowing and we cannot know when the rain will come. In order not to take risks, I have cut down the cows' rations, and the milk has dropped as a result. We cannot risk running out of food, and Heaven alone knows when the rain will come – maybe not until well into next month.

29th March, 1953

Over the weekend eight of our Kikuyu disappeared from the farm overnight. We now have only about six left, apart from the houseboys. There are really very few remaining in the district.

We only have two boys left to work our 200 pigs – the other tribes will not touch pig dung, but we are using women of the Kipsigis tribe who do not seem to mind. The scramble for labour resulting from the exodus (many farms employed 100 per cent Kikuyu) has upset wage rates, and this week I have felt it prudent to increase all wages by five shillings a month, so that our non-Kikuyu labour will not be seduced away. This will cost us £400 a year.

In the past two days the Mau Mau news has been very bad, and it is hard to see what headway the forces of law and order are making against the bandits. The attack on the police armoury at Naivasha had the dash and precision of a Commando raid in the last war, and achieved spectacular success: rifles, sten guns and thousands of rounds of ammunition were taken, and I believe some 150 prisoners were released, including two Mau Mau leaders. On the same night an organised gang of 500 massacred their fellows in the Reserve. It begins to look as though the bandits are becoming better armed and better trained in the arts of hit-and-run warfare.

As a result of Michael Blundell's speech in London, we gather some of you have felt we have not been telling you all the facts about the way we live here. We have consistently shown you the complete picture as it affects us. . . . Rosemary never has a gun on her, and steadfastly refuses to learn to use one. A great many women here are situated where it is necessary to be armed, and many wear their guns where it is quite unnecessary; Rosemary has the greatest contempt for these people and will not become one of them (though sometimes it is because the poor dears have not got any safe place where they can leave their weapons). Michael's wife, Gerry, has been very brave up to a point (she has had several threatening letters) but she now makes rather a fuss. She has four armed guards round the house and a European man sleeping in the house, and if a raid takes place five miles from her she gets upset because she has not been told.

To return to Michael's speech, it is important that he should show the British public, many of whom are pro-native, that their own brothers and sisters are in danger from the very people so many of them want to see in power. But do not apply all he says to us. Rhodora is in an area scheduled as 'Dangerous', but not as 'Very Dangerous'. That means that there are probably no bandit gangs operating in this area.

However, we still have little faith in the administration. The settlers complain that there is a lack of initiative, and too much of the kid glove. We have so often felt that the enemy is one jump ahead – that the policy tends to be defensive, and that even so, the right defensive arrangements are only made after an incident, the stable door being locked after the horse has bolted. Normal peacetime methods of British justice often do not seem to apply when very large numbers are accused, when the accused and the witnesses take it for granted that any lie will do to suit, and the witnesses for the prosecution go in fear of their lives.

As for the military forces out here, we see nothing of them in this district, but the reports we hear are not reassuring. The rank and file, and some of the officers too, are said to be generally left-wing and pro-native in their attitude, and a large number of them are only doing their military service and are, therefore, not very interested in the job. At the same time we have heard tales of serious misconduct on the part of the troops towards the Africans.

I think the feeling of the settlers generally is that very much more severe measures will have to be taken against the Kikuyu if this Mau Mau is to be stamped out. If the present trend of Mau Mau successes goes on, something of the sort may be forced upon the incompetent and lily-livered administration by the weight of public opinion.

We are still hoping to get a new cook from Zanzibar quite soon. We have engaged a man and we now await his arrival. Meanwhile, old Gwara still serves us and we have no reason to doubt his loyalty. His two children help in the kitchen, and another Kikuyu youngster in the pantry, but these are a bit too young for Mau Mau indoctrination. The other Kikuyu we employ is a young and very nice boy in the nursery. He was born and bred on the farm and has no stake in the Reserve. All the same we watch him closely, and so do the other houseboys of the other tribes. So far I think he is loyal, but of course if I had the least suspicion about any of them, I would send them away at once.

5th April 1953

On Wednesday Rosemary and Nancy Laird were sitting on the verandah after tea, while Roy Laird and I were up at the stock. They were looking up in their First Aid books the best method of treating the horribly burnt foot of one of Nancy's African children when Chris Eames came up the garden path. Chris is the twenty-one year old son of J. W. Eames, who was at Harrow with Rosemary's father, and he is our section leader in the Kenya Police Reserve. Being rather young, he gets a bit flurried about giving out orders.

On this occasion he plunged into a long speech, something about 4,000 Kikuyu breaking out of the transit camps at Nakuru, iron rations, and plenty of water at our cowshed. At first Rosemary thought he meant to use the calving boxes for the K.P.R. should an emergency arise, but after a bit she stopped him and asked him to repeat what he had been saying: it was not what she thought, but was far more amusing.

This week is expected to be a sort of D-Day for the Mau Mau, because the result of the Jomo Kenyatta trial will be announced. If there is an emergency the K.P.R. want to move all the men, women and children living in this district into our cowsheds, complete with iron rations and camp beds. It is the most ludicrous plan, for none of the ladies of the district would be pleased to sleep in the cowshed. All would, I am sure, prefer to be assassinated in their own homes. Anyway, Rosemary has firmly told Mrs Mumford and Mrs Ace that should such a situation arise they will have to come into our house and occupy the spare rooms. She told Chris that 'Charity Begins at Home'.

This is what we wrote upon our return from the Coronation in England:

21st June, 1953

Mau Mau has been very quiet in this area lately. The Army is trying to contain the gangs (which are still numerous and sizeable) in the Aberdare and other forests and to starve them out. The gangs are doing all they can to filter out and lie low on farms anywhere, in the hope that the Army will go away and they can start again. However, in this district I do not think anyone is much inclined to take any unknown Kikuyu on their payroll and the authorities are on the lookout for strangers.

On the day I left for England I said to David, 'Now look after Miss Goodwin and the farm for Daddy.' He has taken me quite literally and every day he went up to the stock and asked the head boys if everything was all right. The cheek of it at five and a half! A few days ago he was out riding in the evening with the syce and he saw our head coffee factory boy going towards a neighbouring farm. He called him over and asked him where he was going. On being told, David asked him if he had a pass. The boy produced a piece of paper, and although he could not properly read it, David immediately said it was out of date and the boy had better go home and get a proper pass from the Bwana Manager the next day – and the boy *did as he was told*. I was so shaken by this story that I had David in to the office and told him that whilst I appreciated his looking after things so well, he was a bit young to order the boys about, and when he saw something wrong it would be better to let me know first.

179

10

The summer of 1953 was darkened by the suicide of Roy Laird, that charming neighbour of whom we had become so fond. His ghastly fate was blamed on financial troubles; his wife and family returned to England, with the sympathy of everyone who knew them.

We had to continue despite this depressing reminder of misfortune, and within months we had opened up the crater to a greater extent than before, hugely increased the Rhodora reputation with wins at the Royal Show in Nairobi, and been delighted by a visit from my elder daughter Barbara, who was now eighteen.

Our 2,800 acres was a mere back yard by comparison with some of the Kenyan properties, though these great ranches were, of course, not intensively farmed after the fashion of Rhodora. As Tony wished to prevail on one of the mining companies in the Copper Belt to set up their own farm, he naturally set out to investigate every kind of farming that might be possible, and we were fascinated by our visit to Gilbert Colvile's ranch near Lake Naivasha, where he relied upon the indigenous livestock.

Gilbert Colvile has been immortalised by John Hurt in the film of White Mischief, and before that by the book, and so has a certain way of life among settlers before the war. Our own existence could not have been more different. Tony inspected the farm early every morning and we both walked around, watching out for developments and discussing matters with the staff, every evening; the day between was filled with a long round of duties associated with the livestock and crops and generally running the large enterprise that Rhodora had become. Visitors had by now become such a regular feature of our lives (there were often people for lunch, people to dinner, and yet more people to stay) that Valentine the bull developed his own party trick for entertaining guests. In the early evening he would be on the verandah that ran in front of his loose-box. At feeding time the bull boy used to walk up to the rear of the loose-box to pour the cattle feed through

180

an opening into the manger. Valentine, responding at once to the rattle of the food-bucket would raise the latch on his loose-door with one horn, put his chin over the top and pull the door towards him. In this way he let himself in, and lumbered eagerly towards his supper.

Miss Goodwin left and a replacement arrived from England, but their tenures overlapped: so for a fortnight six-year-old David was privileged to have two governesses. Other staff problems arose, however.

28th June, 1953

I was greeted at 7 am on Friday, by one of the night guards reporting that Gwara, the cook, Gakere, the laundry boy, and Jero, the nursery boy, who are all Kikuyu, had left their huts at 11 pm and returned at 2.30 am. As two gangs have been reported this week, one at Subukia about twenty-five miles away, and one at Dondori, about ten miles away, and as we have been especially warned to look out for people trying to get food to the gangs, I had no option but to take all three of these boys down to the police for questioning. It was unfortunate that there was only the evidence of the one guard against them, but we cannot afford to take risks, and I therefore said that even if the police can get nothing against them, I do not want them back, and they must be repatriated to their Reserve. I brought back from Nakuru with me two boys of the Jaluo tribe, one of whom had done a little laundry work before, and one to help in the nursery; a temporary cook has been found locally.

Ahamed, our head boy, and Ochieng were wonderful, and coped with everything quietly and calmly. Gwara's two little kitchen boys, Simeon his son, and Karuma his nephew, stay on, and that helps a lot with the routine work. Rosemary says we are so lucky to have a capable head boy, because changes of staff out here are no easy matter, and a great deal of training and supervision will inevitably be necessary. She already misses old Gwara at every turn, and as we actually were not able to prove he had done anything wrong, we are keeping his wife and children on the farm. The wife will be paid and will work in the coffee, living in a hut in the small Kikuyu village we

181

still have under constant supervision. She is terrified of going back to the Reserve, where she knows starvation awaits her and her children, so Rosemary feels that until Gwara definitely lets us know that he wants her, the best thing we can do for him is to keep and look after her and the children. As she will not be near the house any longer, there is no danger.

12th July, 1953

On Sunday, 5th July, we woke up to one of our wretched water crises when the pipeline ceased to deliver. Our reserves of water are very meagre, and situated in one awkward place only: consequently, if the pipe fails all the cattle-troughs are quickly empty, we cannot operate the cooler in the dairy, the buildings are waterless and the Aces, in their house, have nothing to cook or wash with. I spent most of the day rushing up and down the four-mile-long pipeline trying unsuccessfully to sort out the problem. When I opened the padlocked box which covers the control cocks for our farm, I found a huge nest of bees hanging on the underside of the lid. Epharesto, our driver, who was with me, was delighted. Quite undeterred he put his hand in amongst them and removed a considerable quantity of dirty brown honeycomb. Then he wiped the bees off the comb and brought it gleefully to show me – I had retired to a safe distance. Some of the cells contained honey, some grubs, and some were empty. Epharesto ate the whole thing there and then on the spot, cells, grubs and all, and only had one sting, on a finger. The Water Bailiff got on to the pipeline at 7 am on Monday and managed to get it running again.

28th August, 1953

We have been rather impressed by the feat of some of our Kipsigis, who are the tribe who form our defence force. Recently a large male baboon was injudicious enough to wander far from the edge of the crater and get into the maize belonging to one of them. A number of them surrounded him, but he broke out once. They ran like hares and somehow got him surrounded again. Then one of them – Brown Eyes, our second head cattleman – jumped in with a knife and killed the baboon with a single blow, a very brave thing to do. They took his body and tied it up on the fence for all the other baboons to see, and since then we have been free of them, though I expect they will be back again soon.

Our second houseboy, Ali, is a nice man and seems to be settling down now he has been with us some months. The other night I asked Ahamed, the head boy, how Ali was getting on.

'Oh, Ali is getting on very well,' he said, 'but he is very frightened of you.'

'How can he be frightened of me? I have always been very nice to him.'

'That is true,' Ali agreed, 'but if he hears you blowing up any of the other boys, he shakes all over.' Poor Ali!

30th August, 1953

Recently I had the District Agricultural Officer up to discuss various problems, the main point being that we are so very short of good ploughable land as a proportion of our total acreage. I told him that no single factor could so improve our economy as the growing of lucerne in the crater, but that we could not find anyone who would lend or hire us a bulldozer to push down the many large fever trees which grow in the area.

He was so impressed with this that within the week we had a bulldozer on the farm supplied by the Soil Conservation Service of the Government, and it is pushing over the trees with great speed. It will stay and help us clear them off the ground; it will build us a small dam to irrigate the land; it will alter the bed of the crater stream to give us a larger ploughable area and will grade a road around. Within a few days we shall be ploughing there, ready to put in the first cover crop to clean the land before the lucerne can be planted. Before it leaves here it is also going to clear another place, higher up in the crater land,

and re-route a road so that we may get about thirty more ploughable acres there. Lastly, it is going to bench-terrace an area of about one acre below our Danish piggery, on the side of a hill, where we may be able to grow tomatoes for Freddie Ward's canning factory. All this is very good news for our farm.

13th September, 1953

After lunch last Sunday we went up to visit the Byng-Halls, taking David (but no governesses). The road is both tortuous and precipitous. When we arrived, we had climbed from less than 6,000 feet to 7,800 feet. Their house is after the style of a Swiss chalet, and is tucked into the side of the hills in a forest of huge cedars. There are fantastic views of the Rift Valley from the front windows. Making a farm out of such surroundings is no easy matter, especially as they have very little capital, but they have obtained a quantity of a new variety of pyrethrum seed which is giving an enormous yield of little white daisy-heads, and their cash return is comparable with that of coffee. They are using the money from this crop to develop the farm. At that altitude, more on account of the cold than of the rainfall, it is possible to establish grass leys using English grasses. I saw some impressive pastures of cocksfoot and meadow fescue. Byng told me that there is one farmer in Kenya who has so developed these grasses (at roughly the same altitude) that his cows give 800 gallons at a lactation without additional concentrates. Byng bought his Guernseys from us when we culled our herd soon after we arrived here.

Up there in the forest they are in grave danger from Mau Mau, and the Army had killed eight on the farm next door only a few days before. The Byng-Hall parents walk about with revolvers strapped to their waists, the daughter of seventeen carries a sporting rifle wherever she goes, and the son of fifteen carries a shotgun. So far their only loss from Mau Mau has been an in-calf Guernsey heifer which was stolen and eaten.

Rosemary and Barbara went down to Nakuru to shop on Wednesday, and called in, on their way back, at a farm and

184

bought eighteen new White Leghorn chickens. Our original chickens long ago died, or were eaten, and we have not been able to arouse much enthusiasm about chickens since. However, eggs are such a dreadful price that we have taken the plunge again. This time, instead of leaving them to Ace to look after, we have handed them over to Ahamed, who is thrilled with his new responsibility and taking it so seriously that I am nearly driven mad. I always thought a chicken more or less got along without being bothered about too much. But not a bit of it! The exact quantity and composition of their food, the sort of nest they like to sit on and the sort of perch they like to roost on, the type of receptacle they like to eat and drink from – all these are matters of moment, which have to be considered from a practical and scientific point of view. And all for eighteen hens! I told Ahamed he must dust them and wash them with soap each day. That hurt his feelings, so he was pleased to be able to tell me yesterday that we had received twelve eggs. (I need scarcely add that Rosemary is a collaborator with Ahamed in all this.)

We had originally named sections of the Rhodora estate after parts of our old farm in England, and parts of Wales farmed and lived in by Tony's family since the Middle Ages. Now we re-organised the farm's geography:

20th September, 1953

Our crater land is so changed that it is scarcely recognisable. We now have a wonderful autobahn on which to drive down there; the top land is jagged across with drainage ditches, and many trees are cleared away. In this section we hope to plough thirty new acres. The fields known as Stroat and Tutshill have been thrown into one which we shall call Tutshill; Penrose and Cowbridge have similarly merged to become Cowbridge. Maesglas is greatly increased in size. Down at the bottom, the scene is extraordinary. Where hundreds of huge trees grew and the undergrowth towered to twenty feet, there is a flat expanse of bare earth. The remains of the trees are piled higgledy-piggledy on the sides of the surrounding hills. In a way it is a sad spectacle, but I shall get over the sadness when we have twenty-five acres of lucerne growing down there. The clearing of that piece has cost about £400; we hope to get some of this back from the sale of logs or charcoal, and the annual value of the lucerne, if it grows as we think it will, should not be less than £1,500. We still have two monstrous bulldozers on the farm but they should finish this week, and leave us with a mass of clearing-up to do and hundreds of yards of new fencing to put up.

11th October, 1953

The beginning of Royal Show week. Our five-ton lorry, followed by Mumford in his car and loaded to the gunwales with three small grade heifers, furniture for the Guernsey Stall, cattle and horse show equipment boxes, cattle and horse food and so on, left for Nairobi at seven in the morning. (Back at home, we were still pumping madly, owing to an interruption in our water supply. Our big frigidaire also decided to go wrong.) After a hasty tea we got into the car, full already of equine equipment, and drove to Nakuru. On the road we passed the three horses, Cellarette, Faith and Gold Lace.

In the goods yard at the station, the truck allotted to Rhodora was eventually found and opened up, and four rather dirty horse-boxes revealed: much scrubbing and disinfection ensued, and the laying of fresh sawdust on the floor.

Then Faith came to the ramp, blew with indignation through her nostrils and entered her compartment with a bang and a clatter. Gold Lace walked in without a murmur. But Cellarette! Oh Cellarette, how true it is that you can take a horse to water but you cannot make it drink! At 6.30, in the twilight, we first led her up to the ramp. As soon as she put her foot on it, although it was well padded, up went her head, back she retreated and nothing would persuade her to take another step forward. We cajoled her with terms of endearment; we tempted her with food; we tried to ride her in – using language which would make any well-bred mare ashamed of herself; we blindfolded her; we linked hands behind her (at great personal risk) and tried to push her in; we brought out Gold Lace and tried to make them walk in together – all to no avail! After two and a half hours of this, the Livestock Officer (a Government official) who takes an interest in our farm, came along full of confidence. For half an hour he tried the same expedients all over again, without success. Then he drew me aside.

'Would you please take Mrs Seys away for ten minutes?'

I took Rosemary, who in the excitement had fallen down and cut her knee, to a discreet distance. Cellarette was taken to the ramp again; she stopped dead in her tracks again; suddenly a knotted rope thwacked upon her startled behind! She shot into the horsebox and the door was closed before she realised what had happened.

Rosemary, Barbara and I sat down to dinner at 10 pm.

At 4.15 next morning the bulls started roaring up at the cowsheds. They are wonderful guards and we always know if someone goes there unexpectedly. The clank of a milk-pail rang through the clear night air and our alarm clock completed the cacophony. Rosemary and I crawled out of bed, drank some tea out of a thermos, put on trousers and thick sweaters and walked up to the dairy buildings in the cool air under a network of tropical stars, with the little forms of Rikki and Red scampering beside us. A light was shining on the loading ramp and Ace was busy tying up Rhodora Beauty's Valentine in the lorry. Valentine himself was already safely in, then Beauty, and then this young bull, Beauty's Valentine, who is a son of those two; next came Vera, a daughter of old Valentine. We watched them loading, each cow led forward on a halter by the light of a lantern as Ace called it. Ace is most efficient and quick and he was away by 5.30 with his precious load of six. We heard the lorry rev up the slope of our drive out onto the Solai road as we turned into the cowshed yard to give instructions to Kipsang for the day's work. Then I went into the office to clear up my desk, and Rosemary finished the last of the packing.

At 8.30 am Rosemary and Barbara left Rhodora, with their car looking like a costermonger's cart. Flowers hung out of one window and Barbara's head out of another as she shouted goodbye; Rosemary was giving Ahamed last-minute instructions and Epharesto, the driver, was hidden on a back seat beneath a tangle of coats, eggs for Ace, and baskets. In spite of all this they arrived safely at the show ground and found Ace already installed and the horses arrived without mishap. There then followed a rapid inspection of Michael Blundell's bull, the main rival. Rosemary was convinced he was a better bull than Valentine. Ace said, to console her, that his feet stretched from here to Timbuktu. . . .

18th October, 1953

The show over, the normal routine of the farm began to work again. I was worried because the lorry had not returned and at about 6 o'clock I set off down the Nairobi road with Mumford. About twenty miles down the road we saw a lot of cars and, down in a hollow off the road, was our lorry. Ace was standing with a bleeding head, a boy was lying on the ground, two more were about to be taken to hospital and the cattle were being caught up and tied to the fence. We had arrived about five minutes after the accident. The lorry had been forced off the road by another car driven by a man who was drunk and who had cut in on it. It overturned and went a complete somersault to land on its wheels again. Ace had a cut over one eye and a cracked rib; four of the five Africans on board had to go to hospital but none was seriously hurt. Four of the seven animals on board were flung out, breaking their halters in the process; two remained in the lorry, one of which was hanging by its halter over the side and had to be cut down. In spite of this, also none of them were seriously hurt, though one or two were suffering from delayed shock. The lorry had the superstructure and wings badly damaged but the engine, chassis, brakes and steering seemed to be all right. I was able to hasten Ace and the Africans to hospital, get hold of the police and reload the lorry

188

and drive it home. Rosemary later went to fetch Ace from hospital and visited those Africans who were also hospitalised. It was a miraculous escape.

1st November, 1953

On Tuesday at dawn Rosemary came down with me to the airstrip at Nakuru and I climbed into a Beechmaster and flew off to Rhodesia. The scheduled services of Central African Airways have been altered so that there was no other way of getting there, and I had to travel 2,500 miles across desolate wastes in a single-engined chartered aircraft. However, the trip went off without incident; I had a very good pilot, who had flown a Hurricane from Biggin Hill during the Battle of Britain. The other directors in the Copper Belt pulled my leg a bit about the cost of the journey, saying that it was a pity to have to close down the mine in order to finance a director's visit, but they also said they thought it was a great risk travelling that way, and so long as the CAA schedule continues to be unhelpful they will try to send up one of their private twin-engined Dove aircraft to fetch me.

That Tuesday morning, as Rosemary turned back from the airstrip towards Nakuru, she realised she had a puncture in one tyre. It was 6.30 am, she had no driver with her, and the main road was desolate. She tried to get the jack in place but the car was in a bad position, and the jack was on a slant. Half an hour later, a lorry stopped, followed by a car. The lorry contained an Indian and about twenty convicts. The Indian said the lorry-driver could help and he unloaded the convicts who thereupon – ignoring the jack – lifted the car with their bare hands, while the driver changed the wheel. The car behind, containing two businessmen in an obvious hurry, drove off. They seemed uncertain whether Rosemary was safe with the prisoners and their guard, but she sent them on their way, saying she felt *perfectly* safe.

8th November, 1953

Yesterday evening we really felt worn out, and were looking forward to a quiet evening. It was not to be. On the verandah at tea-time appeared a certain Mr Cooke, who said he was a stock manager for a huge farm in Tanganyika, and that he had been at the Show and Sale finding out about the availability and prices of Guernseys, with a view to his employers buying some sixty or seventy grade animals and a couple of pedigree bulls. He had already been to see Michael's and Eames's herds, and wanted to see ours.

We took him painstakingly round our stock, and he then came in and settled himself in the sitting room. I gave him a whisky and he just sat, and sat, and stayed. He got through five whiskies, stayed to dinner, and finally, he has spent the night in our spare room. I do not think he knows much about stock, but he is quick, and is picking up tips wherever he can. Certainly he has set about getting a grade herd going in the right way. However we nearly died with laughter when he told us that he knew well Friesians, Ayrshires, Jerseys, Guernseys and *Black* Polls; we suppose he is colour blind. (In spite of this, he announced that he preferred Guernseys.) And although it will be lovely to see the back of him today, his employers probably will take a young bull of ours and as many grade females as we can spare after the clear-out of the Show and Sale – but that will not be until January.

22nd November, 1953

On Tuesday we went to see Mr Gilbert Colvile. He is one of the biggest ranch-owners in Kenya, and I wanted to pick his brains before going to Northern Rhodesia.

He is also well-known because of his wife and his house. His wife, Diana, was formerly married to Sir Delves Broughton, and was involved in the famous murder case which shook Kenya society during the war. The house they live in (one can hardly believe it) is the very house formerly owned by Lord

Erroll, Diana's ex-lover, and it is built after the style of a Moorish palace on the shore of Lake Naivasha. It presents an extraordinary appearance, dead white, with crenellated walls and little minarets on the corners. The front, facing the lake is a broad verandah with rounded arches, mosaics and animal skin rugs on the floor. The garden slopes sharply down to the water and the general effect, when reclining on the verandah on a Fortnum and Mason chaise-longue, is as pleasant as anything we have seen in Kenya. The scene was enhanced by the occasional wild cry of a fish eagle, which conveniently sat on a huge thorn-tree.

Mrs Colvile was quite informal in blue tight-fitting trousers. She possessed as hard a face as one can imagine, was not extraordinarily beautiful, but was amusing and entertaining in her conversation. She gave us an excellent lunch, in spite of the fact that it was cooked on the nursery oil-stove as they were having an Aga installed in their kitchen. Colvile himself was nice, and much older. He obviously adored her. Mrs Colvile took Rosemary through the house to her bedroom and bathroom to wash and tidy. The bathroom was in black marble with a huge bath sunk into the floor. In the bedroom a rather glamorous bed was tucked discreetly in an alcove.

After lunch Mr Colvile took us right across one of the ranches which he has owned for forty years. I asked him a dreadful lot of questions, I fear, but he was kind and did not seem to mind. This ranch was 32,000 acres and had 4,000 head of Boran stock on it. The animals take five and a half years to mature, but they get no hand feeding of any kind from the day they are born, not even hay in the dry weather. The whole organisation seemed awfully easy after dairying, but the capitalisation was high: he estimated it at £5 an acre including land, stock, fencing, water development and so on.

David was quite seriously ill in the later part of the year, but made a full recovery, and went off to the coast to convalesce. We toured Northern Rhodesia in our search for farming information which Tony would write in his report to his fellow-directors:

13th December, 1953

Our first morning in the Monze Hotel began at 5.30 am, after a light sleep punctuated by trains shunting in the railway sidings next door, and the activities of every local tom-cat. Tea was dumped on the floor between our beds, our shoes whisked away for cleaning and any hope of further sleep dispelled by general noise. Rosemary was astonished that she had not shared her bed with any insects; the mere fact of having survived until dawn quite cheered us up.

Mazabuka is forty-one miles from here, and our first call was at the Government Veterinary Headquarters and Research Station there. We had a long talk with the principal Research Officer, Dr Walker, who rather confirmed our impression that no one in this country, except perhaps Woodrow Cross, has the faintest idea how to run a dairy herd efficiently.

We then went to the B.'s farm eighteen miles westwards, where they have a herd of 150 Friesians, seventy in milk. They are sending away 150 gallons a day, but have an awful breeding disease in the herd. They keep no records, other than in their heads, and this is the leading dairyman in the most important farming district in the territory. He told us that he and one other farmer are the only people who bucket-feed their calves, and that farming on the Copper Belt itself will involve a very high mortality of stock. Closely questioned about this, he muttered something about 'climatic conditions' and 'unknown diseases'. We have the impression that African *juju* (witchcraft) seems to affect the white man.

After an indifferent lunch we drove eastwards across the Kaleya valley (opening and shutting ten gates on the way) to a Mr and Mrs Evans. He is Chairman of the Stock Breeders' Council and the only stud breeder of pedigree Afrikander cattle in the country. They live in a white-faced house with a deep thatched roof, with no ceilings inside so that the rooms are like a series of cubicles.

Joseph, their Valentine, looked at us with sleepy eyes, unconcernedly chewing the cud: a superb beast, weighing 1,700 lbs, with a huge hump on his shoulders, enormous dewlap

192

and long swept-back horns. He was in magnificent condition and his shiny Guernsey-coloured coat shone in the sunlight. His young son gambolled around him. The Evanses had been offered 1,000 guineas, they said, for this youngster. He certainly looked a little picture. . . . Will Evans, bombastic but full of enthusiasm, still in his early forties, thinks there is a great future for beef in this country, but could not tell us where to find the land at a ranching price, or the stock. We got back to Monze as the sun was setting.

On Friday we drove over to Ndola to see Mr Kriger, the Provincial Agricultural Officer. We questioned him closely about whether or not we could farm in this area, but he was obviously so keen to get the companies to start a scheme that he made it all sound too easy. Rosemary kept saying 'But where are the snags?' and she said it even more when, in the Chief Surveyor's office, we found two areas, one of about 20,000 acres which could be made adjoining by buying another small bit of land. The first would be divided into dairy farm units and the second, with water on three sides and road and railway on the fourth, would be the ranch.

We lunched at a reasonable hotel in Ndola and set off in Mr Kriger's Jeep to look at part of the proposed ranch. There has been the usual heavy rain, and there was nothing but a wood-cutter's track through the thickly-wooded area. Everything was dripping, and we bounced in and out of potholes. After about five miles Mr Kriger was increasingly doubtful about whether he was on the right road, but eventually we arrived at the clearing he was looking for, where the trees had been cut down, and we were able to study the grass regeneration. Huge millipedes, five or six inches long, slept on the stumps of felled trees. They were rudely awakened by Rosemary, who wanted to see them shake a leg. Small ant-hills, knocked over, revealed millions of little white creatures; all around, insect life abounded, and united in shouting at us that they did not want us to bring order to this decayed, derelict, wasted land. The wild flowers were particularly lovely, but the grass was sparse. The Government are cutting down all the trees in this block for fuel for the mines, and we would try to persuade the stumps to

193

rot quickly by blasting them open with a small charge, and to keep down the regeneration of the undergrowth with thousands of goats. Meanwhile, beef cattle would be introduced in increasing numbers as the grassland thickened and improved. Needless to say the area will have to be fenced, paddocked, and properly laid out with roads and water, but a great advantage is the extensive area lying by the river, which floods in the wet weather and leaves grazing for the animals when the water recedes.

We dined early at the Guest House with a small party and went to see a film called *Laughter in Paradise*.

20th December, 1953

At the close of last week's newsletter we had nearly finished our preliminary investigations in Northern Rhodesia on the subject of agriculture, and this past week was mainly spent by me on mining business, with a long series of board meetings on the Wednesday. We did, however, visit one or two farms, amongst them a rugged place owned by the local town dairyman, an old Scot named Buchanan. We picked him up at his dairy and drove out eight miles to the farm itself. He began by being extremely dour, but warmed up as the afternoon progressed. Next day the wife of one of the mine executives who had met Rosemary went into his shop.

'Do you know,' he said, 'I had two of your directors here yesterday to see the farm? All set, I was, to give them a bit of my mind about what I think of financiers with masses of capital who try to dabble in farming, but I found out that they knew all about it, not only Mr Seys, but the wife too!' (Rosemary was most thrilled with the reference to *two* directors.)

The Dove bought us back. A dead smooth journey as far as Tabora but thereafter we ran into very bad storms and were both horribly sick, as usual. . . . How lovely it always is to come back home! Rhodora is still green and sparkling in the sunshine and the garden a mass of flowers. There is an excellent spirit amongst our labour and all, including houseboys, chauffeur,

194

grooms and milkers have turned out in their spare time to help pick the coffee, which is coming off at the rate of a ton a day. Mumford and Ace co-operated well with each other. Other farms in the district are having terrible trouble with their labour and there have been strikes and walk-outs even on Tom James' farm next door. We think our policy of giving food and amenities to our African employees is proving the right one, and this year they will get both tea and a hot soup stew (made from our own oxen) brought to them in the coffee shamba whilst they are working. Also, we are determined to start building them a club room early in the New Year.

David returns on Tuesday and we are going down to Nairobi to meet him at the airport. We shall be thinking of you all so much over Christmas, and wishing we were with you. We all send our fond love to all of you. . . .

3rd January, 1954

On Sunday Lady Cromer came to see us, accompanied by Pam Scott, her niece, with whom she was staying at Rongai. She seemed very pleased to see Rosemary again and we took her round the garden and the stock. Rosemary amused her by waving her hand towards the rest of the Guernseys whilst patting Valentine and saying 'You see, Lady Cromer, *there* are *my* rhododendrons.'

Lady Cromer was obviously determined not to get a tropical tan, for she arrived wearing a hat and scarf around her face, and carrying a second hat and a parasol. She asked me very seriously whether she should put up her parasol before stepping out from the verandah into the garden. After giving the matter due consideration, I assured her that it would be wise.

Jenny Wren, David's pony, was brought out for her to see and David explained that she was a very nice pony and one could slide off her back and down her tail, or walk between her legs, and she did not mind. Lady Cromer expressed suitable admiration for this amazing pony, so David looked up at her and said,

'Would you like to crawl under her tummy? She won't hurt you.'

On New Year's Eve I did the stock, because Ace had his half-day off. There was a sick grade yearling heifer which had been in a hospital box since the previous evening. I took her temperature and it was 107°. I concluded she had a local fever named 'three-day sickness' which is not very serious, and for which it is better to give no medicine.

Next morning, she was dead.

There were no outward symptoms, except that her ears had turned very black and we could not read the tattoo number in them. Ace had her carried into the coffee, did a post-mortem, and buried her. He thought she had died of heartwater. The next morning we sent the blood slides and samples of the spleen down to the vet for examination, and a few hours later, to our dismay, he rang up to say it was anthrax.

The spores of this dread disease are only killed by heat (212°) and they can live in the ground for at least twenty years. We inoculate all animals over six months against it every year, but this heifer had been just under six months last year, and we were about to commence our annual inoculations. The fever is readily transmitted to humans and we are anxious about Ace and four Africans who handled it during the post-mortem; Ace, in particular, had several cuts and sores on his hands. All the bedding of the animal has been burnt and its box has been cleaned out with a blow-lamp. Meanwhile, we immediately got up some fresh vaccine and inoculated all our stock again. We are now wondering what to do with the patch in the coffee where we buried it. . . . Rosemary shudders when she remembers that the blood-slides sat on our tea-trolley on the verandah for some three hours, but there is really no danger, for they were well wrapped.

10th January, 1954

Water, sufficient to pulp our coffee and at the same time to water our stock (and ourselves) has been the main problem again this week. It has necessitated the strictest control of all water points. Recently, whilst David and Miss Smith were at the coffee factory where the washing and pulping of the crop takes place, a *bibi* came to the tap to draw water and afterwards began to wash herself. This was altogether too much for our head boy at the factory.

'What are you doing there?' he bellowed. 'You cannot use water to wash and make yourself beautiful these days. Do you think you are a European?'

The coffee picking is nearly over; we have picked thirty tons and there is not much left on the trees. This week we had an inter-tribal fight amongst the pickers, which is a very rare occurrence. The Kipsigis and the Jaluo fell out and I was fetched in haste by a terrified Headman. When I got there, I found a lot of jabbering and one man with a hole in his head (not serious). I tried to talk to them like a Dutch Uncle while pointing out the advantages of *Pax Britannica*. I must say, I think if I had to stand out in the blazing sun from 7 am until 5 pm picking coffee, I should feel like fighting with someone!

On Friday we had a police raid on our labour lines to find out if all was in order, which it was, except that the following day I found a radio set in working order with dry battery, hidden in a hollow in the ground. Africans around here do not *buy* radio sets. This one had been stolen and hidden outside a hut when the police came.

14th February, 1954

Whilst I was in England in February, I had to go to hospital and Tudor Ace, back on leave, came and told me this story which, of course, had been kept from me.

'Mr Seys and Douglas Skett went riding into the crater. Luckily Douglas had mentioned that they would be back around 11.00 am. Towards 12.30–1.00 pm I started to feel alarmed. Taking some Kipsigis I walked to the crater to see if I

197

could spot them. We could see or hear nothing. I returned to the office and informed Tim Mumford, as the Mau Mau trouble was on and I was worried in case they had been ambushed.

'We decided to call the police but their transport was out of action so I drove to Solai police station and picked up two policemen, and together with some of the boys we walked right into the middle of the crater. There we found hoof marks but no sign of the horses or the men.

'By this time the heat was horrific and we were really worried. I returned to the house and called up the Air Wing of the Kenya Police and went back into the crater waiting for the plane which arrived just before dusk. It circled round and then came back to us dropping a note to say "Follow me and when I dip my wings you will know where they are."

'Having been given this sign and knowing we could not find them in the last of the daylight we went back to the house to collect drinks and food. I told Ahamed what I wanted and then went up to the *duka* (shop) for a supply of torches. When I got back I found Ahamed sitting in the back of the car, all dressed for waiting at table, with a crystal bowl of peaches on a large silver tray. When I asked him where he was going to take them he said "To the Bwana". I said "Don't be silly, Ahamed, you would smash them before you got ten yards into the crater." By then I was very thirsty and hungry so I ate the lot.

'We proceeded in to the crater (minus Ahamed) and reached them at about 9.00 pm. Mr Seys was thirsty but otherwise in good shape; Douglas Skett was in a bad way (dehydrated). I made them as comfortable as possible. At sunrise we walked out and were very thankful to see the lorry waiting to take us home.'

14th March, 1954

On Friday morning Rosemary was much occupied with a little niece of Arap Chuma, our wonderful head bull boy. His brother had sent the child to him from the reserve, and Arap

Chuma asked Rosemary if she would take her to our doctor as she had a bit of stick showing out of her leg. Rosemary, in a great hurry, popped the child in the car without looking at the leg. When the doctor opened up the bandage he found a compound fracture; the piece of stick was the bone sticking out. Later, in the African hospital, the child told the orderlies that her leg was first broken by accident by a *panga* (chopping knife) and the mother had then broken it again several times, to try and help the child to walk.

Because Arap Chuma was away with Rosemary for the morning, Kipsang, our head boy, helped with the daily walking of the bulls. Beauty's Valentine, the Champion who is the son of old Valentine, got him down and when I arrived on the scene he was thought to be dying. This was mainly because he had lost his speech, owing to shock. I rushed him to the doctor and we had an X-ray done, but fortunately, it was nothing much and he is already back at work.

21st March, 1954

Kipsang has been having a good deal of pain from the bruises he sustained when he was gored by the bull. Rosemary asked him to come to the house for her to rub them with Grandma Leopold de Rothschild's magic Viennese lotion. He seemed rather unwilling, and we soon discovered why: he had cut all his bruises open with a knife. Just an old native custom.

Another breath of Darkest Africa came to me through the medium of Manasseh, our second head boy amongst the Jaluo. He has been complaining of pains in various parts of his body for some time, and has run a bit of a temperature. We have been giving him a course of M&B. On Monday the temperature was normal, but he looked like a dying duck and complained of pains in his legs. The Headman approached me and stated that Manasseh wished to have a *maneno* (palaver) with me. To my astonishment I was informed that he knew he was suffering from an illness that only the witch doctor on the Reserve could cure. He must go home at once or he would die! I pointed out that he now had no temperature and was quite well; but home he must go, and home he went.

4th April, 1954

There has been a slight crisis amongst the Kipsigis. Brown Eyes, our second head cattleman, clasped the wife of another man around the waist with a view to taking her to his hut. The husband objected, not for any reason connected with the affections, but because he said he had paid for her, and she was his investment, and Brown Eyes had no right to try to take that away from him. . . .

11th April, 1954

These last few days there have been locusts on the farm, and we have been thankful to have sold off so many animals. They are not yet in such numbers as to do serious damage but it is unpleasant to see them all the same. I stood with my horse on the edge of the crater the other morning and they were driving towards me silently, just like light snow, with their white wings and brown bodies. As I continued my ride around the farm there was a little white cloud getting up in front of me all the time. Old Cellarette did not like it much and was inclined to shy. The same morning I came upon the biggest snake I have yet seen, sitting at the entrance to an ant-bear hole, flicking his forked tongue in and out. Cellarette and I stood rooted to the spot, eyeing him whilst he eyed us. Eventually he decided to retreat down his hole, and I am looking forward to a date with him with my shotgun in the near future.

11

One of Kenya's twenty-minute hailstorms had cost us £23,000 in a devastated coffee crop, and we must have been pretty down in the mouth about it at the time, but we carried on nonetheless, hoping for a good crop the following year – weather, locusts and a bit of luck permitting! In between supervising the staff, organising our comings and goings and the daily life of the farm, and entertaining visitors, we led an increasingly busy social and public life. Tony was elected to the County Council. Our relationship with the Blundells was still very cordial, although our enthusiasm for Michael's political stance had cooled off considerably. We were by now actively resisting some of the worst Mau Mau incursions into the Highlands.

My darling mother Mariloo visited us for the first time; David went off to a prep school; and we made the best we could of a Royal Show restricted, for us, to horse and produce, because of foot-and-mouth amongst up-country cattle.

Tony travelled regularly to the Copper Belt on business in the mining company's Dove light aircraft. The plane used to circle over Rhodora to signal its arrival, and we would drive down to the airstrip at Nakuru to bring back the pilot and co-pilot. They would have dinner with us, and stay the night, and in the morning I would drive them back to the plane with Tony. (Sometimes I flew down to Ndola with him and once we took, as a favour to a friend, two large deerhound puppies for export. The pilots protested furiously and there was a long delay before take-off while we found muzzles, at their insistence.) The Bancroft Mine farm was doing very well indeed, much to our gratification, since Tony had been instrumental in setting it up. We travelled at this time to Southern Rhodesia and, once again, to Johannesburg:

25th April, 1954

Our first call in the morning was again at the Rand Show, where we watched some of the Hereford cattle from the Oppenheimer's ranch come under the auctioneer's hammer. Then we motored into town and visited one or two shops to buy Easter eggs, before ending up at 44 Main Street, the enormous building which houses Anglo-American Corporation. We went up to the first floor, to Sir Ernest's office, and there we were shown his private collection of diamonds. It was treasure such as one would not believe could exist. White diamonds of fantastic size, cut in various shapes – I picked one up at random and its value was estimated at £58,000 (wholesale!). There was an enormous blue diamond, the value of which could not be assessed, and a wonderful deep yellow one. Beside the showcase were two strings of pearls, one of white and one of black pearls.

All these diamonds and pearls had just returned from the Ideal Home Exhibition in London, and it was luck that they were not on the Comet which crashed. Up on the top floor of the building we had a drink with various directors of Anglo-American and then we went off to lunch at a restaurant in town. In the evening there was another dinner party.

On Saturday we drove off towards Pretoria until we reached the Premier mine, which is the largest and most up-to-date diamond mine in the world. The General Manager received us and showed us specimen rocks with diamonds sticking out of them. Then we saw a copy of the Cullinan diamond, which was found here. From his office we went to the sorting office where there were four cardboard boxes on a table in an inner room surrounded by steel bars. These boxes contained one week's production from the mine. Production is four to five thousand carats of diamonds per day (the average diamond ring sold in America is one third of a carat). The uncut stones just looked like small pieces of silicate or glass, mostly dirty brown in colour, and ranging in size from dust particles to small marbles.

During the tour of the plant we saw the famous grease system

202

for finding the stones. This is done by passing the crushed ore over layers of grease which impales the diamonds, however large or small, but allows the ore to pass on. We were told that the proportion of ore to diamond is twelve and a half million to one: so you see, it is not easy to find a diamond.

We had lunch in the Manager's house and afterwards he and his wife took us underground for two hours. Here we saw the famous 'blue ground' in which diamonds are found, and stood at the bottom of a 600 foot hole where open-cast mining was done in the early years.

We rushed back to change quickly before going out to an exhibition of floodlit jumping, men versus women (they managed to make it a tie) at the Rand Show. We dined at a table overlooking the arena in company with Bridget and Harry, Mary and Nicky – their two children – and Harry's racehorse trainer. It was all most pleasant.

Sunday morning was spent quietly, except that just before lunch we looked in on a twenty-first birthday party – a flashy and rather awful affair. Then we went to a lunch party, where the principal guest was General de Guingand who was Montgomery's Chief-of-Staff during the war. At teatime I had another game of squash with Harry, then off to a quick cocktail with the Marshall Clarkes (he co-ordinates the Anglo-American copper interests). Finally, we ended this 'quiet' day with a dinner party at Sir Ernest Oppenheimer's house. Rosemary sat next to Sir Ernest and Sir Ulick Alexander and had a most interesting time while I was next to Lady Oppenheimer and Mrs Marshall Clarke. After dinner we were both cornered by Lady Oppenheimer who wanted to know just how to set about importing a Jersey bull and two heifers. She is a remarkable personality and looks as if she had just stepped out of a fairy story; tonight she was dressed in a Hardy Amies short white lace evening dress. She is in her early fifties, and for many years her hair has been snow white. The effect of this white hair, her clear, fresh complexion, and her white dress set off by rows of magnificent pearls and sparkling diamonds made one blink and wonder if she was real.

On Tuesday Bridget took us to the airport where we

regretfully said goodbye. The plane was quite steady and we reached Salisbury after three and three-quarter hours without a stop. There on the tarmac was Sir Ellis Robins waiting for us, and as he is Chairman of the airline on which we were travelling, there was not much delay in going through the Customs. He whisked us off to 'June Hill', built by the British South Africa Company for its resident director (which he is). It was plastered with pictures of Rhodes and with other relics of early Rhodesia. His son-in-law, who is head of the Military Mission to the Federation, and Mr and Mrs Robert Bruce (he is another co-director of mine) came to dinner. Sir Ellis is charming, and we are very fond of him, and Lady Robins is very nice, under a rough and forbidding exterior. She is, however, most amusing in her ordering of the house: notices are pinned on the lavatory door exhorting one to lock the door and pull the chain gently, while in our chest of drawers was a washing list, like that in a hotel, and a notice informing us that all washing would have to go to the laundry and would take three days unless asked for urgently!

On Thursday, back at Rhodora, there was a lot of settling in and sorting out to do, especially as we had to go to Nairobi on Friday for the day. David had to have another fitting for his clothes for England and I went to see the nutrition expert, Dr French. Then there was a Kennel Club meeting in the evening, at which I was made Chairman of their Show Committee. We sent David and Miss Smith back early after lunch at the Club and Rosemary and I arrived back at dinner time. That was the day when the government here imposed a nasty Budget upon us. We can scarcely expect anything else with this Mau Mau trouble, the cost of which is astronomic. Apart from the increases in income tax, personal tax, duties on wines, spirits, beers and sugar, there is also a vicious export tax of 12.5% on coffee. Most upsetting, and we hope the Inland Revenue and the locusts between them will leave us a little something to live on.

2nd May, 1954

The rain is good and the farm is clothed in green. The coffee trees which were so damaged by the hail are shooting out tentative little leaves from their denuded branches. The grass has grown enough for us to put the cows out on pastures and we hope they are beginning to stoke up again with the vitamins and nutrients which they have been lacking in the dry weather; anyway, our butter has already become more yellow in colour. Our planting programme is far ahead of last year, and already the maize and oats are showing well.

What marvellous news all this has been to the large baboon colony in the crater! They swarm over the edge onto our fields, first in one place and then in another. If one goes out without a gun, they nearly sit on the bonnet of the car; if one has a gun, one never sees them. This year I have lost patience with them, and at my urgent request an official of the Game Department has been here and has allocated us two armed guards as a short-term deterrent to the invaders. His long-term plan, which we are going to adopt, is ingenious. He says we shall never catch a baboon by simply putting out poisoned food, however tempting. They are much too clever for that; so clever, in fact, that one must treat them like small naughty boys. So we are to build two maize cribs on the edge of the crater and store maize in them, but leave a hole in the wire, as if by mistake. The baboons would not go in by the door, but if they think we have made a stupid mistake they will find their way in and start stealing the maize. Once they have got used to this we can start poisoning the maize.

If this plan fails we are going to ask permission to shut the official of the Game Department in a crib, and poison *him*.

A man from the Meat Commission came to see us and we have sold all our steers and surplus oxen to him. This will mean some forty-seven fewer mouths to feed if the locusts come. I took him down to the crater and he climbed up some of the rocky hillside, which has grass growing on it. He gave it as his opinion that we could run at least 1,000 Boran steers in the crater, and that this would bring us a net income of some £2,000

a year with a minimum of trouble. These Borans are extraordinary animals. They can climb hills like mountain goats,
need to be watered only once in two days, and can graze up to
three miles from the water-point. They live on virtually
nothing when there is a drought; this year in the Kamasia
Reserve, the Africans have been cutting down trees and feeding
the bark to these cattle to keep them alive.

15th August, 1954

We have decided on a major change in our farm policy. We
have now been keeping pigs for five years and they have shown
a very small return for a lot of work. Admittedly, we have been
feeding them on bought-in foods, because we did not have the
arable acres to produce our own food and that is a very
expensive way of keeping them. But now that we have
developed more of the farm, there is a good prospect in a
normal year of having some surplus maize and a field or two of
barley, yet we do not know the results of a home-grown mix on
the setting qualities of the baconers: so we have decided to
reduce our pigs to three sows and a boar, feed them and their
progeny on food mostly grown on the farm, and watch the
results carefully before allowing the numbers to increase.

In the meantime we have decided to start a flock of sheep.
Two years ago we bought a small experimental flock of a dozen
Romney Marsh, and kept them for eighteen months before we
sold them all to the butcher. They did very well here and
showed a much higher profit ratio than the pigs; they required
no bought-in food. The only criticism was that they became too
fat. We think perhaps they were the wrong breed for our
climate. Accordingly, we have decided to embark on a flock of
Corriedales, which are smaller animals, from Australia – the
product of a cross made at the turn of the century between the
Lincoln Longwool and the Merino. They carry better-quality
wool than the Romney, but the carcasses are smaller, and the
weight of the fleece is less. Yesterday we went up to see a well-
known breeder at Molo and placed an order for fifty ewes and

two rams. We shall go up to select them in early October and take delivery after shearing, in early November.

Whilst we were up there David found two chameleons. One was about two inches long, with a tail of one and a half inches, horned, and of a bright colour, whilst the other was smaller and more mud-coloured. They came back with us in the car, precariously balanced on a stick, rolling their eyes at each other and changing colour as they felt inclined. David announced that he had named them John and Cinderella. They were put on a small tree near the nursery while David had his afternoon rest, but there was dismay when he awoke to find that they had gone. Eventually they were found hidden in the stem of a flower on the border of the lawn, locked in a loving embrace. David wanted to know exactly what they were up to, so we told him that we might have some babies from John and Cinderella if he just left them to get on with it. . . . But he was quite sure that Cinderella had had quite enough of John, and in any case he wanted to take one of them up to the cowshed, so he somehow managed to prise John off with a stick. He is busy finding flies for their breakfast as I write.

22nd August, 1954

The chameleon stud has thriven all week. A black-and-white stranger appeared while I was away, and hissed so continuously at David, John and Cinderella that when it disappeared, no one felt inclined to put out a search party for it. Another one, jet black, put in an appearance just as Rosemary and David were off to Nairobi to fetch me, but David decided against keeping it and magnanimously gave it to the garden boy. In the meantime, Ochieng was left in charge of John and Cinderella, with the inevitable result that on our return John had disappeared. Cinderella is still with us and perches on David's hand quite happily whenever he wants to take her from point to point. They seem devoted to each other and he sometimes says soulfully to his mother,

'Don't you think Cinderella has a beautiful face?'

26th September, 1954

Last Sunday, as you know, David went to school. We kept him late in bed that morning and he came into our bed after breakfast and read an exciting new book that Rosemary had found him. Then we all dressed and went up to Kabazi to Freddie and Vi. Just before lunch Rosemary changed David into his school uniform: grey shorts, white poplin shirt with long sleeves, grey socks, brown shoes, red and grey school tie, red blazer with school crest on pocket, grey felt hat with red and grey hatband. The blazer fascinated David, and he had to wear it at lunch.

While we were having coffee he came and sat rather close to Rosemary but went on reading his exciting book, and at two o'clock sharp the Blundells arrived with Susan, their little daughter, and Denis Ireland. So we had three little red blazers milling round chatting to each other while we popped David's last few oddments into the car. Rosemary had lollipops for each child to suck, and a small toy for each one, and while they were looking at all these things Michael and Gerry drove them quietly away so that the good-byes were hardly noticed.

On Monday evening Rosemary rang up Mrs Lavers, the headmistress, and was told that David had settled down nicely.

We feel rather flat, first because there is no David, and secondly because we cannot show the cattle or pigs on account of foot-and-mouth. Nevertheless, we have had a busy week. The Rhodora Exhibit which we are displaying at the show is quite complicated. We have been allotted a space six feet by four feet, and we are going to put a back board to display photographs; we have a selection of about twenty, showing various prizewinning animals and different activities and aspects of the farm. Production figures also have to be quoted. (It reminds me of Speech Day at school.)

Here are some of the items we are displaying, all produced on the farm:

oranges	lemons	cut stone
oat hay	lucerne hay	grass hay

mangolds	kale	vegetables
canna	coffee	butter
milk	cream	bacon
pork	silage	maize
grass seed	building sand	charcoal
firewood	eggs	dressed bird
peaches	coffee trees	maize meal
calfskin	oats	bananas

All these things have to be arranged and displayed. Ace has been enormously ingenious in the production of miniature bales of the various hays. We know there is some competition in this class, and we are making a great effort to win it – it is one of the few forms of advertising open to us.

Apart from the Rhodora Exhibit, we have entered for the following individual classes of farm and dairy produce:

Twenty cobs of fresh season's white maize.
One bale of lucerne hay.
One bale of oat hay.
One bale any other variety hay.
One glass jar, 4 lbs with lid, of silage.
One sod in a container, exhibiting a ley.
One bundle of green oats.
20 lbs farm-produced stockfeed roots (mangolds).
Rhodes grass seed – one half sack.
Three growing plants, any kale family, in a container.
Coffee in parchment, naturally dried, 10 lbs.
3 lbs sweet cream butter.
3 lbs ripened cream butter.

In the poultry section we have a white Leghorn hen and a dish of one dozen eggs.

In the horse section, Gold Lace is ridden by Liza Long in the Hack Under Fifteen Hands class and Faith is in the same class, ridden by Skett. Jenny Wren is in the Leading-Rein class with little Peter Ace, aged two, on her back (me leading), and she is also in the Child's Pony class with a little girl of eleven riding her, whom we have not yet met.

28th September, 1954

Liza and Douglas Skett had taken Gold Lace and Faith off to the exercising ground to school them, while Rosemary and Arap Genich were coping with Jenny Wren, when Osman the Ostrich strolled across with his usual supercilious stare. (He was picked up by the Kenya Regiment when he was a chick, and now draws a little carriage and is a great hit with the crowd in the arena events.) The horses took one look at him and nearly died of fright. Osman, quite unaware of the sensation he was causing, took a great interest in Douglas' and Liza's work, and followed them about all over the place. They roundly cursed him and he turned his attention to Rosemary, Arap Genich and Jenny, chasing them – in a majestic fashion – off the field. Eventually the Chief Steward got Osman locked up in a stallion box, where his near presence terrified only the stallions. He is a most upsetting factor in the Show Horse world.

10th October, 1954

Although we were very busy with the backlog of show week to clear up I had to spend a whole afternoon with Mr Phillips Price, Socialist MP for Gloucestershire West, who is touring Kenya in a private capacity in order to advise the Labour Party on the agricultural aspects of their colonial policy. He was brought out here by one of the Government Agricultural Officers. He is a right-wing Socialist, and not too rabid – rather pompous. Of course he wanted to know all about the wages we pay and the food we give to the Africans. Then we had to go down to our labour lines, and I have never seen an African gape with quite so much astonishment as when Mr Price took off his hat, bowed to him twice, and shook him warmly by the hand before going into his hut.

On Wednesday I made long and tiring trips into the Reserve over indifferent and dusty roads. Most of the land is a Garden of Eden: lovely green valleys with clear, flowing streams, the Africans apparently happy and very polite. Every square inch was cultivated and both men and women were working hard on their small patches. The area is vast and the population dense. I contacted three Chiefs. (Each Chief rules a location consisting of about 5,000 families. He is appointed by the tribe, but the appointment has to have the approval of the Government, which also pays him a salary.) Those I contacted were Chief Melchisedek Nindo, Chief Zephaniah Abungo and Chief William. I was extremely well-received everywhere and my visit will, I think, result in a steady flow of labour coming to the farm ready for the large crop of coffee we hope to have in 1955.

On Thursday at eight in the evening, when I was in my bath, a houseboy came to tell me that Mutiso, an old Mkamba of ours, wanted to see me. I went out and he told me that there were two Mau Mau terrorists in his hut asking for food. He had left a relative of his to entertain them while he came for me. I sent him back and told him to keep them entertained. Then I phoned the police, seized my rifle and set off.

On my way down to the hut I collected a Kipsigis and was joined by Ace, who had his shotgun. We surrounded the hut silently and I then kicked open the door and went in. One terrorist was just inside the doorway and seemed to be unarmed. Mutiso indicated that the other was hiding behind a partition. I ordered him out, but he did not come, so I put a bullet through the partition and then he did. I prodded them both out of the hut with the barrel of my rifle and searched them whilst Ace held them covered. They had nothing on them of any importance. The Kipsigis was by now sobbing with excitement and – had I not restrained him – would have killed the men on the spot. As it was we marched them back to the office and later, when the police turned up, put the handcuffs on them.

There followed a period of questioning (together with a certain amount of persuasion) of the two terrorists. For skilful lying you cannot beat the Kikuyu. However, after about two

211

hours, one of them broke down, and admitted that the rest of the gang were encamped in our crater land. He said that there were only two others, and that they were unarmed and he would show us where they were.

I posted Kipsang and another Kipsigis on our verandah to guard Rosemary, and two other men to guard Mrs Ace. We set off again, and at the top of the crater land I told the European policeman and his African *askaris* that it was no good their coming any further because of the noise they made with their huge boots. I then selected Brown Eyes (our second head herd boy) and two other trusted Kipsigis, and I made them strip naked, for their black bodies were the best camouflage at night. Brown Eyes carried a bow and arrow, and the other two carried chopping knives. Ace and I put on dark blue police raincoats.

We started slowly, with the informer amongst us, and we reached Howard Bridge and filed around the edge of a ploughed field. It was a dead still night, with the moon occasionally obscured by cloud. The crater stream was gurgling deep in its bed on our right.

At the bottom of the field we climbed through a barbed wire fence and into thick bush. Suddenly, ahead of us we heard somebody chopping wood. We crept forward. I felt that every twig which snapped might give us away, and the gang would either run off or start hunting us.

Our direction was now down towards the stream. Through the trees I saw the red glow of a fire. Step by step we came nearer, and what noise we made was covered by the noise of the water. I was in front with the others in single file behind, the handcuffed informer in the middle. (Brown Eyes, in his excitement, jabbed one of his arrows into the back of my head.) At last I could see the fire clearly.

My heart sank, for there were not two men but four around it, and because they were on the opposite bank we would lose time in the attack as we struggled across the stream. I would have liked to have gone back and organised a bigger party to surround them, but we were now so near that it was a miracle we had not been detected, and I dared not risk a withdrawal. In any case one of the gang was peering suspiciously in our direction. We stood motionless in the bush about fifteen yards from them, separated from them by the stream. We could see all four of them clearly illuminated by the moon and the fire, on which was a large cooking pot.

It seemed like an age whilst Ace, with infinite caution, moved up beside me. We raised our guns together. I aimed at a man on the left, and he aimed at a man with his back to us in the centre. I shouted 'Fire!'

All hell broke loose. As soon as my gun went off I was knocked headlong into the stream by Brown Eyes, who was in a hurry to get after the fleeing terrorists. When I climbed out on the other side I expected to find one, and possibly two, bodies lying near the fire. To my great disappointment there was not one. Meanwhile the Africans were tearing about, yelling in a most bloodthirsty manner. We searched all the bush in the near vicinity with the help of my torch.

Finding nothing we returned to the camp and found that they had left behind two home-made guns with .303 bullets in the breech, seven other rounds of .303 ammunition in two clips, two strangling ropes, and a book in Kikuyu, which was either a diary, or a detail of Mau Mau ceremonies. We had disturbed them before they had eaten, and there was a freshly killed sheep, masses of beans and maize, numerous cooking pots and some clothing. Ace and I could not believe that we had not seriously wounded at least one of them. Even if I missed with a bullet, how could he miss with SSG shot in his 12 bore at fifteen yards?

Hearing the shots the police arrived again, but not before our Kipsigis had beaten the informer with the rhino-hide whip until he was nearly dead, because he had said there were only two men when there were four – and because he had said they were unarmed, when they had guns. Later that night all our Kipsigis turned out and searched, but we found no more than a few hide-outs which the gang obviously used to lie up in by day.

The point where we found them was within two hundred yards of where Rosemary and I had been that same evening, looking at the lucerne.

We got to bed at 3 am, tracker dogs were on the farm at

dawn, a spotter plane was over the crater, and forty of our Kipsigis turned out to search. A very large hide-out was found, with considerable stores of maize, and the police say they think the gang has been living at Rhodora since last June. No trace of the fugitives has yet been found.

The Chief of Police at Nakuru rang up and congratulated me on the engagement. He also authorised me to pay fifty shillings to Mutiso (who gave the first information) on behalf of the Government, and this man may be entitled to a further 700 shillings, because the information he gave led to the discovery of arms and ammunition.

Rosemary and I went out to a nice play this evening at Nakuru.

We returned after a pre-Christmas visit to England:

12th December, 1954

First thing in the morning we drove around the farm. All is very well. The coffee is ripening and serious picking starts tomorrow; the trees are in very good order. The maize is being harvested, and both here and throughout the Valley is giving a better yield than ever before. The oats came off well. The lucerne is growing. The farm is tidy, with hay bulging everywhere in barns or in neatly thatched stacks. We have enough hay and silage for two years. The rain has surpassed the annual average, and Rhodora is green and beautiful, with ample grass in the paddocks so that the cattle and horses, pigs and sheep, dogs and poultry are sleek and well. The gallonage of milk is up.

As for the Mau Mau, there has been no sign of it during our absence and the district is quiet.

On Friday we got up full of excitement, set off in good time, and arrived at St Andrew's School to find the hall already crowded with parents. The lights went out, the curtain went up and the play began. Every one of the 160 children appeared at some stage. At last David came, the leader of a band of tiny tots, and he addressed the proud Caliph in his high, piping voice as follows:

'Sailors from the coast of Azania are here, and bring you gifts from the land of Zenje!'

That was his only line! We were rather struck by the school song, set to an attractive tune and made up by the children themselves especially for the occasion. Here are the first two verses:

> *Kenya, Kenya, where I belong,*
> *Kenya, Kenya, this is my song –*
> *Coral coast where the palm trees grow,*
> *Mountain tops that are white with snow.*
>
> *Leafy forests and spreading plains.*
> *Golden fields of ripening grain,*
> *White pyrethrum and graceful maize,*
> *I will serve thee, all my days.*

2nd January, 1955

The farm has been settling down after the Christmas festivities. Several of the Kipsigis were so much under the influence of *tembo* (beer) one evening that they either did not appear at all for work, or had to be laid out on the floor in the cattle-feed room whilst Ace hosed them with cold water. A tractor driver was found sitting beside his machine, groaning, with his head in his hands; the see-saw effect of discing across the lines of coffee had proved too much for him.

One of our sheep came home in the evening, having spent the day in the Kipsigis village, so much afflicted that it weaved all over the place and had obviously no idea whether it was coming or going. When we opened its mouth a strong smell of beer wafted up to us.

In general a good time was had by all – and there was some astonishment and dismay when I put my foot down a few days ago and said that Christmas was over. . . .

215

13th February, 1955

Last Sunday we and Mariloo were invited to lunch with Lord and Lady Claud Hamilton at Nderit. After entering their property, we rolled across the rain-swept plain leading to their house and saw not only herds of huge Boran cattle but also zebra and gazelles. This 28,500 acre farm is so vast that they say they cannot cope with any part of it in detail, but we spent a considerable time on the way home (as we often have before) wondering whether it would be possible to clear it and make large, clean paddocks and have a first-class beef herd there. The land is, for the most part, flat and bare of trees, and one feels it could be greatly more productive if it were ploughed and cultivated in rotation with good leys; but they say it is short of rain, and that there are only two water-points on the property. And anyway, Genessie likes it as 'Africa'.

They had just arrived home after a few days away, so we left soon after lunch, Claud very kindly taking us first to see the flamingos on Lake Nakuru. This is always an interesting spectacle. Mariloo was intrigued by the various hawks, kites, buzzards, kestrels and eagles we saw, and thrilled with a small family of Sykes monkeys.

On Monday morning a car drove up and out stepped a prospective buyer of bulls, an old gentleman named Mr Oswald Bentley. His nickname is Pink Gin Bentley, and he maintains (so it is said) a succession of glamorous continental girl-friends. He peered with rheumy eyes at everything we had to show him and was most interested. His fancy was taken by a young bull whose dam was named Marlene, and no doubt it was the continental flavour of her name which persuaded him to buy the bull. He has since written a charming letter to thank Rosemary for the lunch we gave him, saying he keeps thinking about the lovely Marlene cow we showed him, and cannot wait for us to send him up the young Marlene bull. . . .

On Friday we drove Mariloo down to Nairobi to the airport. The plane was late in from Johannesburg, and as a car had been shot at a few nights before on the escarpment, we decided not to wait to see her off, but said our sad good-byes and returned immediately. We rang the airport and were told the plane would leave at ten-thirty, and just after that time, we heard it approaching (the main plane route to London passes almost over Rhodora). Rosemary rushed out onto the lawn and saw the outline of the huge aircraft clearly silhouetted against the moon. It was all lit up; one could almost see Mariloo settling down for the night in her seat. It disappeared over the hills into the darkness, and Rosemary and I were very sad to see it go.

27th February, 1955

An atmosphere of gloom attended the meeting of Kenya's Coffee Marketing Board, which I went to on Friday. When Brazil devalued her currency about six weeks ago the world coffee market became very uneasy and the price fell steadily until a low point (representing a drop of about £160 a ton) was reached ten days ago. Unfortunately the Kenya crop is later than usual, and the fall in price coincided with large offerings at Nairobi, and in the auction only ten lots were sold out of 150. The remainder did not reach the reserve, although the Chairman of the Marketing Board offered them for sale by private treaty afterwards and all but thirty-one are now sold.

Meanwhile, sales of about 500 tons go on each week, and the big decision we had to make was whether to allow our coffee to go forward and meet the market, or whether to hold it off. We decided that we have no right to gamble with the growers' coffee, and will meet the market for better or worse. The dealers are living from hand to mouth, holding a minimum of stock, and waiting to see whether Brazil will make another move.

It is just sad that this fall in price should come in the first year that we have to suffer the twelve and a half per cent export tax, to help pay for the Emergency.

On Saturday morning while we were shopping the sky was obscured by a cloud and people came out of their offices onto the rooftops to watch the locusts go over the city. They passed for some twenty minutes and I heard several people round me say,

'Those are worse than the Mau Mau.'

20th March, 1955

Thursday night was definitely unpleasant. Our dog boy was walking back to bed at 11 pm when he encountered a gang of five terrorists sitting on the grass beside our doggery, within fifty yards of the house. The gang fled into the coffee and the dog boy fled to tell his friend, the head sheep boy. These two went round the outside of the coffee shamba and saw the gang emerge, travelling north.

For some reason they did not come to tell us until 1 am, when we were awakened by the familiar sound of the dog boy's voice on our verandah. Ajax lazily opened one eye, decided that he knew the intruder, and went on sleeping. I phoned the police and at 6 am next morning a patrol arrived with a tracker dog. The man in charge of the dog said he would not put it into the coffee because the tracks were not well enough defined, and the dog was being ruined by many disappointments when it assiduously followed a scent, only to find it had completed a circle and was back at the Headman's hut. Anyway the dog looked as if it could not have cared less. It was a mean-looking cross between a Doberman and an Alsatian, and just stood and looked around with bloodshot eyes. Further police patrols went out into the crater during the day but found nothing.

On Wednesday evening everyone trooped down to the Town Hall to Michael Blundell's vote of confidence meeting. The crowd was the biggest I have yet seen in Kenya and even the window-frames were thronged. We arrived very early to get a seat. People seemed in high spirits. The first resolution was on the subject of the surrender terms: it was carried by only eight votes, and Rosemary and I voted against it. Michael's vote of confidence was carried by 204 votes to 90. He made a bad speech and seemed nervous, whereas Humphrey Slade, in opposition, spoke coolly and to the point.

17th April, 1955

Sunday morning again. We three are sitting in a row in our bed. Breakfast, on three trays, has just been removed. Rosemary is now immersed in the Book Society Choice of the Month, and David is well stuck into Robinson Crusoe. We have heard about the terrible hurricane and the cave with the roof crumbling in. Any moment now Man Friday is going to appear on the scene.

Earlier, wrapping myself in a dressing-gown, I went out onto the lawn with the two Alsatians, Ajax and Diana, to meet the dog boy, Kiplangat, with the four Shelties. We watched all these dogs drink their morning milk, laced with calcium, and then they all went off with Kiplangat for a walk round the top of the farm. How lovely and fresh it was outside, with the lawn greening fast after the rain we have had this week. As I stood there, with the dogs lapping the milk, I could hear the noises of the cattle and the ring of the pails up at the cowshed. One of our tractors went chugging down the road to finish planting yellow maize in the Stroat field, for we had a little bit left over last night. From the bottom spare room, where Mortimer (our friend and adviser from the English Guernsey Council) was sleeping it off, having got in late after a day on Geoffrey Ireland's farm, there was no sound. As I walked back into our bedroom I noticed that the house martins have returned to occupy the nest over the door.

24th April, 1955

On Sunday Mortimer spent the day with Ace, and we three went up to Sheila and Andy Reynard on the North Kinangop. David enjoyed every second of it all, playing with the three children, the youngest of whom is at his school. Sheila and her husband have built really rather a lovely house up there, almost on top of the world, for the Kinangop is a huge plateau about 8,000 feet up, surrounded by the Aberdares, which tower above it. The house is a solid, English type of house, built round a courtyard, with none of the usual Kenya flimsiness. Even the doors in the hall are made of heavy mahogany imported from their bombed house in Yorkshire.

8th May, 1955

Thursday was my first meeting of the County Council, and I was amused to find everyone pompously referring to each other as *Councillor* Smith or whatever. The American foreign aid representatives have been here, and have offered to provide a comparatively small sum of money, provided that the Council telescopes its five-year social welfare plan (for Africans only) into two years. This means the Council will have to borrow large sums of money and greatly increase the rates. I opposed this strongly, saying that I thought the five-year plan was excellent, but that the acceleration of it was mad, just when the personal incomes of the farmers (i.e. ratepayers) were likely to be reduced by world events. They would not listen, and passed the plan by a majority vote.

Later, I was put on the Finance Committee and the Roads Committee.

12

A ghastly double murder in Nakuru chilled our small community to the marrow. The poor man whose wife and daughter were murdered was well known to us, being the respected manager of the chemist's shop Howse & McGeorge. It was not thought to be the work of Mau Mau but of their African house boys, not Kikuyu, who had been smoking a drug called 'bhang'. For a few weeks Tony was engaged on front-line duty against terrorists. And yet official feeling seemed to be that the Mau Mau were on the decline; the British Army involvement was gradually wound down. Everywhere one heard quite serious discussion of how Kenya was to be governed once the Mau Mau were wiped out, and certainly the intelligence reports we received indicated that morale was very low amongst them.

Our social life was livelier than ever. Susan, my younger daughter, now aged eighteen, visited us; we went to the Congo with my brother Leo, and we were thrilled to receive an international phone call from Barbara – what a rare event an international call was in those days! And what momentous news: she was to be married.

We had even greater success than usual at the Royal Show, and at Nakuru I judged the Jerseys. I was by now on the Management Board of the Nakuru Memorial Hospital.

21st June, 1955

On Friday I had a County Council meeting in the morning in Nakuru, and in the afternoon Rosemary had a hospital meeting. Sheila Reynard arrived to stay two nights, but I had to go out from dusk to dawn as there were signs that our hide-out was being occupied. Sure enough, it was, and after a long chase, one of our Kipsigis caught a so-called Mau Mau

General, who spent the night being interrogated – first in our pantry and then on the back verandah. Sheila, an old hand at this sort of business, went to bed, but Rosemary spent most of the night dressed in a pair of slacks doling out tea and biscuits for the various police patrols which kept milling in and out of the house. We had a lot of ambushes laid.

On Saturday Rosemary and Sheila went up to Sports Day at St Andrew's School, and found David and Bill well but full of the 'Turi cold'. Rosemary and I went up again on Sunday and had a picnic lunch with them. That evening the only incident in the ambushes happened to a young man who heard noises by a water trough and hit what he thought was a Mau Mau. It turned out to be an ant-bear, and he had killed it stone dead with one shot. This is the first one we have ever managed to shoot on the farm.

Last night, Monday, we came back from Nairobi, where I had a Coffee Board meeting, to find our Kipsigis were wanted again on ambush. Rosemary quickly cut them meat sandwiches and boiled them an egg each, and at dusk they went off with the fully armed African police to various points. I had just got into the bath when Ace rushed unceremoniously into the room and said that one of the ambush parties had met a gang of twenty-two or more and had fired on them. They had slipped over the edge of the crater and disappeared. Another night of activity – but Rosemary slept most of the time, leaving Ali on guard over the sitting-room, telephone and fire. This morning (Tuesday) there is a general service unit in the crater. The Mau Mau General got co-operative at about eight last night and said that the four of Saturday night were about to join up with the big gang of last night; he had been sent by the head man ('Field Marshal' Dedan Kimathi) to meet them. Please do not start to worry, because the house is not in danger, the cattle are specially guarded and the farm is stiff with police.

We were keeping the whole truth from our families at home. The situation was much more alarming than we said and we heard many stories of atrocities near the farm. One night, with more bravado than good sense, I accompanied Tony and Ace on an ambush. We crept out of the house in pitch darkness and made our way silently to a ploughed field called Cowbridge, about a quarter of a mile away. We dropped to the ground and inched forward on our stomachs until we had reached the bed of a dry waterfall, where we lay noiselessly staring into the African night. I could feel mosquito-bites swelling on every inch of my neck and face and hands. Still we lay in silence. After a while I saw something small and bright glowing in the dark ahead of me. Then another little, bright, pin-prick of light. And more. They were everywhere, swaying and rustling in the blackness, and so dark was it that I could not estimate how far away they were. Was I watching torches across a distant field? Or bright little eyes, much closer, and watching me as I was watching them? Fear made me stiffen, and I whispered softly to Tony.

'There's somebody there.'

'Where?'

'Look!'

He looked and hissed 'Fireflies.'

I hoped I did not hear Ace suppress a snigger. At least it was dark so my blushes could not be seen. I lay on my front for another half an hour. My neck was stiff and my arms ached. I thought longingly of bed. Then I made a courageous decision: I would get up and go home. And so I stumbled, fearful and unaccompanied, across the ploughed field under Africa's huge black sky.

26th June, 1955

Rosemary and I – after much thought – have decided to tell you about the Mau Mau here in detail, because if these newsletters are to be an accurate record we must write the facts. This past week everything has been subordinated to operational requirements; visits to Nairobi have been cancelled, as have most other engagements off the farm.

The gangs, at this stage of the Emergency, are not aggressive. They are very much on the run and on the defensive, and they are short of arms and ammunition. Risk, for a European, only arises if one happens to run into a gang in some lonely place, or is wounded when contact is made. The chances of

223

Mau Mau attacking our house are negligible, even at night, but the police have been anxious that they might take reprisals against our cattle, and we have been keeping the pedigrees in at night under guard.

I think there is little doubt that the track around the edge of the crater is a highway for gangs moving between Njoro and the Aberdares, and that there are hide-outs in the 300 foot cliff which bounds our farm on the edge of the crater, and at the foot of this cliff, and out in the bush and rocks of the crater itself. These hide-outs are used as staging-points for the gangs, and they lie out in the crater by day, but come into the cliff face by night to light their fires in order to cook their food. They get their water from our cattle-troughs.

We might never have known about this state of affairs (which has persisted for some considerable time) had I not happened to stumble upon one of the hide-outs on the cliff face, by the grace of God unoccupied at the time, while Rosemary was in Paris. From that moment I had a tracker watching all the known tracks on the farm and one day he took me up to our cattle-trough in Boverton field and showed me – without any possibility of a doubt – that two men, one with large feet and one with small, had come for water in the night and retired down the precipitous track towards the hide-out.

The approach to the hide-out makes it impossible to surprise it by day and dangerous to attack it by night. Accordingly, we decided to ambush the water-trough, which is some 400 yards from the entrance to the hide-out tracks, that night. I led a party of about twenty Kipsigis up there at dusk; a policeman and a few armed *askaris* came up behind. We approached the trough through some trees and as we broke cover to get into position – there were three terrorists, coming over the skyline towards us.

We froze.

We were around the trough, but three Kipsigis had already begun to work their way around in a flanking movement. It was not quite dark. In a moment the terrorists began to notice that there was something wrong. They hesitated, came on a bit, then stopped. They said to each other in Kikuyu,

224

'Who are these men?'

At that moment we all rose, and they fled. None of us, except for the three men on the flank, had a chance of catching them, for they had a start of about 150 yards. Two tall terrorists (the ones with big feet!) ran back to the crater's edge. One of them had four arrows in his back by the time he got there. Further along the edge, a European whom we had placed in ambush loosed off his sten gun, though he really could not distinguish friend from foe. The excitement was terrific, with Kipsigis emitting blood-curdling yells and rushing off in all directions.

Meanwhile, Arap Genich, our head *syce*, who was on the flank, chopped at the legs of one of the fleeing terrorists, and in so doing his panga fell out of his hand. Notwithstanding that he was unarmed, he set out in pursuit, having thrown off his blanket; the terrorist (the short one with small feet) was deflected from the crater by the sten gun burst. They raced across Boverton and Arbon Grove – about half a mile – before Arap Genich caught his man, and he held onto him until two more Kipsigis turned up to help them – although the terrorist had cut Arap Genich's arm with a knife, severing several tendons. It was by then pitch dark and a very black night. I came up, blowing like a whale, some time afterwards to find that my orders to take the man alive were being obeyed more in the spirit than in the observance. It is extraordinary how excited and worked-up Africans become on these occasions.

We brought our captive back to our headquarters in the trees and questioned him by the light of a torch. He was at first unwilling to talk but, with a little persuasion, he loosened up. He said he was a Mau Mau General who formerly led a gang of sixty, but at the moment he was on a special mission, and was accompanied by six others with four precision weapons between them. We reinforced our 'stops' on each side of the hide-out at the foot of the cliff, and left in our ambush parties. Our 'general' was then led up to the house for further questioning (in the pantry and on the back verandah). The next morning, just before first light, I crept down the baboon track with a policeman with a Patchett gun behind me and the Kipsigis behind him. There was no one in the hide-out and we went on to the foot of the cliff and searched the area without success.

Next night and the following night we intensified our ambushes to four. . . . Nothing happened and everyone got terribly tired, for it is frightfully cold lying out all night and we all have to do our milking and run our farms by day. The ambush party usually consists of one European (a local farmer) armed with a sten gun or rifle – in my case I prefer my old 16 bore shotgun and a revolver – three police *askaris* with rifles, and one or two Kipsigis with spears or bows and arrows. We also have a guard on the crater edge by day.

The next night was black and moonless, like all the other nights, and we had not enough Europeans for all the ambush parties; the ambush on Hill Top track was commanded by an African corporal. We really had no luck. At about 7.30 they suddenly saw what seemed to be a huge force bearing silently down upon them in columns of three. They panicked, stood up, and fired off every round in their magazines at random. The large gang (which, from subsequent information, we estimate at twenty-two strong) disappeared into the crater. We could do nothing that night except reinforce our ambush parties, and at 4 am a special commando went down the baboon track, but they made no contact. That morning at dawn I sat on the edge of the crater with a Bren gun, and could hear the Mau Mau giving their distinctive bird's cry call from several places, but I could see no one.

At noon the Army appeared with three-inch mortars, and gave a wonderful display of inefficiency: first by refusing to take our advice, and firing into the wrong corner of the crater; then by putting two shells about 15° off-line and nearly wiping out our grade herd in Inchmery field; and finally, by dropping one shell about 100° off-line within fifty yards of Ace's house.

For the last two nights there has been no sign of Mau Mau and we have lifted our ambushes whilst continuing to watch the tracks. In any case, the large gang may have been virtually destroyed, for our captive 'general' led a striking force to two hide-outs in the Dundori forest, about ten miles from here, and

226

they killed five and wounded at least five more. Quite a number of home-made guns were captured.

10th July, 1955

Bruce McKenzie is the largest Friesian farmer in the country, and his farm is next door to ours, also on the edge of the crater but round the corner a bit from us. He has been keeping his nineteen bulls tethered in an area of about one-fifth of an acre at night, with a guard in the middle. On Wednesday night, at 3 am, the guard woke up to find a bull lose and fighting with another. He went to fetch Bruce, but by the time they returned the bull had disappeared. They could not find it, so they concluded that it must have gone off to visit a lady friend somewhere.

The next morning its remains were found. It had been slaughtered by the Mau Mau for food, and the tracks revealed a gang of about ten, which had come from the direction of our farm and gone off towards the Bahati Forest. In view of this incident (and there have been others like it recently) we have decided to bring in our cattle at night to the three paddocks behind the house. Some of the Guernseys are in the buildings at night and the oxen are in a night paddock beside the Kipsigis village. This plan adds the cattle guards to the house and maize store guards, so there are now more guards near the house.

The news about Bruce came to me in Nakuru on Thursday morning at a Stud Book meeting. Rosemary and Susan were about to join me for lunch, and then we were going on to Nairobi to spend the night. We decided not to change our plans and arrived in Nairobi in time to attend the Annual General Meeting of the Alsatian League. Then we all went to the Club and changed, had dinner and hastened off to the National Theatre, where *Chu Chin Chow* was being performed. All tickets had long ago been sold, but we got hold of the manager and told a long story, which moved him so much that he had three picnic chairs put up for us at the back of the auditorium. It was our first visit to the National Theatre, which is hideous outside but nice inside. The staging of the play was superb and could hardly have been bettered in London. The costumes especially were remarkable, and one could see from the acknowledgements printed in the programme that the Indian community had assisted with many priceless silks. We all enjoyed it and returned to Rhodora on Friday in time for lunch.

17th July, 1955

On Tuesday the vet came up to stitch Ajax's ear, which he tore on some barbed wire whilst ragging with Diana. Giving him the anaesthetic was not easy, because as soon as he felt any pain, he wanted to eat everyone in sight. All that night he lay on blankets in our lavatory, moaning and groaning and keeping us awake, and it was really not until the next morning that he came round sufficiently to stagger about the lawn in a drunken fashion. He is developing into a magnificent dog and we are both very attached to him. Although barely nine months, he weighs eighty pounds and eats two and a half pounds of meat and drinks two and a half pints of whole milk with an egg in it every day.

31st July, 1955

As usual there has always appeared to be rain falling anywhere else but here – and noticeably so this year on a farm next door. This is mainly because when rain is scarce, it is also very local, but we are also very suspicious of a nearby farmer who has hired a large aircraft, at great expense, and goes up every day *making* rain. He says that by this means he has been getting some rain every day on his crops. Now he has got some balloons which will carry some kind of magic to make rain right up in the clouds, whenever there are rain clouds overhead. I only hope the wind blows the balloon over our farm first.

Last Sunday we had lunch at Michael Blundell's and

General Heyman, the Chief of Staff, was there. I had a talk with him and he said that they had not captured anyone for some time who had been less than six months in the forest: in other words, the terrorists are not getting recruits. With casualties still running at around fifty a week, he thought it would all be over in about a year's time. He did, however, think that there might soon be a fresh manifestation of Mau Mau amongst the Nyanza tribes, on the edge of Lake Victoria, next door to Uganda – where there is also a good deal of unrest.

We took my daughter Sue to the Amboseli Game Park:

7th August, 1955

As we write this Rosemary and I are sitting on a tiny verandah in front of our *banda* which consists of a *makuti* thatched hut, with a double bedroom and bathroom off. It has a concrete floor, two iron beds with Dunlopillo mattresses (very comfortable), a few wooden shelves, curtained off, and wire netting, instead of a ceiling, to prevent the monkeys coming through. David and Susan are sharing a replica of our *banda*, about twenty yards away, and we can hear them giggling and talking as they sit on Sue's bed surrounded by balls of coloured wool, from which they are knitting a patchwork blanket.

We arrived here on Friday just as it was getting dark after a seven-hour journey from Rhodora. We four travelled in our Ford Zephyr. In the Peugeot behind came our driver, the cook, and Ochieng, Rosemary's boy. We unpacked the food in the nice little kitchen provided, made up the beds, sorted out the clothes, and generally set up camp.

From our verandah we look out onto the very wildness of Africa, fever trees and stunted bush and the shimmering heat on the grass. A herd of wildebeest has just passed across our view and a giraffe is alternately nibbling the top of a thorn tree and taking a peep at us. At night one hears hyenas howling, the squeals of the zebra and grunts and roars of the lions. The whole vast reserve, of nearly 1,300 square miles, is teeming with game.

There are twelve *bandas*, a shop and a garage in this government-run camp. Two game wardens have their own houses. It was originally built by the film company which made *Where No Vultures Fly*. The charge is ten shillings per head per night. No radios or gramophones are allowed so that it is dead quiet except for the sounds of the animals, the songs of the birds and a murmur of human voices.

Next door to us is a tented camp for another film unit, which is arriving any moment for a stay of six weeks. (Sue is dying to know who the stars are going to be.) Further down the road is a small government camp for Indians, and beyond that, tucked away in the middle of some large fever trees, is Gethin's famous rhino camp, where we have stayed several times before, but it is much more expensive and far less comfortable than here.

We get up at 5.45 am, have a cup of tea and a biscuit, pick up a picturesque Mkamba game ranger and set out in the car, armed with binoculars and cameras, to spot the animals. We come back for breakfast at nine, and spend the rest of the morning in useful pursuits such as writing newsletters, or catching lizards. . . . Sleep overwhelms us and most of the wild animals during the afternoon. We have tea at four, and set out again for the evening trip.

The highlights so far have been a herd of female elephants with their young, a lioness which ignored us, two bull buffaloes on the edge of the swamp, a rhino with its child (which had no ears and only half a tail), and a wonderful collection of birds, including the sacred ibis, the Egyptian goose, flamingos, toucans and the lilac-breasted roller. Rosemary and I have promised each other we will come down and watch these quietly one week-end.

Family visitors were generally deputed to write a newsletter home, and my daughter Sue was no exception:

14th August, 1955

. . . . David and I rode whilst Mummy and Tony showed the two Frenchmen round the farm. They came back full of excitement, having found a garment belonging to a Mau Mau. Tony took the Frenchmen back to Nairobi after lunch, as he had a Dog Show Committee meeting in the afternoon. At teatime the police turned up in a truck, and inside was a Mau Mau. He had been sleeping on Peter Howard's land right on our boundary. He looked a dreadful wreck with hair sticking out everywhere, a tin cap, a hide over his shoulders, very dilapidated trousers and a blue bandage on one of his toes. He was still holding his home-made gun, and in the truck was his water-bottle and a sling. He could speak English quite well. A little later he was brought up to the stock because the policeman wanted to speak to Mummy, so the truck was soon surrounded by myself and Linda Ace, and a mass of Kipsigis who had left milking the cows and feeding the horses in order to gape at the Mau Mau. I wanted to know what had induced him to become one, as he had only been one for nineteen months, and he said he had heard it was 'a good thing.'

Tony again:

21st August, 1955

As dusk fell last Sunday night Rosemary and Sue came out to the police lorries beside the tractor sheds and saw Ace and myself and three other Europeans, each with a small patrol of four *askaris*, move off to various remote parts of the farm on all-night ambush. It poured with rain early in the night, but I was lucky as my ambush was in the lucerne, which enabled me and my party to shelter in the new open-sided drying shed. The others were soaked and had to stay wet through, lying on the wet ground all night.

At the house, Anne Fitzmaurice was staying overnight in the double spare room and Sue and David were asleep in the

231

nursery wing. At 4 am Rosemary was awakened by a night guard calling into her window. She jumped up at once and went to see what the matter was.

'Mau Mau, Memsahib,' he mumbled in Swahili. 'By the maize store.'

She didn't recognize his voice and peered into the darkness. She could see him clearly and knew she had not seen him before.

'Are you the night guard?' she asked doubtfully.

'Yes, Memsahib. The Mau Mau are over there.'

The maize store is only 200 yards from our bedroom so she had to do something quickly. She rang Kipsang on the internal telephone which runs from our bathroom to Ace's house and thence to Kipsang's hut. He answered her immediately and promised to come at once with a party of Kipsigis.

The dogs were in the bedroom but the night guard had vanished from the verandah. Rosemary was extremely uneasy as the minutes ticked by since she was sure she had never seen him before, and outside was silence broken only by the usual noises of the Kenyan night. She dressed and stood near the window. Time went on and there was no sign of Kipsang at all. A host of possibilities occurred to her, each one more horrible than the last. If she left the room to cross to the nursery wing and there really were Mau Mau out there her life would be in danger. But she had to restrain the thought that Sue and David might at any moment be murdered in their beds.

It was after six in the morning when first light broke and we returned after a fruitless night to see Rosemary marching down the path towards us demanding to know where we had been when we needed her. Of course, Kipsang had arrived at once after her call, checked the place thoroughly, reassured the night guards and taken his party of Kipsigis to protect the maize store. But it hadn't occurred to him to let Rosemary know what they had done.

When I got to the maize store I found them examining tracks which led away from it into the coffee. Nothing had been taken, as the robbers had been surprised by the guard who woke up, but a tracker dog was brought and we were able to follow a trail of two men from our maize store for about a mile and a half. They had avoided all the ambushes and we lost the trail on the edge of the crater. One was very big with a footprint an inch longer than mine; he is said to be someone with a price on his head, whom the police have been looking for since the Emergency began.

Some interesting work has been going on in the crater based on the farm of our neighbour, Bruce McKenzie. A certain Intelligence Officer has been making trips into the crater for periods of several days. He goes alone, with a party of terrorists who have previously been captured. He blacks his face, and dresses and lives as a terrorist. It is extremely dangerous work, for the terrorists he goes with (about ten of them) are completely free, and even armed, so that they could turn on him and kill him at any moment. They have a very good reason for wanting to kill him, because he takes with him a Patchett gun (submachine-gun) which any terrorist would like to possess.

The whole plan sounds mad, but it has produced surprising results. On his first trip he came back with his whole gang and three more captives, and on his second trip with two more. On this journey he was in the crater for three days and nights, during which he did not dare sleep or relax for a moment; and the two men he captured said they shadowed his party for a day and a half before they approached it. When they were seen, the Intelligence Officer turned away and pretended to be doing something. The new arrivals went round shaking hands with the 'friendly' gang, but when they came to him he swung round and they found themselves looking down the barrel of the Patchett.

These new captives confirm that there are about thirty terrorists on our side of the crater, and the same Intelligence Officer, accompanied by our local policeman and their band of 'friendly' terrorists, are going in before dawn tomorrow morning to try and contact and capture them.

At night now our arrangements resemble mediaeval times when all the animals were driven into the castle at night and the drawbridge raised until morning. Between our house and Ace's we now have all our animals in small paddocks, including the oxen. The sheep are in a paddock between us and the cowshed, and the bulls remain in their pens. Each unit has its guard, and the stores and implement sheds are within the area. The guards are armed with chopping knives and whistles, and the guards on the milking herds also have thunder-flashes. To complete the security there is the telephone across to Ace's house and going on to the Kipsigis camp. In all we have nine guards between the cowshed and Ace's house (a distance of some 400 yards) with our house roughly in the middle. I only wish we had a wall and a moat.

28th August, 1955

A little before noon last Sunday the Kipsigis arrived on the lawn to dance for Sue, as it was her last Sunday. Forming a ring under the big pepper tree, they started beating their drum and singing. Nearby, their women, dressed in colourful cottons, together with their many small children, grouped themselves and we sat on the lawn amongst them. At about lunchtime Rosemary fetched some sweets for the children and we gave the men Coca-Cola and cigarettes and told them we were going in for lunch. They stayed on under the tree idly strumming a primitive guitar and quietly pounding away on the drum, and when we reappeared they started up again. Eventually they decided it was getting near milking time so they departed in single file chanting 'Kwa heri, Memsahib ... Kwa heri, Memsahib ...'

On Thursday morning I had a meeting of the County Council, and on my way out of the farm I thought I would take a look at our main labour gang, which was cleaning the lucerne. On my way down the crater road, the gang came running towards me in a state of high excitement and fear.

'Bwana, three bad men, all armed with guns, came out of the crater! They are sitting in the lucerne! They are asking for you!'

I told them that if the men were asking for me there was surely nothing to fear. They should go back to the bad men and tell them that if they would give up their guns the Bwana would come. Trembling, they returned to the terrorists who were squatting in the lucerne, whilst I walked up slowly behind. Eventually, I got close enough to recognise our local police-man, all got up like a wandering minstrel, who had emerged from the crater with two of his 'friendly' terrorists because they were short of water. I took them up to the house, and we gave the policeman a meal and supplies, and later he and his men went back to the crater to rejoin the main party.

After dark that evening I again had a call to the lucerne, and the whole party emerged. They went back to Bruce McKenzie's farm for refreshment, and descended once more into the crater at dawn the next morning from Peter Howard's farm. They finally came out on Wednesday evening, wet and exhausted, having failed to contact any Mau Mau.

11th September, 1955

Ajax and Diana occupied one large double bench at the show, sitting on a rust-coloured blanket, and they had many admirers from the crowd which thronged by in the afternoon. Never having been to anything like this before, and being still very young (eleven and nine months respectively), they did not behave as well as they should have done. Nevertheless, in large classes, Ajax got two Seconds and two Thirds against mature imported dogs, and Diana excelled herself (chiefly, we think, because she behaved a little better than Ajax) by getting two Firsts and one Second and the Reserve Challenge Certificate.

Kiplangat, the dog boy, who has been with us for the past year, was a tower of strength and never left his charges all day long. He told us afterwards that a great many people enquired what we fed the dogs on, and he always replied that he had no idea, as the Memsahib always saw to their food. He added,

'Had I told them, they would feed their dogs as we do ours, and then perhaps win next time instead of us!'

We were much amused at this subtle thinking.

25th September, 1955

Monday, Tuesday and Wednesday were spent on the farm in a whirl of preparation for the Royal Show. On Thursday I had an all-day session at the County Council. Rosemary, accompanied by Arap Genich and the driver, and armed with a saddle and bridle and an inadequate map, set off for a farm belonging to a Mr Pardoe, situated between Gilgil and Naivasha, in order to try out a prospective show hack named Golden Planet. Owing to the inadequacy of the map and Rosemary's inability to read one, she motored for a good ten miles around the district before she found the place. Amongst a shambles of buildings, animals and Africans she eventually found the so-called manager, who said Mr Pardoe would like to see her – but he was in bed.

Another quarter of an hour was wasted talking to the manager while Mr Pardoe got up, and then another half hour while he talked about the iniquities of Mau Mau. At last Rosemary persuaded him to let her see the horse, which on first appearance looked rather nice. On closer inspection she saw he had a swollen front leg and a split back hoof. Standing amongst a collection of bulls, a mob of other horses, various dogs and some goggling Africans, she managed to get him saddled up, and Arap Genich got up and tried to make him go. Nothing doing. He merely bucked, walked a few steps and bucked again.

Then it came out that he had been with the Kenya Regiment on patrol against Mau Mau. Any horse that survives that is a tough horse indeed, but Rosemary could not quite see how they got him to chase Mau Mau, because all he wanted to do was go home.

She drove off to Nairobi with Arap Genich shaking his head in the back of the car all the way from there to the city.

5th October, 1955

The judge from the English Guernsey Cattle Society arrived from London; his name is John Brittain. I met him on the show ground and soon discovered that he went to Oundle. Further questioning revealed that he occupied exactly the same position (hooker) in the Rugger XV in 1933 as I did in 1931. After that he and I were away to a good start and got on like a house on fire.

For some time during the morning Rosemary and I watched the sheep judging because this is a new venture for us, and we have a lot to learn. Our non-pedigree ram, George, was definitely not up to it, and should not have been shown; we have since decided to sell him and buy a pedigree ram instead. Our three ewes were not bad, but we made the unforgiveable error of washing their behinds, which spoils the wool, and the judges would not look at them. Also, we should have put canvas rugs on them for weeks beforehand in order to get their wool to knit together. Last in the judging came our pen of three fat lambs, and here we got a First – and later, a large cup.

Throughout the day many members of the Guernsey Society came to the stall which Rosemary had, as usual, set up most elegantly. The walls are off-white, the floor polished a rust red; there are wicker chairs and tables and a pretty screen, Guernsey literature on the big table and a huge copper bowl filled with wonderful velvet-like flowers of a glorious deep rust-red like the floor. The flowers were donated by a leading Nairobi florist whose husband happens to breed Guernseys. There were lunch boxes and free drinks and we took down little Ali, our Comorien houseboy, to look after the place.

On Friday Rosemary and I had lunch in the President's tent, and I sat next to a woman from Nanyuki who told me how terrible the Mau Mau had been, and how she had lost 250 sheep. I looked at her with deep sympathy, feeling sure she must be nearly bankrupt, but later discovered that she had a mere 10,000 sheep left! In the afternoon I showed the Governor around the Guernsey exhibits, and if he felt as bored as he looked I am sorry for him. . . .

Leo, my brother, arrived (with a motley collection of luggage about which, it is recorded, I made certain scathing remarks) and of course we asked him to write home. . . .

237

15th October, 1955

We were on our way to Rhodora, climbing up the edge of the escarpment and down along the straight tarmac road over the floor of the valley, skirting Longonot's sloping shoulder, through the fever trees bordering Lake Naivasha, round the rocky bends overlooking Lake Elmenteita and up the graded, dusty section of branch road towards Solai Valley. It was all so familiar that I felt I had barely been out of the country for four weeks, let alone four years; only the rains had made everything a softer green than I can remember, and the Kenya sky was at its best – a clear blue, dotted with luminous white clouds such as some Dutch Masters liked to paint.

After a bath, lunch and sleep, I was shown round some of the outstanding changes that have taken place since my last visit: the rearrangement of flower beds and growing of plants and shrubs, the garden wall, and of course the new road around the edge of the crater and re-routing of the road into it, with the wide clearing for lucerne at the bottom, dramatically dominated by a sheer wall of red rock at one end.

On Sunday I admired the stock, still in super-prime condition from the Royal Show, as well the wall of rosettes and shelf-full of cups collected over the past years and displayed in the farm office. In the evening the Blundells came to dinner and brought Granville Roberts (now adviser on Kenyan Affairs to the Colonial Office) with them. He said that the British Government are now expressing much more confidence in Kenya and in his opinion, the colony is in for a period of economic expansion. The Mau Mau threat, while still present from scattered gangs who have been chased out of the forests, is diminishing and things have been fairly quiet recently. The African-European problem remains, however, and the only solution seems to be an inter-racial government with the balance of power heavily weighted in favour of the whites.

On Monday at lunchtime a sharp fall of hail occurred with some really unpleasantly large stones, which soon covered the lawn in a sheet of white and reduced poor Tony to a state of near-nervous collapse, only alleviated by a quick visit to the

238

nearest coffee shamba to assure himself that the entire coffee crop was not scattered on the ground. In fact the damage, though not as severe as it might have been, is estimated at five tons – and with the price at around £350 a ton, this is not altogether a laughing matter.

The next day was taken up with a safari to Nairobi. Those of you who have been out here know the form – hideously early start in the cold Kenya dawn, hurtling down the road at a quite astonishing speed, very welcome breakfast at Njoro Inn, separation of Tony to Coffee Marketing Board and of Rosemary to dress and various other clothing establishments, a visit (this time) to the Belgian Consulate to obtain Congo visas, more hectic shopping, meeting for a hurried lunch at the Club which always lasts longer than it should, followed by joint visits to the cleaners and the market and a final separation, with Tony going off to what proved to be a troublesome meeting of the Kenya Kennel Club whilst Rosemary and I started for home.

The day ended with everyone in a pleasantly comatose state around the fire after one of Onyango's excellent dinners.

Leo on our visit to the Congo:

24th October, 1955

We flew down from Nakuru to Kitwe in Northern Rhodesia in the Anglo-American Dove on Sunday – a smooth journey except for the last fifteen minutes. We landed in blazing equatorial heat as the rains are expected shortly and are always presaged by almost intolerably stifling weather conditions. We were met by the General Manager and his wife, Mr and Mrs Bennett, and put up in the company's superbly comfortable guest house under the supervision of the housekeeper, the very Scottish Mrs English, whose cuisine is certainly not calculated to make one tighten one's belt.

The Belgian Congo border lies about forty miles away,

reached by an excellent tarmac road cutting through the endless wastes of shabby, sandy-floored forests which cover most of the Rhodesias. After the border the road undergoes an abrupt transition, and degenerates into a third-rate cart track, potholes and all. This continues through exactly the same oppressive, tree-infested country, for the whole remaining 100 miles to Elisabethville – and in fact, as we were to discover only too well, over the whole of the province of Katanga. A surprising state of affairs, considering the immense wealth of the country as a whole and the highly industrialised state of this particular province. Anyway, we bumped and banged our way to Elisabethville, arriving hot, shaken and exhausted as well as two hours late. We called on the Manager of Banque Lambert's Cold Storage Company, a Mr Denruyter, who had drawn up an itinerary for us. He seemed pleased to see us, but surprised at our comments on the condition of the road.

Elisabethville, at 4,500 feet, normally enjoys a reasonably temperate climate. But of course we had struck it at the worst moment, just before the rains break, and the atmosphere was heavy and unpleasant. The hotel, although reasonably modern, is very badly run, and neither food nor service lived up to the standards one might expect from Belgians. In fact there was really no standard at all. No-one moved faster than a crawl; the rooms were dirty and stuffy, and the food was off – either off the menu, or off colour. The city itself has pleasant residential quarters where all the villas look like a tropical version of Le Zoute; but the dominating feature, as in most mining towns, is the belching chimney of Union Minière's foundry. In fact we were told that the whole Congo is dominated by three factors: Union Minière, the Church, and the State, in that order.

Union Minière is, as its name suggests, a virtual mining monopoly, and as the huge ore deposits in the Congo include copper four times as pure as that found in Rhodesia, uranium, and diamonds, the company is not exactly insolvent. During our stay in the Congo we were alternately in their hands, or those of the various Lambert representatives. A Colonel de Ryckman showed us round the local foundry. Built in 1911, and acknowledged to be somewhat old-fashioned, it presents nevertheless an awe-inspiring spectacle as the copper travels in its molten form from one furnace to another during the various refining processes. We learnt that labour relations are somewhat easier than in Rhodesia. European labour, of which there is an absolute minimum, is engaged on a three-year contract, after which they are automatically sent home; only if they are proven non-troublemakers is the contract renewed. Add to this the complete absence of any African union and you have a situation which would make most Rhodesian Copper Belt managers contented men.

Early next morning, as instructed, we presented ourselves at Elisabethville airport, where Union Minière had arranged for an aeroplane to take us to Kolwezi, the actual mining centre, about 230 miles west. After about a half-hour's wait, the pilot appeared with a long face: we were overweight, and would have to shed 100 kilos of luggage. Although we were none of us exactly travelling light, we reckoned that to do this would leave us with one handkerchief each: so we firmly dug our toes in and said that it was impossible. Much moustache stroking and hurried mathematics ensued, with the result that half the plane's fuel was taken out, and we took off. Of course we were late, and Union Minière's representative at the other end wore a haggard look until he had got us safely to our destination, which was Le Marinel dam, about 120 kilometres away.

This is one of four being built to supplement power, of which both the Congo and Rhodesian copper companies are becoming increasingly short. Part of the output from this station will, in fact, find its way into the Rhodesias over a 500 kilometre power line. Everything here was just about to be completed, and we were lucky to see it looking like a sectioned model with the lid off, as it were. Thus we (not Rosemary!) were able to walk along the pipes down which the water will eventually pour on its final precipitation to the turbines, and we saw the turbines with their outsides off, so we could see exactly where the water would go to make the blades revolve.

The river is dammed – not by concrete, but by clay and stones – on one side of a mountain, while the power station is on the other side, in a valley lower than the level of the riverbed, producing the necessary drop. Later on we drove in a car inside the twenty-foot-diameter tunnel that will convey the water from the dam about one and a half miles through a mountain-side to the power station.

Next day Tony and I inspected the vast open-cast copper mine near Kolwezi. It looked like a gigantic sand-pit, with railways and roads running around its perimeter at different levels. The ore is extracted by excavators which bite into the earth and disgorge enormous mouthfuls of it into trucks and lorries, which whisk it to the concentrator, where a preliminary refining process takes place. The gentleness and precision with which the excavators are handled and the ease with which the great boulders and tons of earth are moved with only the flick of a wrist is breathtaking.

That afternoon a car came to fetch us from Biano where another Lambert subsidiary, Grelco, have a 165,000 acre ranch. Within two hours we were transported to a different world. We had climbed out of the stuffy, wooded regions, onto a high, grass-covered plateau, where huge plains roll away as far as the eye can see – fine open country, and a welcome relief climatically, for the rains had broken here and the coolness was delicious.

The director of the ranch is a Swiss, Mr Lutz, and he and his Italian wife looked after us very handsomely, particularly from a culinary point of view, during our two-day visit. The actual guest house was somewhat primitive (no details) and the beds had lumps in the most unlikely places. But what we saw on the ranch proved an eye-opener. After seven months of drought, the cattle, bred from Afrikander bulls, all appeared (though thin) in excellent condition. There was hardly any fresh grass, no hay and they had been fed very little silage. We must have travelled over 100 miles in one morning, looking at the scattered herds, and we did not see a single sick animal. Rosemary and Tony were in their element, and Mr Lutz was obviously pleased to find people who could take a knowledge-able interest. He is due to retire in two years and his wife is not relishing the prospect of returning to Europe, where she dreads the servant problem. She does not like the idea of leaving Africa, where she has created a comfortable home out of inhospitable territory. Her father actually founded the ranch when, in 1911, he brought the first herd of cattle up from Livingstone on foot, having taken one year to do so.

We enjoyed every minute of our stay. On our last morning we found one herd of cattle with some quite tame zebra in its midst. We saw several small antelope and some large birds – hornbills, secretary birds and various cranes – but most of the big game had been killed off during the construction of the railway which runs through part of the ranch.

13

1956 brought a series of gloomy events in our lives. The incurable Rift Valley Fever passed through the stock; Ace broke his leg; water on the farm was a continuing worry; Michael Blundell, with all his policies which we found so wrong-headed, was returned at the elections to Legco; and we finally faced the fact that we might have to leave Kenya.

Accordingly, we set in motion negotiations for the sale of Rhodora (they were to come to nothing at this stage) and the purchase of a farm in England, and began to send our things back to Europe. We had bought a 100-acre farm, Hardwick Court Farm, in Surrey, with a lovely Elizabethan farmhouse. We spent some time at Hardwick every year from now on.

Tony thought long and hard about any political future he might have in Kenya: he was not at all opposed to moves that the Africans were making towards greater integration; he simply felt that any hurried transfer of political power might result in a desire to seize economic power in an anarchic and damaging way.

We received Mau Mau intelligence straight from the horse's mouth:

5th December, 1955

One evening early in the week Rosemary and I were walking back from milking when a jeep drew up and we discerned in the dusk a local policeman, another European and an African. The policeman said they had come to tell us that a 'friendly' gang of Mau Mau was about to go into the crater, and we were to warn our baboon guards not to get too excited if they should see any suspicious characters about. We asked them in for a drink and discovered that the second European was the almost mythical

244

character, Whately, who for some months now has been operating with the Mau Mau in this district. The things he told us were extraordinary and this week we thought, as we have no special news, you would like to hear some of his stories.

We have mentioned in a previous letter that a number of these 'friendly' gangs are now at work. They consist of captured Mau Mau who have been through a short course at a special police school, and who as a result are willing to operate against their erstwhile friends. The gang has one of two proven Kikuyu loyalists with it, and sometimes is accompanied by a European disguised as one of them (blackened face and hands, filthy verminous clothing, stinking provisions, etc.). They carry the usual pangas, perhaps a few spears, a gun or two – home-made or a shotgun – with very few rounds of ammunition; the European carries a knife and a powerful automatic weapon which he keeps hidden in his clothing. They go out into the forest for several days at a time, and the ex-Mau Mau get onto the payroll after three successful engagements. The treachery of these people is such that they will tell the authorities all they know, and co-operate in every way they can in catching or killing other terrorists. There has been only one case of the system breaking down, when two of them ran back into the forest with a fresh captive, but that was not in this district, and does not seem to have done any harm so far.

The gang generally wanders about in the forest until they contact other terrorists, and when some of these approach, the European hides under a blanket or pretends to be occupied with something else. Africans are great handshakers, and when the gangs meet each man goes around shaking everyone by the hand. As soon as the terrorists are well in amongst them the 'friendly' gang dash to one side and the European springs up or turns sharply round and sprays the terrorists with his automatic weapon. You might think the Mau Mau would be alive to all this by now and wary of approaching strange gangs, but apparently not.

At Subukia recently one of the 'friendly' gangs met upon a single terrorist who came up to talk to them. He said he was a 'General', and had a party of six, who were away foraging for

245

food. He was told he was now a captive, and what about coming over to our side? The General agreed, and sat down there and then, and wrote a letter to his gang saying he would be back next day at noon. The postbox was under a large stone.

Then they all went back to the police station. The following day, accompanied by Europeans, they picked up the remainder of the General's men at the appointed place and at the time arranged.

Another incident was a few days ago in the crater near the foot of the cliff, on Bruce McKenzie's farm next door. The 'friendly' gang was this time operating with two Europeans. Four terrorists came up and were received by binding their arms behind them. The Europeans then told their African colleagues to have a talk to them. They not only talked to them but also administered some sort of oath that they would now remain on our side, upon which their hands were untied, they were given the stores to carry, and the whole party emerged from the crater in a completely amicable mood. The next day these four led the police to a hide-out where the remaining five members of their gang were located, so all nine are now behind wire.

It sounds too easy to be true, doesn't it? You can imagine that we feel we owe a lot to these exceptionally brave men, like Whately, who have planned these campaigns and carry them out, going into the forest with the ex-Mau Mau gangs. The rigours of living with Mau Mau are terrible, and of course during the whole time they are out, the Europeans dare not sleep for one minute.

18th December, 1955

David is home. We fetched him on 10th December after a peaceful picnic lunch together on the way up to his school. At 2.30 pm the school play started. Forty little boys blackened from head to waist with boot polish appeared on stage as '*Shamba* (garden) boys to the King and Queen of Fairyland.' Behind the scenes their two matrons were storming with indignation:

246

'It's awful, it's dreadful, *why* couldn't Mrs Lavers have had a *sensible* Shakespeare play! It's going to take us all night to get these children clean. We don't know *when* they will be ready to go home.'

The play continued despite their protests. The little girls of the school, dressed as flowers, danced delightfully. Much singing by all, during which the Kenya accent cut one with a knife (it has to be heard to be believed) and the hard chairs added to one's torture. Nevertheless, it was enjoyed by children and parents and, in spite of the matrons' gloom, the forty little 'black boys' were clean and changed in time to return to their homes for the night.

25th December, 1955

The Labour Officer sent us up four lorry-loads of 250 workers from Nakuru township for coffee picking. They, plus seventy from the forest, twenty from the stone quarries, and our own labour force, made the coffee shamba sound like bedlam, but in spite of all this we are not getting the crop off as fast as we should and considerable quantities are drying out on the trees.

Christmas Eve was upon us before we knew where we were. As dusk fell we drove down to Nakuru – Rosemary, David, Mrs Lloyd, myself, Linda and Ian Ace, Mary and Annette Mumford and Geoffrey Ireland with his son Denis. Around the large illuminated Christmas tree, by the lamp which was imported from the old Waterloo Bridge in London, we joined the Nakuru township people in singing carols. Soft rain came down and drove us for a while under the shop verandahs, but most of the time we were able to gather around the tree itself. At the top was a huge star, and hundreds of fairy lights were fixed on its branches all the way down. The parson led the singing from a small dais, and the Clerk to the County Council, with his spectacles on the end of his nose, played the harmonium.

At Malindi after Christmas:

247

8th January, 1956

The hotel is perfect. We have a room and balcony upstairs within fifty yards of the sea at full tide. David sleeps on the balcony, and it is so arranged that one can have a permanent through draught to the back, and there is a constant cooling breeze. It is tropical; the sea is warm to bathe in; there are vast stretches of golden sand at low tide, and in front of the hotel, great waves for surfing.

The town of Malindi is ancient and truly Arab in character. A notice is displayed in the main hotels (Sinbad, Eden Roc and Blue Marlin) on behalf of the District Commissioner, asking people not to go into the town in short bathing dresses or sunsuits, because the Arabs think it is discourteous for women not to be fully covered.

We go to the swimming pool at the Eden Roc Hotel where David has learnt to plunge in off the diving board, bobbing up like a bit of cork, and swimming the length with a lot of other eight-year-olds like a puppy dog. The pool overlooks the beach, and it is like being in a ship. Alternatively, we go out to the Blue Lagoon, a fairy place with white sands and crystal clear water, big black rocks with exciting caves around one side of the lagoon and sand around the other.

The days slip by amazingly quickly, considering one does nothing useful. . . .

29th January, 1956

We motored up to John and Pam Ward for lunch. They are finalising their plans to build a £40,000 canning factory in Nakuru this year. After much exchange of gossip and pleasant talk, we motored next door to tea with Gerry and Michael Blundell. He is already beginning to think about his re-election at the national elections here next September. Many people, including ourselves, feel he is forcing the pace of progress towards a multi-racial state. It is quite likely that at least one candidate will appear to oppose him, but though speculation is rife, there is nothing definite yet.

5th February, 1956

. . . . This short account of our doings conceals the hectic activity which has really been going on at Rhodora. A flush of coffee has come on with a rush, and for the first time this year, the picking rate per man has begun to go up. I have been dashing round everywhere organising pickers. (One farmer in the Valley estimates that he has been losing three tons of coffee a day, dropping off his trees – at least £1,000 a day! – because he cannot pick it.) We have had lorry-loads of Kikuyu arriving from various forest camps, and from Nakuru. But the best news of all came yesterday, when the Administration, after much prodding, announced that they would bring three hundred Kikuyu women up from the Reserve, with two or three tribal policemen to look after them, to live on the farms until the crisis is over. They come on Tuesday and we hope to get a hundred and fifteen. Fortunately, we have a lot of stone huts available in the Jaluo village. This extra labour force, in addition to those coming from outside, should just turn the scales. At present we are picking about a ton a day, including Sundays. But while all this is going on – with all its problems of administration and cartage – our maize harvest still has to be picked, our cattle to be looked after, our fields to be ploughed and a thousand and one other things. Just at the moment we are really stretched to the limit.

12th February, 1956

Nakuru Municipality proudly opened its Motor Racing Track, the first in Kenya, on Sunday. Rosemary and I saw His Worship the Mayor arrive, cut the tape, then drive in state once around the mile circuit. After that, racing cars of various sorts made nasty noises and Rosemary and I would have been

249

rather bored, had we not by then taken up our positions at the receipt of custom: that is, we sat at the end of the refreshment tent run voluntarily by the Appeal Committee of the Nakuru War Memorial Hospital. Everyone shuffled along in a queue, taking what they wanted from the various trays, then arrived at me, where I assessed the value and Rosemary gave change. There were 3,000 lunches, so our heads were spinning by the end, and our throats were parched, for one side of the marquee was open, and dust blew up in a continuous fine white cloud. The food was sold out by 2.30. The cars were still roaring round the track, the crowd still cheering, and the loudspeaker still burbling away, but having done our jobs we thankfully packed up and returned home, to wash layers of dust from ourselves and our clothes.

Although I was very busy on the farm, next day I had to go to the local Farmers' Association to tell them about County Council matters. Michael Blundell was also billed to talk to them on political affairs, and he came here to lunch first. His main purpose in coming was to find out whether I would stand against him in the forthcoming elections in September, and when he heard I would not, he put forward three propositions:

(1) that I should, perhaps, stand for a constituency, possibly Nairobi North, where there has been a sitting candidate who has been there many years;

(2) that I should organise the whole of his election campaign in this Rift Valley constituency, with a view to taking his place here if he should ever give it up – which he says (but I do not believe) he will do some day;

(3) that I should organise the Solai Ward of his constituency during the election.

I told him I would think over these three suggestions, and meanwhile he will find out more about the prospects in Nairobi North. But I doubt if anything will come of it.

Next day seventy-two Kikuyu women arrived from Kiambu in lorries to help us with the coffee. They came late in the evening and we were all ready with rations (maize meal, maize, sugar, beans, salt) and blankets and cooking pots for them.

250

Then we showed them to their huts – five to a hut. The following day, thirty-four more came.

With their help, the coffee pick has climbed to about 1,000 *debbies* – one and a half tons – a day. The high rate has shown signs of straining our water resources for pulping and washing. We are also picking maize. We started work at 6.30 am on Thursday and I did not get out of the maize field until 8.45 pm – we were working in the headlight of the tractor. Mumford was at the coffee factory until 11 pm.

28th February, 1956

Rosemary and I went into Nakuru for a political meeting on Thursday. It represented the first shots fired in the elections due in September this year. The principal speaker was a certain Major Roberts, who is the chairman of an organisation called the Federal Independence Party which is strongly opposed to the policy of racial integration of which Michael Blundell is the leading exponent. Major Roberts wants Kenya split up into provinces, with the white settlers entirely responsible for their own province, the Africans controlled by the Colonial Office in their provinces and the Asians to be excluded from all executive participation in the Government.

The opening of the meeting was a sort of comic opera. The Chairman told us all, no less than three times, that we were all Going Down the Drain. Then the first speaker, by name one Carr Hartley, who catches big game for foreign zoos and would obviously have been happier riding on the back of a rhino than facing an audience, read his speech – that is, when he was able to read his own writing. He also failed to notice any punctuation, and it was with the greatest difficulty that we were able to understand one word of what he said. The second speaker – an old settler, vintage 1900, complete with hearing aid and a loud sniff after every few words – proved conclusively that the party was formed by the earliest missionaries who toiled their way up to Uganda on foot. Then we had Major Roberts, who spoke like a prima donna in her prime, and finally, the

Chairman asked if there were any questions. As nobody got up, and the meeting was about to end rather flatly, I walked out in front of the crowd and started to pull his policy to bits. His hecklers did not let me get very far, and at one time I was compelled to tell them that they were not nearly so good as the hecklers in the East End where I was taught to speak politically in my days in Conservative Central Office before the war.

Since this meeting I have been besieged by people wanting to talk politics to me, until I am quite fed up with the subject. Kenya is certainly going through a period of intense political thinking. Few people agree with Major Roberts' policy of autonomous provinces, but there is widespread suspicion of Michael Blundell.

5th March, 1956

We have spent two days out at Bancroft Mine examining the progress of the mine farm and the mine itself. The little farm is most encouraging. The small Jersey herd, having survived the dry weather, has now all but survived the wet. They look well, are milking well, and there have been no serious troubles. Many hundreds of poultry, ducks and turkeys are thriving. The fish-ponds are well stocked and will soon be producing many tons of fish (though there has been a bit of trouble with two marauding hippos). The small flock of sheep is well. Lastly, the land is producing so much succulent food of many different kinds that the vegetable requirements of the mine are met, and there is a large surplus of food suitable for the stock. All this has been achieved where farming has never been practised before, and where the experts said it was quite impossible either to keep stock alive, or to grow the food for it.

On Wednesday we left early for Nairobi and while Rosemary visited Mr Nino, the hairdresser, I went to a Coffee Marketing Board meeting. It was rather an historic occasion because Africans were included in the meeting for the first time. It has been the policy of the Government for some years to encourage coffee growing by Africans in the Reserves (one hundred trees per family) and, now that their production is rapidly rising, it is important that they should have a say in the marketing of the national crop.

25th March, 1956

Mr Milton, who is the manager of Howse & McGeorge chemist's shop in Nakuru, has been staying with us. Recently his wife and small daughter were murdered: you may remember from the Press that he returned home for his lunch to be confronted with the ghastly scene. He was a completely devoted husband and father and the shock has had a great effect on him, though he is very courageous. Now he is quite alone.

17th June, 1956

At the beginning of last week we went down to Nakuru to shop and found that an air of gaiety and festivity was apparent all through the little town: flags and bunting everywhere, shop windows specially decorated to compete for the Best Dressed Shop in Nakuru, and people thronging the streets as if it were a holiday. As we were rather tied to the farm, we did not see all the activities, but they included a *concours d'élégance* with cars and beautiful ladies, a public health display, a horse race meeting, a car hill climb, films and plays, and a wonderful procession of floats, which passed through the town on Saturday afternoon and ended up in the main arena of the show.

On Friday, being Show Chairman, I had to receive the Provincial Commissioner and the Mayor, and we started on a tour of the exhibits. At lunchtime I entertained visitors from the Deputy Governor downwards at an official lunch; Rosemary was supposed to join me, but got delayed in the cattle ring, and decided that as she was late she was best out of it all! She gave away prizes in the evening for the best African herdsman of each breed, and the best European herdsman in the show. Much to her embarrassment, when the whole thing had been judged, she found herself giving away a prize to Kipsang for Best African Guernsey Herdsman, and another to Ace for Best European Herdsman in the show.

After dinner at home we took our visitors down to see the Nakuru Players' production of *Blithe Spirit*, which was really excellent.

On Saturday the outstanding event in the arena was the procession of festival floats, preceded by some twenty-five old crocks which had motored up from Nairobi. The leading old crock was Smuts' safari car, and the driver was wearing Smuts' hat, and waving his spear. Among the floats the big firms had made great efforts: each one was a pageant in itself. Our five-ton lorry was used by the hospital, with a huge stork on the cab roof and a maternity ward, complete with patient and twin cots, on the main float; partitioned off at the back, our doctor played the distracted father, unshaven, with tie askew, incessant cigarettes, much beer and a gramophone. The winner was the Motor Mart and Exchange, whose float carried a new car done up in cellophane with a bow on top to look like an Easter Egg. The whole display was greatly enlivened by some funny men in a little car with its hubs off centre, which bumped along alarmingly at great speed and had placards on it saying NJORO ROAD. (Njoro Road is one of the worst blots on the achievement record of the County Council's Roads Committee. . . .)

David's pony, Sir Echo, had broken his leg:

11th September, 1956

Brian Sherriff arrived in the evening, looked at Sir Echo and thought we might save him; the fracture would heal and it was an even chance as to whether he would be lame afterwards. Brian brought up a wonderful sling from the race-course and in no time, Ace had it hanging from the beams in the roof. Sir Echo was coaxed into it. This means he has his weight off his legs and can sleep. Normally, a horse with a broken leg is afraid to lie down, and eventually collapses from fatigue. Now Sir Echo can rest peacefully in this sling for a month or more, until the fracture is mended. He is the best little patient one could wish for, full of common sense and intelligence, and we have put one of the best *syces*, Kiptano, to sleep in his box and stay with him day and night, as it is safe not to leave him alone. Of course, he has to be hand-fed.

16th September, 1956

The household staff have suffered a setback by the departure on leave for one week of Macahawa, our completely goofy but charming pantry boy. He asked for leave because some time ago his wife was reclaimed by his in-laws, on the grounds that he had failed to pay an instalment of the bride price. Now, armed with 200 shillings (some of which is a loan from us), he hopes to buy three skinny cows with which to pay the instalment and then recover his wife. Appallingly dopey, Macahawa had been given up as a bad job by all the neighbouring housewives, including Mrs Ace, but he persists in coming back to Rhodora, and has been driving Ahamed, Ali and Saidi quite demented with his stupidity. However, now that he is not here, much to our amusement they groan at the amount of work they have to do and miss him quite a lot. Macahawa is in *our* good books, because he is devoted to a small white kitten, which he keeps in the houseboys' camp and even feeds from time to time. Affection for animals is very rare in Africans.

Our staff have unwittingly caused Rosemary quite some little pique in the past few months. When we got back from England in the summer we discovered that Genessie Hamilton had taken advantage of our absence to approach Varley about taking Ali into her own household. Naturally, he told her she must ask us on our return. Rosemary wrote to her as soon as she

255

heard about it, remarking, rather acidly I thought, that Ali was not available and in any case has only one eye and breaks everything, left, right and centre.

I suspect that Genessie was trying to take her revenge. She is quite shameless sometimes. I'm sure we haven't told you about the way she tried to use Rosemary as a kind of publicist for her book. She heard that we were having Will May and his wife to stay after the dog show in Nairobi last March, and she happened to know that he was connected with publishing in New York. So she planned a kind of charade which she quite seriously expected Rosemary to play out at lunch. Her book was to lie temptingly upon the piano, and Rosemary was to draw Will's attention to it – you can imagine the kind of thing that might be dropped into the conversation.

'Yes, the sky *is* blue, isn't it? It almost matches the dust cover of THIS BOOK, by my dear friend LADY CLAUD HAMILTON. Have you read it?'

She rang us with several afterthoughts to add to this *completely* uncontrived script on the very day the couple were expected. Of course Rosemary had great fun at lunch, recounting the entire episode.

Barbara and Sandy arrive up from the Copper Belt on Wednesday evening and we are very much looking forward to having them here. They will have the unique experience of moving from one country in a State of Emergency to another in the same state.

Every four years a Gold Medal was awarded to the Best Farm in Kenya over 750 Acres. Naturally this award carried with it enormous prestige. We had received the Silver medal in 1952 (being pipped at the post by Geoffrey Ireland) and had made many improvements since – so now we were even more determined to have everything absolutely perfect when the judge arrived.

5th October, 1956

On Tuesday afternoon peace reigned at Rhodora. The only

sound was the family eating tea. Saidi appeared.

'There is a Bwana to see you.'

'Bet that's the Gold Medal judges!' cracked Sandy, knowing full well we did not expect them for another two days. I went out to the back amidst laughter and what did I see? The judges! Chaos and confusion. Rosemary puce in the face, myself pale, Barbara and Sandy repressing giggles. Tea-cups and plates hastily brought in order to gain time to warn Ace to get the cows, their tails washed and the buildings tidy. We all found ourselves thinking of the uncompleted programme of beautification: the verges at the top of the farm not yet cut; one field not quite ploughed; the weeds on the drive. . . . All this was to have been ready by Thursday, and here were these dismal experts two days early.

They spent thirty-five minutes on the place, during which time they managed to pick up the one musty piece of silage in the silage pit, complain that our barley field was slightly dirty, and remark that it was now considered out of date to grow roots. By the time they reached our *pièce de résistance*, the cowshed, it was raining.

When they left a wail went up from all concerned, and you can imagine how high we now rate our chances of winning. To add to our depression, Bruce McKenzie called in to tell us about a farm in Limuru which has wonderful pyrethrum, pigs, Friesians. . . . The Limuru farm is on the short-list as well as ours and Peter Howard's.

13th October, 1956

After lunch at the Muthaiga Club we went off to the Races, where we sat in great comfort in Robin and Liza Long's box. We left before the last two races (which was lucky, because by that time we were all out of pocket) and made our début at Government House in time for tea. As we were ushered in our knees shook at the size of the tea-party which met our eyes. There seemed to be an enormous house-party. However, we gradually got used to it, and mostly they were people of

257

Barbara and Sandy's age. Besides Sir Evelyn and Lady Mary Baring and their elder daughter, Catherine, there were three ADCs (Peter Carthew, Colin Campbell, and Peregrine Pollen); Peregrine's Aunt, Maria Newall; Lady Mary's niece, Ann Dawnay; and two of Catherine's girlfriends from England, Fiona Middleton and Marion Bevan. After tea all the young people played tennis and we talked to Lady Mary. The Barings are charming and the party the greatest fun.

Government House is huge. Our bedroom was nearly as large as the whole house at Rhodora. I had a spacious dressing room leading through to a bathroom. Everything had just been painted, so Rosemary ran for her anti-allergy pills, and unfortunately we were just over the main entrance, where a searchlight kept our room illuminated like daylight all night. There were also two sentries below, and although they wore gym shoes at night, they would cough and spit. We did not sleep too well.

Just down the corridor was the suite of rooms prepared for Princess Margaret, all done up in green with a touch of pink here and there, and lovely green chintz with flowers. The sitting room has a huge balcony, looking across extensive and lovely gardens, and lawns which have been watered to an emerald green. Of course, there was a piano. We heard she is travelling with an entourage of thirteen, which (apart from secretaries) includes two ladies-in-waiting, four lady's maids (called 'dressers'), a butler, a footman and a hairdresser. When they all went down to Mombasa to see her pass through on her way to Mauritius, the Princess was in great form, and Sir Evelyn told us that as she took leave of him, she said 'See you later, Alligator!', at which he was non-plussed. His ADCs have now bought him the requisite Rock'n Roll record and he is primed to say, 'In a while, Crocodile!'

On Tuesday, Rosemary had occasion to go over and see our neighbours, the Howards, and she mentioned that we were waiting anxiously to hear the result of the Gold Medal Competition. 'Haven't you heard?' they said, 'We have won it!' With a tremendous effort she warmly congratulated them and later we heard from Bruce Mackenzie that we have the Silver

Medal again. Now we must wait another four years for the next time the Competition is held. Third time lucky!

14

As befitted a year of underlying gloom, we had been horrified and saddened at the end of 1956 by the sudden death of little Denis Ireland, David's playmate since our arrival in Kenya. He died in the course of an operation at Nakuru Hospital.

A series of relatively trivial misfortunes befell us. David was unhappy at school; the loss of his close friend undoubtedly affected him. Tony was diagnosed as having an ulcer. And our vet seemed to be losing his battle with alcohol, though help was at hand in the veterinary department in the form of Peter Larkin and Michael and Doreen Gahan, all of whom became firm friends. Amid these troubles, although we still expected to sell Rhodora, we took on more public duties than ever before, and continued enthusiastically to show our animals. (Even Ajax finally won the Championship which had eluded him on several previous occasions.) So we were very busy indeed. We noticed, too, the very beginnings of social integration between the races in Kenya, a phenomenon which would slowly gain ground as the years went by.

We returned from a short break in the UK. . . .

16th December, 1956

We had a good journey back, flying to schedule. All the staff were well. Ace is really pleased because we are bringing out the new bull, Gillcray Pauline's Monty, for him; Mumford is as inscrutable as ever, but steadily getting things done. Varley Everett was at the coast, because the ship in which his son serves had called at Mombasa. No trouble with the Africans, who have been working well, although there have been one or two cases of assault. When Rosemary and Ahamed were working on the severed finger of a boy last night, Ahamed could not resist remarking quietly, 'The Kipsigis like their meat raw.' The finger had been *bitten off*. . . .

The harvest is coming on. The barley is off, and accepted as a malting sample by the brewery, which means we get a much higher price for it. The oats are good, and with these in the store we are now able to mix our own concentrate feed again, instead of having to buy dairy meal. The oat hay is mediocre, because of the drizzle when they were making it. The sunflower is stooked in the field. The kale and roots are fair, and we have scarcely begun to use them yet. Now we are bringing in the maize, and it is the heaviest crop we have ever seen – which is lucky, because we have a small acreage this year, and there was some doubt as to whether we would have enough to feed our labour over the next twelve months.

Above all, the stock are in wonderful order with glossy coats, and often we rub our eyes at the fine spectacle of this bloom, compared with the rough winter coats which the English cattle now have. We send away 130 gallons a day, and still have enough kept back for sixty calves and the large labour force (the ration strength is at present 207); we have never been able to produce the milk so cheaply.

The rain has stopped, and the farm is beginning to turn golden brown, so we have opened the silage pit.

30th December, 1956

This week I was in the Peugeot with Ace, near the top of the farm, when we saw a huge cobra. I accelerated and got the off-side front tyre on the middle of its body. It then reared up beside the wing, looking most menacing, and when I opened the door it spat onto my bare arm. Ace got out on the passenger side but could not get near it because it kept spitting – trying to spit into his eyes. We managed to find a long pole, but it was quite a battle and took us about twenty minutes to kill it. It measured more than six feet along its body, and there were marks on the tyre where it had tried to bite its way out.

13th January, 1957

On Wednesday night (much to the concern of the houseboys, who thought our marriage was breaking up) I was relegated to the spare room to sleep, because I was to get up at 4 am next morning to go down to Lake Nakuru for a duck shoot.

We waded in just before dawn, with mild apprehension, because the hippos were grunting and snorting. They sounded much nearer than they really were. At first light, about six o'clock, I found myself in a rather inadequate hide in the middle of the lake, up to my knees in water. The duck were flighting well and I had some wonderful shots, most of which I missed. Dawn was beautiful, with the hills around the lake changing colour as the sun rose. It might have been anywhere in the British Isles, except for the lovely colouring of the flamingos (which I did not shoot at) as they passed overhead, or the graceful flight of the sacred ibis, the noise of the hippos and the strange sound of the giant hornbills – like someone tuning a bass drum. I shall long remember the unfortunate misfire which I had as an Egyptian goose came honking right over me, flying low. We emerged from the water at about nine o'clock, and counted twenty-six duck in our bag, and we were four guns (I only shot four). The others seemed to think it had not been a very good day, but I enjoyed the sport immensely. Amongst the bag we had such curious birds as Cape Widgeon, Hottentot Teal, Gargany, European Shoveller and African Pochard. Breakfast tasted good after that. . . .

27th January, 1957

This past week has been almost entirely occupied for me with meetings, and for Rosemary with puppies. The pack (eight balls of fluffy fur) is now putting on weight at the rate of a quarter of a pound per pup per day. As the main provider, Diana, the mother, looks daily more worn and a little fed up, whilst Rosemary, the foster-mother, gets busier and busier and spends nearly the whole day giving each puppy its individual meal, or preparing food for the next meal. They are becoming very mobile, refusing to sit in their warm box and preferring to crawl about on the cold stone floor, or nestling just under the door when one is trying to open it.

Monday and Tuesday we had to spend in Nairobi. On the way down we inspected (on behalf of the Guernsey Society) a newly imported young bull at Lady McMillan's farm. After that Rosemary had a Kennel Club meeting; the next morning I had a meeting of the Coffee Marketing Board. We returned via Broomhill Estate, in Kiambu, where Rosemary inspected twelve animals entered in the grading-up scheme and I earmarked them. On Wednesday we had a Council meeting of the Guernsey Society at Nakuru. This was followed on Thursday by a whole day with the Finance and General Purposes committee of the County Council, of which I am Chairman. On Friday there was the annual meeting of the members of the Royal Agricultural Society of Kenya who reside in Nakuru District. I was re-elected Chairman, and this automatically carries with it the Vice-Presidency. Following this I was again in the Chair for the first Show Committee meeting of the County Show to be held in June.

Interspersed with meetings and puppies we have again had numerous visitors to the herd, and Rosemary has started a Visitors' Book up at the cowshed. The most interesting were a man and his wife from the Belgian Congo. He is running three establishments there for the improvement of indigenous stock by the use of exotic bulls of various breeds, and has promised to send us some special elephant grass from the Cameroons, which he says carries more leaf and has a higher sugar content than any other known variety. . . . I was down at the County Council meeting when they arrived, and Rosemary had Doreen Gahan here for the day. She got them some tea, and you can imagine what an uneasy party it was, because Madame Desbuleaux could not speak a word of English, and Doreen Gahan could not speak a word of French.

263

5th February, 1957

Donald and Kathini Graham, who live near here, invited us to dine on Thursday to help entertain three Asians from Nakuru. They also had an elderly cousin out from England. We arrived at 7.00, having been told by Donald to come at that time. Consternation in the household; no one was ready! Kathini was expecting us at 8.15. . . . The Asians turned out to be two men and a woman. They were quite nice and the party went reasonably well. The one next to me kept talking about interest rates, discounts and margins of profit! The other one was a grandson of Nakuru's very first settler, who opened a hotel in Nakuru in 1899. This grandson was a nice type of man and Rosemary discovered that his wife holds a university degree and was very pleasant to talk to.

After dinner things did not go quite so well. One of the Indians was in the middle of an involved story about a Sikh when, to my horror, I saw the cousin from England fall asleep on the sofa. Soon after that I told Rosemary it was time to leave, and the party broke up, bidding good night to the cousin from England, who, having woken up with a start, was madly trying to pin up her hair, which had fallen down in strands at the back.

The next day, Saturday, Miss Bradbury, a former President of our Kennel Club, arrived with a Miss Weatherill who is a famous breeder of bull-terriers in England. She also runs the kennels of Raymond Oppenheimer, and was on her way home after a long stay with Bridget and Harry in Johannesburg. They came at 11.30 am and stayed to tea.

No sooner had they left than three Americans from the Consulate, all with impossible names, descended upon us. One was a Consul, and an economist; another was Agricultural Attaché; the third was Head of the US Information Service in Kenya. The economist had been in Salisbury, and he told us how, on their first day in the city, he and his wife took the children to the municipal park. They found the swings, and told the children to have a good time while they went for a walk. When they got back the children were all sitting on the bench.

'Did you have a nice swing?' they asked.

'No,' was the answer. 'We didn't use the swings, because we saw a notice: EUROPEANS ONLY – and we are Americans.'

17th February, 1957

The biggest fire since we have been here started this week in the stone quarries above our land, and rapidly swept down upon the crater that adjoins Rhodora. Had we not harvested the yellow maize from Stroat field, we should have lost it all. As it is, everything below Howard Bridge is a blackened waste, except the lucerne. I myself went down to the lucerne drier and ringed it with a belt before the main fire arrived. Then I waited there whilst a strong wind carried the fire straight towards me. It was most dramatic, but except for the loss of a few fencing posts, it did us no harm. In fact it cleared all Stroat (about 55 acres) of old maize *stova*, which meant that instead of hours of discing before ploughing we were able to put the plough through like a knife through butter.

After it had finished with Rhodora it passed on to our neighbours around the crater's edge. On the second night Menengai was a blaze of light, like the pier at Blackpool, and they had to turn out the Army and the police to put out the conflagration.

While this was going on last week a leopard took a ewe, one of last year's drop. It is our practice to fold the sheep over the pastures in the little wire-netting enclosures during the night. A man sleeps with them, and a lantern is left burning. On this occasion, the sheep, sensing the leopard, panicked and broke out of the wire.

We recovered what was left of the corpse from the foot of the crater cliff.

The next night we put the sheep near our house, but the marks of two leopards could be seen along the road. We think they have cubs. Ace shot some buck on Friday and left them on the trails which the leopards use to come up the cliff. One of the buck was taken, so last night we set up a trap, in the form of a thorn fence around a dead buck. There are two entrances; one conceals a gin trap, and the other is covered by my shotgun, which automatically discharges. Ajax has given us some anxiety, because he thought he would help kill the bait, and to his great glee, ran a buck to earth in the coffee. His glee, however, was nothing to that of some Jaluo, who were working nearby and recovered the body and took it back for lunch. Ajax now thinks he should go hunting all the time and we are afraid he may find the leopard trap, so we watch him carefully.

At Malindi. . . .

17th April, 1957

From our cottage we walk about a hundred yards to the hotel for our meals, and David goes there to spend hours in the swimming pool with masses of other children. The swimming pool is overlooked by a long, open verandah, with a bar behind, and the local inhabitants sit sipping their iced drinks while watching the prowess of others on the diving boards. They are a mixed crowd in the hotel, some from up-country, some from Rhodesia – but the star turn is the local public hangman, who is presumably having a well-earned rest with his family after the exertions of the Emergency. I noticed that Rosemary could not help flinching a little when he was talking to her the other day.

The sea is below and in front of our cottage, a vast expanse of the Indian Ocean stretching unbroken before us, but there are usually a few little fishing smacks with a single brown sail dotted about. In Malindi harbour, we can see numerous private boats and schooners riding at anchor, and there is the long line of the reef, with the sea breaking over it even at high tide. At night the lighthouse at Vasco da Gama Point winks at us; beyond is another at Kasserine Point.

Surfing is all the rage. I have a large surfboard and David has a little one. You wade out to sea roughly to the point where the waves are breaking, and you wait until a nice one, say ten feet high, is about to break over you. Then, gripping the turned-up end of the surfboard with both hands and tucking it under the length of your body, you leap forward with the wave, and it carries you at a fast pace all the way to the shore. It is a grand sensation, and David loves it all the more because he is better at it than I am, and likes to show me how to do it.

We had planned a day's fishing, and in order to make the arrangements a young man came out to see us who is making his living out of catching sharks. They are caught in a nylon tangle net with four-inch mesh, and his best catch has been one of 2,000 lbs. The meat is sold to local Africans, the liver is sold for the oil and the fins and tail are shipped to Hong Kong for processing. Rather an interesting occupation, we thought.

We decided to take the train back from Mombasa, partly because David had developed an abscess in his ear and partly because the rains had broken and the roads were reported to be in a bad state. We drove the seventy-eight miles to Mombasa, confirmed our reservations at the station and then had lunch at the Carlton Hotel. Afterwards, as there were no vacant bedrooms, we found a sofa and some armchairs on a fairly cool and large landing on the first floor, and there we settled down to pass the time until our train left at 6.00 pm. Just as all was quiet, we heard a key inserted in the lock of one of the rooms off where we were sitting. There followed a lot of fiddling, pushing and banging from which we concluded that someone could not get out of their bedroom. I went over to try and help and shouted instructions through a grille which obviously connected with the bathroom. Muffled replies from inside. Rosemary then called an African houseboy who was sauntering by on his afternoon rounds. He tried to help but also without success. By now Rosemary and David were thoroughly enjoying the fun and could not wait to see what sort of a person would eventually emerge from the room. Finally, the manager was sent for but by then I had got the door open to find an aged, white-haired and rather frightened couple inside. Much discussion and gesticulation ensued and then the room boy and the manager went into the bedroom to show the couple how simple it all was . . . but the next thing we heard was the manager wildly trying to get himself and all the inmates out. I obliged by opening the door again and setting them free!

Back at Rhodora . . .

28th April, 1957

Rhodora is wearing her beautiful clothes again. If there has been any crisis, it is between our lorry driver, Kwambai, and our best tractor driver, Kumunia. I was brought into it this week. It seems that Kwambai went into town with his wife and Kumunia's wife came too. Like so many Africans the first thing they did was to have their photographs (*pikshers*) taken, and of course, the print showed a smiling Kwambai flanked by *two* women. This infuriated Kumunia, who said he had purchased his wife, and Kwambai had no right to pose in a photograph with her as if she were his. 'After all,' he said to me, 'would you like the Memsahib to have her photo taken with another man, as if she belonged to him?'

In his rage Kumunia rushed off to Kwambai's hut and seized the photo, which he now threatens to destroy. This would be a serious matter, because Kwambai paid five shillings towards the cost of it, and that is a lot of money.

Kwambai and Kumunia tell me they will kill each other. All I could say to them was that where a man's investments (wife) were concerned, I really could not interfere. But I felt I was being singularly unhelpful.

Rosemary has had a severe allergic attack coupled, I think, with some kind of flu. She made me mad by insisting on going down to Nakuru on Friday morning just when she was at her worst and should have been in bed. Later I discovered why. At teatime the most wonderful birthday cake appeared for me! It had been specially made to Rosemary's specifications by the French chef at the bakery in Nakuru, and consisted of a large (and very good) sponge cake, iced to represent a chess-board, with all thirty-two pieces beautifully executed.

268

12th May, 1957

Daily, interspersed with sunny periods, the rain keeps steadily
on. Roads are waterlogged; the green grass is fresh and
delicious; trees which have been dormant during the winter are
covered with sprouting leaves. The rows and rows of coffee
trees, which looked like bare little skeletons after their drastic
pruning, are now covered with pale green, baby foliage at the
tips of every branch, and this will soon make a dense shady
cover for the huge crop which they are bearing. The crop itself
has passed from the heady, sweet-smelling, flowering stage to
little pinhead groups of cherry, with larger beans from earlier
flowerings mixed in amongst them.

Every evening, long after his work is finished, as dusk falls
Mumford's car can be found parked somewhere beside the
trees, whilst he prowls about amongst them, keeping an ever-
watchful eye on the condition of the crop. Everything grows for
him, from coffee to bougainvillea cuttings, from the vegetable
garden to tiny kei apple plants for filling the blanks in the
hedges. In spite of his interest in anything of this sort, however,
the poor man looked rather taken aback when we told him
(earlier this year) to grow an experimental *acre* of tomatoes for
Kabazi's canning factory.

4th August, 1957

Having had our suspicions for some time that our cows were
being milked during the night, we managed to catch the culprit
at about midnight, just as he was carrying the milk home.
Tudor, in his pyjamas, interviewed him on the verandah of his
house, and as he is inclined to be rather rough and ready in his
method of dispensing justice, the wretched culprit was soon
stretched out cold on the floor. Tudor, looking around to get a
jug of cold water to revive him, could find nothing better than
his small son's potty . . . this seemed to us the classic case of
adding insult to injury!

28th August, 1957

Slowly, assisted by good rains, our coffee crop is ripening, and as the beans swell and become more apparent we are quite sure that the quality will be better than ever before. The price we shall receive is, as usual, unknown. The season that has ended saw Brazil with three million bags retained in store, in order that the market should not be swamped. This coming season, production in Brazil is expected to exceed that of last year by six million bags and in the following year, it may go up by another six million. Will the Brazilian Government go on subsidising its coffee industry by holding the surplus off the market, or will it risk ruining the industry by letting the price find its own level in a free market? Is it not tragic that there seems no way that this vast surplus can be supplied to the millions of undernourished people in India and China and other parts of the world?

A Dr and Mrs Wallace visited us. He is a Harley Street skin specialist out here on holiday: a tiny, hunchbacked little man, with a very small, quiet wife who is also a doctor. They arrived sitting at the back of a bus marked AFRICAN TOURS. They were the only passengers. We gave them the usual medicine for people just out from England: view of crater, description of Mau Mau, and visit inside African hut. Incidentally, just to show you how truly colonial we are, we discovered that David does not know what coal is – only charcoal.

At last we tried a really adventurous way of getting to Malindi and back . . .

4th September, 1957

David was vastly excited as we set out in the Peugeot station waggon with our luggage piled in the back. We motored down to Nakuru airstrip, right into a huge hangar, and stopped beside the diminutive aircraft with its single engine. Then we stowed the luggage in the hold.

There was another passenger with the pilot in the two front seats, so the Seys family all climbed into the back seat, together with David's butterfly net. The engine started and we were soon taxi-ing out, and trundling down the rough grass runway to a good take-off.

We ambled down the line of the Nairobi Road and David was able to have a good look at his school at Gilgil. Then there was dense cloud and we climbed to 11,500 feet to get above it. From there on, past Nairobi to the coast (which we reached in two and a half hours), the little plane seemed to float steadily on a sea of sunlit cotton-wool. All we saw were the snow-clad peaks of Mount Kenya to port, and Mount Kilimanjaro to starboard. There was a great betting match as to who would see the sea first (which David was allowed to win) before the cloud disappeared and the sparkling blue sea and its white line of sand lay beneath us. Geoff Baker, the pilot, very kindly took us in over the sea to lose height, instead of bumping down through the clouds, and we cruised up and down for ten minutes identifying the places we knew at Malindi. Finally we skimmed in over the heads of waving bathers to make a good landing.

A car was waiting, and the journey had been so smooth that we all felt like lunch.

17th September, 1957

I was quite relieved when the engine of the little plane finally stopped in the hangar at Nakuru; however much one sneers at superstition, one cannot get it out of one's mind when the whole of one's family is travelling in a single-engined plane on Friday the Thirteenth.

We were sorry to leave the hotel; some of the other guests were fascinating. I remember particularly a little American girl of eleven, who came to children's supper, and told me that she had spent her day reading. When I asked her what she had read, she said,

'Oh, the usual story of husband-snatching.'

The following day, when we were all agog for further entertainment, she told us that the full moon denoted Romance, according to her Love Comics. We gathered that she was thrilled to be allowed to stay up for the dancing that night, with her room-mate, aged fifteen; the point being that her room-mate had a boyfriend at an adjacent hotel; but it was all so exciting, because the boyfriend would not be allowed across by his parents to see her until later in the evening – so in the interval, she would have plenty of opportunity of finding other boyfriends. . . .

We had a day to settle down at home and then two visitors arrived from Government House, in the shape of Jacob Rothschild and Nicholas Baring, who is a distant relative of the Governor and who is acting as ADC for the time being. Jacob has been in Kenya for about a month and is shortly returning to England to continue his studies at Oxford; Nicholas has completed his university training. We gave them the full tour – forest, flamingos, farm, etc.; they could not have been nicer guests and we found them both quite delightful. Jacob is a modest person and we were quite amused by the following example of humility, which was said in a perfectly genuine fashion. It arose when I was asking him about his military service and he told me that he had been in an armoured car unit – 'Why don't you tell them that you were in the Life Guards?' said Nicholas. They motored off back to Government House on Monday, armed with samples of Rhodora coffee.

22nd September, 1957

On Thursday morning I was greeted by a long-faced Ace. Ten of our sixty-six sheep had been slaughtered by a leopard in the night. Since the last sheep-murder we have housed the flock in the old boar house, a stone building with a *makuti* (palm-frond) roof and wire netting right up to the eaves. The cunning brute had climbed onto the roof, torn its way through, and dropped down onto the sheep. It even managed to pull one of its victims through the hole it had made and to carry it away.

Each animal had its neck broken, and the only marks on it were where the leopard's teeth had bitten it under the chin, piercing the jugular vein and sucking the blood. No meat was eaten from the nine sheep left behind.

The following night, Amdurhaman, our Boran baboon guard, an intelligent and ferocious-looking man from the north-west frontier near Abyssinia, slept amongst the flock with his gun, in the hope that the murderer would return. Tracks revealed in the morning that the leopard came as far as the door itself, but the odour of Amdurhaman was more powerful than that of the flock, and he departed. The next night we removed the sheep, and left a rotting corpse with a trap-gun at the door; but this time there were no tracks at all in the morning.

Last night I left two old ewes in the house with the corpse (which was by now putrid) and again, the trap-gun. Our Sunday morning peace was disturbed by Ace at the window telling us 'The leopard has been killed!' Rosemary and I got up hurriedly and went up to the sheep house.

Lying full length on the ground outside was a magnificent young male leopard, a little longer than Ajax and at least twice as heavy. His skin had such bloom on it, and his muscles were as hard as iron; the pads of his feet were enormous and his teeth surprisingly white and menacing. Even in death, he seemed immensely powerful and compact, and one realised that nothing would have a chance if he attacked. Masses of little red ticks were busy abandoning the ship.

As we write he is being skinned in the butchery, and perhaps – when you next come to stay with us – you will find him on the floor, in the form of a rug.

Rosemary and Ace are suffering from Show Fever. Stimulated by the Best of Breed and Reserve Best in the show at Chertsey, they have decided they will not be outdone at the Royal Show at Nairobi. I can get no sense out of them. Any questions I ask are either lost in the noise of the automatic clippers, or discounted in the preoccupation of filing horns and hooves, assembling show equipment and generally fussing. . . . Everything will be loaded into a pantechnicon with trailer (rather like Noah's Ark on wheels), to trundle down to Mitchell Park Showground. The four horses (Satan, Faith, Jenny Wren and Prydus) leave this afternoon on the lorry and will be loaded by Rosemary and Ace onto the exhibitors' special train from Nakuru.

Christmas Day always began with a thrilling present-opening session . . .

26th December, 1957

After these tremendous excitements and after breakfast, Kipsang and Manasseh, the two Headmen, called in and had a glass of beer on the verandah with us. The Gahans (Michael and Doreen, with Antony their baby) appeared next, and at about midday we all went up to Kabazi for a very rowdy Christmas lunch. Pam and John had made a model railway amongst a snow scene in the corner of the dining-room. It was Harrods Toy Fair at its best. The little train went round and round through a tunnel and out again, cotton-wool smoke coming out of its funnel. A church, numerous houses, stations, fields with sheep and cows in them, all snow-clad and sparkling were there on the mountain side. It was really beautifully done.

We left again at three o'clock sharp, as we were expecting the staff in for the usual Christmas tea party at Rhodora. This year Rosemary had bought two tiny little Christmas trees: one she had put in a silver flower-pot and the other in a gold one. They stood beside the window of our bedroom, each on a table decorated with little bells and silver fluffy pieces on the branches. David thought they were 'mingy' compared with last year's big tree, but the general opinion was how sweet they looked, with the Christmas cards hung from the pictures behind them on long strands of ribbon, and red bougainvillea as a carpet round the tables, and the staff presents piled up in the middle.

Doreen and Michael stayed to dinner and left at about ten,

274

and Rosemary and I sank thankfully into bed, with a thought for each of you before we fell asleep.

Ahamed was such a rock of strength helping Rosemary with all the parcels beforehand that we felt we must do something special for him, so we got an old sock of mine and stuffed it full of oddments such as handkerchiefs, a smart red tie, a pair of socks, and a large piece of smelly bath soap – tying it up with a huge red ribbon. We presented him with this as he said goodnight to us on Christmas Eve, and it did one good to see his face. He was simply delighted.

The head boys in each department all had half a month's pay, and the main labour, nearly 300 strong at the moment, got 2 lbs of meat each for the occasion from the slaughter of two oxen and a cow, together with sugar, extra posho (maize meal) and cigarettes. They seemed very happy and contented and no one got too drunk.

I had been visiting England, and Tony was coming to collect me from the airport:

23rd March, 1958

I proceeded with speed to the new aerodrome at Embakasi. It is seven miles south of Nairobi along Princess Elizabeth Highway, which is probably the most beautiful carriageway in the Commonwealth: it is flanked with hedges of brilliant bougainvillea interspersed with blue petraea every few yards – and in front of this hedge, there are broad mown grass verges with exotic tropical trees, flowering shrubs, and more bougainvillea grown high into a pyramid. There are occasional roundabouts planted as rock gardens in a solid mass of colour, and strips of border plants dividing the streams of traffic.

The airport is off the road to Mombasa and so far largely unbuilt; it looks like a Meccano model abandoned by a bored child.

When the huge plane came in I went through on a special

275

pass to the passenger lounge, so that I was very close when Rosemary appeared, smiling, at the top of the gangway. She had not liked the Britannia because of its tail wobble, and the effect it gave of being too big and unbalanced, yet she survived the trip very well. I had seen the Customs and Immigration Authorities before so she passed through first amongst all the passengers and talked for a little while to her old friend, Jean Guepin, whose husband is on a tour of oil installations in Africa (in his capacity as Chairman of Royal Dutch Shell), while I loaded the luggage into the car.

For the first few days she has found the change in temperature very marked, and has wanted to turn off the central heating and open the windows – and has then realised, with a shock, that all the windows are open and there is no central heating.

David has written regularly from school and he is well. I went to the school play last night, but Rosemary could not come because they are in quarantine for mumps, which she has not had. When I arrived, a small boy informed me that David had a part in *HMS Pinafore*. I asked how he was doing and he said, 'All right', adding that he looked 'very sweet'. I gathered from this that he was taking the part of a girl, and so he was: he was a member of a sort of female chorus of sisters, aunties and cousins. At half-time David told me that he got the part because another boy said, when he was issued with his costume, that he would not wear that 'rotten dress'.

'I think it is a lovely dress, don't you, Daddy?' enquired David, and I warmly agreed. It was a blue and white gingham affair and he wore a white bonnet with a blue bow on one side, whilst his hair was pulled down to a fringe showing under the front of the bonnet. He was an undeniably attractive-looking piece, and reminded me strongly of a typical female Rothschild! He was quite at home on stage and acted the part to the best of his ability.

Mariloo was visiting us again, so it was her turn to write.

13th April, 1958

This evening Tony came into my room brandishing a wad of scrap paper and said,

'There you are, Mariloo. It's your turn this week, and be sure to make it funny!'

It is a curious fact that whenever one is asked to say something funny, ideas scramble out of one's head like grasshoppers.

But hark! What is that laughter mingled with shrieks emanating from David's bathroom? Believe it or not, a frog was sitting in David's lavatory pan winking at him. This is no ordinary English frog but his African brother, about three times as big. All the family tried to pull him out. Ochieng arrived with a stick with a nail on it, but a frog is a slippery customer and, fixing a beady eye on his pursuers, evaded capture. The plug was pulled: down went the frog, only to reappear a few moment later when the rush of water subsided.

As my bathroom is next to David's I have visions of a melodramatic evening meeting with this fellow round the bend by candlelight (as the electricity is turned off at 10 pm).

Now all is quiet and it is 9 pm, which reminds me that I have only one hour left to tell you of the week's happenings . . .

The most exciting news is that rain has come, bringing relief to the parched fields – you should see the smile on the face of the tiger (I mean Tony). It is as though a million pounds had been put into his pocket. Did I say a million? No, only half a million; for there is some trouble up at the dairy. For some reason or other a percentage of the milk is not passing the test, and is being rejected. Consternation! Endless discussion. All milk experts in the district have been contacted. . . .

The only inhabitants of Rhodora who do not seem concerned are Ajax, Diana and their two flea-sized companions, Della and Rikki. They bark, gambol and eat huge meals. Both Alsatians are on the look-out for some poor unfortunate, a stranger to them, so that they can take a large chunk out of his trousers – and maybe his leg!

We had a wonderful drive up to Michael Blundell and his

277

wife in order to see their attractive garden. No rain today, so the hills were pale blue-grey against a deep blue sky dotted with mother-of-pearl clouds. We met a few Africans wearing highly-coloured garments – unbelievable ultramarine shirts, or orange ones. The *bibis* too, although sometimes clad in rags, were wearing the brightest possible wraps, their backs laden with their *totos* and their heads surmounted by heavy loads. The men, of course, walked in front of them empty-handed. Birds of every kind and hue sang and fluttered about.

We received a warm welcome from Michael and Gerry.

'It is cold,' said Gerry. 'Would you like a coat?'

To me the temperature is what we would get on a fine English day in mid-June.

Michael took me to see his famous garden, showing me, with great pride – his *foxgloves*. I must say, this left me a bit cold; but what should I see nearby but maidenhair fern, growing in profusion. The garden is full of these anomalies: common English garden flowers grow cheek-by-jowl with tropical beauties, only they grow twice the size. Orchids grow in the forks of trees. Alstroemaria cover the ground. As for the lilies. . . ! There are arums, regale, longiflorum, henryi. Magnolia and camellia flourish, and nearby the petraea and tacoma stans are covered with blooms. The Exbury nerines are doing very well.

6th May, 1958

This year we are planting wheat, the first time for many years, because at this altitude one can grow a 'hard' wheat which the millers like, and for which there is a premium of five shillings per bag.

It is the season when the white ants make their annual mating flight. They emerge from the ground with long wings folded back, then take off with their four wings, making them look like obsolete biplanes. They never make much height, and after a few minutes they come to ground, their wings drop off, and they seem to disappear. The next morning there are little piles of white wings all over the place.

15

For the third time during our time in Kenya, those close to us suffered tragic misfortune. Mr and Mrs Ace lost their baby son in a drowning accident. It was a harrowing time for their entire family, but they bore it bravely.

Tony was elected President of the Royal Agricultural Society of Kenya and we bought and sold horses and cattle, improved the house, congratulated each other on the coffee crop, and won prizes at shows, as if it had never crossed our minds to leave. We even felt a degree of optimism politically.

Nonetheless, at this time it seemed possible that Tony might accept a job in Southern Rhodesia. We even began to look for somewhere to live in Salisbury. The plan fell through, largely because of its tax disadvantages, but nothing dimmed our fervent admiration for Sir Roy Welensky, then Prime Minister of the Federation. . . .

8th October, 1958

We first met him at a dinner last Tuesday night, given in his honour at the Muthaiga Club by the President of the Royal Agricultural Society of Kenya, Sir Charles Markham. Lady Welensky was with him, a large woman, without an H to her name, down-to-earth and with a grand sense of humour.

The next day (as he had started his career as an engine-driver) he drove one of our largest locomotives up to the show ground from Nairobi and then spent the day with us there. He is massive, weighing about eighteen stone, and whilst having enormous charm, also has a tremendously strong character.

The speech he made at the opening of the show was a

rallying cry to the Europeans. It came like a bottle of champagne to the community here, which is somewhat dispirited and lacking in confidence just now. He made it quite clear that in 1960 the Federation will have Dominion status, whether the British Government likes it or not. During and after his speech he received an ovation such as has never been heard at a show before. I was sitting next to Lady Welensky and Rosemary leaned forward from behind and asked her to lend Kenya her husband for a bit.

' 'E'll 'ave to pay off 'is debts back 'ome before you can 'ave 'im,' she said.

Our Governor, Sir Evelyn Baring, sat looking pretty glum throughout the speech. It is said he and Welensky do not get on, and Welensky taunts him, calling him the 'Kaffir-loving Governor'.

Afterwards, going round the show, Sir Roy told several stories of how little boys are fascinated by meeting an engine-driver. He said that when he went up to Scotland to stay with Lord Dalhousie (before Lord D was appointed Governor-General) his small son asked him many questions about railway engines, and eventually summoned up courage to say that he could not understand how Sir Roy could have left engine-driving in order to become Prime Minister.

I met him again at a cocktail party at Government House, and the last thing he said to me, looking me straight in the eye, was,

'When you came to Rhodesia, I want you to come and see me and I mean that, you know.'

His visit to Kenya was an unqualified success. He charmed everyone he met, and did a great deal to cement better relations between Kenya and the Federation. He also showed up some of our lily-livered politicians, whose sole expedient is to retreat with increasing speed before the mounting demands of African nationalism.

Quite soon we were, indeed, to visit Southern Rhodesia:

280

2nd November, 1958

Keith Acutt told another story about the Welenskys. It seems that long ago Lady Welensky worked as a waitress in a restaurant owned by Mrs MacIntyre, who is the wife of the present Federal Finance Minister. They did not meet for many years, and by then both had got on in the world. When their paths eventually crossed again, Mrs MacIntyre said,

'How very nice to see you again, *Mrs* Welensky.'

'The pleasure is all mine, *Lady* MacIntyre,' replied Lady Welensky. When she told Keith this story she added, 'and I 'ad no further trouble from 'er!'

Next day I had board meetings and an official lunch, whilst Rosemary was again lent one of the Anglo-American cars to do what she liked (needless to say, she landed up at the hairdresser). We invited Davies and his wife to dinner at the Colony Restaurant. Then on Friday morning early, a nice man named David Worthington called for us and drove us down to Charter Ranch, about sixty miles from Salisbury, where he is manager. This property is owned by a group of eminent and very Conservative peers in England. Worthington was trained in the Argentine and seemed to know his job.

It was at this ranch that we first met General and Mrs Shapland, who were our hosts for the next five days. He is the manager for all the Willoughby ranches, comprising over half a million acres, and he runs them from a central office in Bulawayo. She is very definitely the manager of General Shapland! We visited three of these ranches (one of them a mere *three hundred and ninety thousand acres*). On one of them we stayed the night in a sumptuous guest house, but for the rest, we were based in the Shapland's comfortable house in Bulawayo – comfortable except for a profusion of spiders the size of small mice.

On Sunday they most kindly took us out to Matopos, where Cecil Rhodes is buried, and we brought back a piece of the Resurrection Plant, which we picked about 100 yards from his grave. We enclose a tiny bit in your letters. They say that if you keep it even for a year, it will come out green when you put it in

281

water. Matopos is extraordinary – the highest of a mass of little hills like great pimples. Rhodes himself decided that he wanted to be buried there. He used to call it 'World's View'.

Bulawayo is in Matabele country – in fact Lobengula's kraal is still preserved in the grounds of Government House. We saw the table-shaped hill, with perpendicular sides, where he held court, and where those who were condemned were thrown to their deaths over the cliff; we saw the Wilson Memorial, commemorating the band of men who, when attacked by the Matabele, fired off all their ammunition and then sang 'God Save the Queen' while waiting to be slaughtered.

Back at Rhodora. . . .

9th November, 1958

Sorcery has afflicted us this week. One evening a mother and child were waiting by the office. The child was apparently asleep, and she said it had been in that condition since midday; a man had come to the hut and cast a spell upon it. I assumed a grave appearance and summoned a chief who is employed by the Government in the district. There was a long conference (which I got out of attending) and the result is that Karioki, one of the junior Kikuyu headmen, has been taken away for questioning. If it is proved that he is indeed a wizard, he will get a heavy term of imprisonment. Meanwhile I sent the mother to hospital, and she now tells me that her child, having received several injections, has quite recovered.

The other main excitement is a case of smallpox in the camp, so about 150 of our labour were vaccinated yesterday.

Most evenings just now, when up at the stock, Rosemary has a chair brought from the office, and sits in the field beside the stables, watching and helping with the schooling of my new horse, Thunder Flash. We only have him in a snaffle so far, and he has to learn to take the bit. He must be taught all the aids to stop and walk, and trot and canter, and back; he must walk

282

away from other horses, and pass them without faltering. In about a month we shall put him in a double bridle. He has a superb temperament, and is fast putting on condition. Arap Genich, our head *syce*, is intelligent and learns from studying good riders. He has been with us ever since we first introduced horses onto Rhodora, and is now quite a proficient rider himself.

As we walk back from the stock we are lost in admiration of the early jacaranda trees, now in full bloom – a mass of blue flowers, the colour of bluebells, forming a lacy outline against a cloudless sky. Nearby is a markhamia, dark green and yellow in contrast. Looking from the verandah in the early mornings, the great beauty of this jacaranda tree stands out against the cobalt blue of Menengai mountain. What a lovely country this is!

16th November, 1958

We had lunch with Charles Markham, who told us something of the constitutional crisis which is again showing signs of arising here. Briefly, the Lennox Boyd Constitution, under which we are at present governed, has never been accepted by the elected African members – although numerous nominated African members *have* accepted it, with its principle of partnership between the races, and are working with the Government, even up to Ministerial rank. In order to draw attention to their grievance, the elected Africans deliberately walked out in a body whilst the Governor was speaking at the opening of Legco. For this unseemly conduct they were suspended for three days by the Speaker, but since then they have not resumed their seats, and there are rumours that they will all resign. There is a possibility that the Asian (Hindu) Members will also resign. The Africans are, of course, asking for greatly increased representation – and they will not stop until they get a majority. Yet not one of them has any experience of government, they do not understand the meaning of democracy, and their sole knowledge of administration is in organising their wives and children to till their smallholdings.

Those political difficulties loom against a background of increasing financial stringency. Revenue is falling but the Government, having wonderful plans for development, finds it hard to make economies.

Broomhill, where we arrived in time for tea, is a beautiful estate. It is in Kiambu, fifteen miles from Nairobi, and it comprises 200 acres of coffee and 650 acres of arable land. The coffee is the best in Kenya for quality. It is grown under the shade of huge grovillea trees, and the average rainfall is about fifty-three inches. The arable is nearly all Kikuyu grass pasture, and they run a nice herd of Guernseys to catch the high-priced Nairobi milk market. The quiet dark forest of the coffee contrasts with the emerald green of the pastures, and there are views all round. Dinner was a most congenial meal, with several other friends from the Guernsey Society present.

4th January, 1959

You may remember we told you that our old cat, Caramello, was very ill. Fortunately, he has made a good recovery. But no sooner was he better than one morning the pantry boy opened the door of the shed where he sleeps and the two Alsatians, Ajax and Diana, got in. Only my timely intervention prevented them from tearing him in half. Now we are determined to teach these two unruly hounds that cats must be respected, for the farm is nearly denuded of them, and we are becoming overrun with rodents.

As a first step we have acquired two tiny kittens, half Burmese, half any-old-tabby, and they are enchanting. Rosemary says they are the plainest kittens she has ever seen, but she adores them all the same. It is a good time to start them off, because the big dogs have to be shut up at the cowshed. Diana is in an 'interesting condition' just now, and Ajax is better near her than tearing the house apart trying to get to her. The two kittens play all day and are a source of constant delight. Della and Rikki, the little dogs, cannot make them out at all and are rather frightened. I have had Ajax with them once or twice, secured on a lead. He drooled at the mouth as he thought what a delicious meal each of them would make, but I gave him no chance, though he had quite a lot to put up with – one stood in front of him and spat in his face while the other played with his tail.

David is extremely well and can fit into none of the clothes he wore before he left here last June. His school report was excellent. We have found a new grey pony for him which he insists on calling Miss Molesworth (the female counterpart of a character in a book some of you will know). He has taken to Miss Molesworth in a big way.

We have turned half the old doggery across the garden into a study for him. It consists of one fairly large room and two tiny ones, these latter being used as a workshop and a collecting room. At present he is busy fitting it out and, of course, he is thrilled with it. We have made it a rule that during the holidays we will not go there except by invitation.

At the dairy all is chaotic because we are busy installing refrigerated cooling and a cold room. The hot weather is on top of us and we want to be sure of getting first grade for our evening milk. Coffee-picking is nearly over and we have picked over 100 tons. I wonder if we shall ever get such a crop again – yet the trees are in wonderful condition and at this moment there is a tremendous flowering on them for the next crop. We ended 1958 with fifty-two inches of rain, against our usual average of thirty-six inches, so no wonder the coffee does well.

19th January, 1959

The hot weather is really here. All the grass is turning brown, and in the evening the wind gets up, with whirling dust-storms. We have hastily left the coffee and turned the whole labour force on to harvesting the maize, for in this heat a fire out in the fields could sweep through the whole crop in no time. The cattle are being hand-fed in a shady paddock near the sheds. As a matter of fact, we have finished picking all the clean coffee;

only the stripping of *mbuni* remains. We have at least 105 tons, and it may work out better.

Up at the dairy, the new refrigeration plant is in operation, and it is Ace's ghastly threat to the milkers that anyone who misbehaves will be shut in the cold room for half an hour. Outside, the temperature is over 100°; inside it is about 85°; in the cold room it is 46°. Any anxieties about keeping the milk are now over. We are sending around 230 gallons a day to the dairy.

22nd March, 1959

The Guernsey Society Field Day was held here on Friday. It involved a good deal of organisation, for there were about 130 people, black and white, and they were given lunch and tea. At the same time we had three couples staying in the house. The work involved in preparing the animals, arranging the catering (taken over by Mrs Ace and her friends), the office work in producing a programme and sending out invitations and so on, painting signboards, and countless other things, was quite considerable; we could never have done it without the wonderful co-operation of the people who work here.

The proceedings started with the Annual General Meeting of the Society in the grade cowshed. Bales of hay were put in mangers, and everyone sat happily around, with the cows peering through the doorways. At noon I talked for an hour in the main yard about the farm and the stock and methods of management. I had Valentine and Monty out, and then groups of four of their daughters, and of the daughters of the three Rhodora bulls standing at the Artificial Insemination Centre. Ace had each group of four trained to walk abreast on one pole.

There followed a buffet lunch in the pedigree cowshed, during which a girl gave a demonstration of hand-milking, dressed in a 150-year-old costume, sent specially from Guernsey Island. After lunch Rosemary, Denis Whetham and Mike Barratt conducted a judging contest, and then the people wandered about inspecting the 270 head of stock which we had put in small paddocks round about. Every female had a number on it which showed which bull it was sired by.

People left after tea, and there was a good deal to clear up. It was nice to see so many European breeders, most of whom we know well, but African farmers also came from Nandi, Elgeyo and Meru Reserves. By the next morning all was in order again, and Rhodora sank back with a sigh of relief to ordinary routine affairs.

5th April, 1959

Ramadan is nearly through (thanks be to Allah, says Rosemary). For a month our Comorien houseboys, who are Mohammedans, have grown daily thinner and more irritable, and never have we been so busy in the house. They eat only at sunset and at 2 am. The result is that they have insufficient sleep, and have to work all day on empty stomachs. In four days' time I shall see Ahamed waiting at dusk at the end of our store-sheds for a glimpse of the new moon. The fast is not broken until the crescent is seen.

Easter has come and gone. We had a lot of people staying, which we always find a strain: it is so difficult to sit around and be polite, when one knows a thousand and one things await one on the farm. Billy Whittaker and Bill Pike and his wife were staying in the house, and other people drifted in and out for drinks or meals. Always in the background was Diana's litter of puppies, now on four supplementary feeds per day – each puppy separately fed. Mumford arrived back from hospital on Friday, having had glandular fever, and went off next day to his brother in Kiambu to recuperate. David came home on Saturday. What with flu and measles he missed six weeks' schooling last term, yet came second in his class at the end of it.

On March 26th we went down to Nairobi for the AGM of the Royal Agricultural Society of Kenya, together with many supporters from the locality. My nomination for the Presidency was contested by a man from Western Kenya, but I defeated him in a secret ballot, so for one year I have hard labour.

3rd May, 1959

Early last November I told you that a woman had complained that her child had had a spell cast upon it by a certain Karioki, who is a junior Kikuyu headman here. At that time Karioki was closely questioned, but nothing could be proved against him.

Now the whole question is reopened because our cook's twenty-year-old daughter, Waidja, has died. For months she had been pining, and several doctors had seen her, including our own. There were no symptoms and there was no diagnosis, but we are having a post-mortem done. Her father is convinced that she has died from a spell laid on her by Karioki. The District Officer is investigating the case.

I accompanied Tony on a flying visit to the mines in Northern Rhodesia:

15th May, 1959

Breakfast at 7.30 sharp, and at 8 am we set off with Sir Ellis Robins to look at Bancroft. Rosemary had brought a book, and when we got out to look at some particularly dull part, she occupied herself more profitably. However, she was amused to watch for a while a party at the shaft head waiting to go down below. The African miners, fine figures of men, in their yellow oilskins and brown steel helmets, each with a lamp fixed to the front, the Europeans, in white overalls and blue helmets, with firm chiselled faces, and the shift boss, with his red helmet, made a group that stood out against the grim, grey surroundings, like a snatch of a film.

We left Bancroft at 11 am and returned via Nchanga. Here, after a cup of tea in the General Manager's office, we drove out to see the open-cast pit. Rosemary was fascinated by the vast machinery, like prehistoric monsters, moving across the face of the land, lifting thousands of tons of earth in one day, and creating a vast hole whilst building a mountain where the earth is deposited. One single colossal digger from Germany, with its component parts, cost one and a half *million* pounds. There is a cabin in this machine which is worked by one single man on an eight-hour shift. The machine does the work of many hundreds of men, and in consequence it will soon pay for itself. Lunch at one o'clock, Ellis looking at his watch to see that we finished in time to leave for the show ground at 2 pm. . . . We had a quick look at the Kenya Exhibit which the Royal Agricultural Society of Kenya was preparing for the Copper Belt Agricultural and Industrial Show. Then we dropped Rosemary back for a rest, and went off to see Chibuluma Mine. In the evening there was a large dinner of about twenty-five people at the General Manager's house next door.

The Nanyuki Show later in the year – an as-it-happens account:

9th August, 1959

Wednesday, 8.30 am: the sides are on the new lorry, the ramp is on the back, and four horses, rugged and bandaged, are loaded side by side, facing forward, all squashed in tight. The Show Box is in with them, behind their hooves, and so are the various sacks containing oats, bran, maize, lucerne meal, salt, chaff, barley, molasses. The hay is stacked in front of the horses so that they will not knock their knees, and the *syces* hold them, sitting on the bales. The saddles, bridles, girths and other tack are on the front seat beside the driver, for it might rain and there is no top to the lorry.

The engine starts, the horses rear a little, and one sees the whites of their eyes; the lorry moves forward and their hooves scrape as they get a grip; the sides bulge as they lean against each other, going round the corners out of the yard. At last they are clear and, with our hearts in our mouths, we wave good-bye.

They are off to the Nanyuki Hunter Trials and Horse Show. The journey is over 100 miles and it will take four hours.

8.50 am: A local farm manager rings me up to say that the lorry is stationary four miles down the road, and that one of the mares is playing up. I rush off in the car to find the ramp down, all the kit off, and the temperamental Star Sight unloaded. She had managed to get Faith down in the truck and the *syces* had a very anxious time. The only damage is a slight abrasion on one of Star Sight's hocks, above the bandages. I repack the lorry and it sets off again, this time with three *good* horses. Star Sight walks back in disgrace to Rhodora.

9.30 am: David and I leave for Nanyuki in the Peugeot. We pass the lorry on the way and check that all is well.

10.30 am: Rosemary and a charming horsey friend, Mrs Leaver, leave with Ochieng and the luggage in the new Ford Sedan.

1.30 pm: We all join up at Nanyuki Sports Club. David and I have already seen the horses off and into their stables. We are very cramped for space – four stables for four horses and no room for the kit. We rig up a saddle room in little Miss Molesworth's stable; she is so good and does not seem to mind the continual coming and going to get food, saddles, cleaning kit. We lunch and I set off in the lorry to fetch Star Sight. David and Rosemary go up to the Mawingo Hotel and take possession of our rooms. This hotel was once a private house, built by a Frenchman. The rooms are quite lovely, facing Mount Kenya. We have a large bedroom, a little room off for David and a bathroom; it is absolutely first class, well run and deluxe.

Half way home I run into heavy rain and the road becomes a sea of mud. The lorry gets bogged down and I have to walk several miles with no coat to a farm to get help. The farmer gets out his tractor and I ride on the back of the lorry. He pulls me up the hill and we complete the rest of the journey in six hours.

I ring Rosemary and tell her I cannot get through the next day until the sun has been on the road for some time. She tells me that Jane Bamber, who is to ride one of our horses, has got flu.

Thursday, 1 pm: I arrive with Star Sight. She behaves well considering the road is so sticky that in places we proceed sideways like a crab, with our engine roaring and all our wheels spinning.

Rosemary has been at the farrier's all morning with May Queen and Faith. Sergeant Coffey of the Army Transport Company (pack mules, etc.) is the only European farrier in Kenya; but that is not all, for he is also a Master Farrier, and has been Champion of All England. So he is quite an important man, as you can imagine, and everyone clamours for his services. Rosemary, having made an appointment some time ago with Captain Bulmer, his CO, has been lucky to get so much time with him during the morning, and she also has a date to shoe Star Sight (who has been lame all the week with a torn frog and strained shoulder) during the afternoon.

Jane arrived for lunch, full of flu but determined to be at the show. She and David then go off exercising the horses.

3 pm: Rosemary and I go along to the forge, and wait half an hour for Sergeant Coffey to finish his siesta. When he arrives we tell him several times that Star Sight is a *young* mare and very 'fly' with her hind legs. He laughs it off and tells us of all his experience with many sorts of horses. For a quarter of an hour he handles her legs; she lashes out at first, then gets quieter. He makes her fore shoes at the anvil, and fits them. When it comes to driving in the nails, she pulls her foot away sharply and throws him to the ground. He rolls clear as she is coming round with her hind legs. We beg him to put a twitch on her, but he pays no attention to us. He tries again; she throws him again.

With determination, he takes up her foreleg for the third time; and with equal determination she throws him once more. To our consternation this time he gets up holding his arm and says,

'My arm is broken!'

His face is contorted with pain, and with his arm held by Rosemary, we get him sitting on the ground while I rush for help. Eventually the Orderly Officer arrives and, ignoring my protests, says sharply,

'Now come along Sergeant Coffey, get up and walk over to my jeep and we will drive round to the Medical Officer.'

We can almost hear the bones moving as, half fainting with pain, the brave Sergeant walks off.

When he has gone we put a twitch on Star Sight and one of

the three African Army farriers finishes the nailing of the shoes.

20th September, 1959

There are definite signs in this country of a revival of confidence. The Army is now coming out here in a big way and, as a first step, is spending £4 million on new barracks outside Nairobi. The Air Force is greatly expanding and four new squadrons are arriving. Shell have decided to build a refinery at Mombasa, Cow & Gate are building a factory at Eldoret, the world prices of primary products are showing a tendency to improve, and death duties have been abolished. The Emergency is likely soon to be ended (although I am not certain that all is quiet amongst the Kikuyu), the African Nationalists are fighting amongst themselves, the appointment of the new Governor, Sir Patrick Renison, is generally approved of, and we have hopes that the Conservatives will win the General Election in Britain. We are all crossing our fingers that this trend will continue, and encourage more capital to flow into the country.

20th October, 1959

Sir Evelyn Baring, the Governor, left us this week, after seven eventful years in office. We went down to the farewell celebration.

It was a perfect evening and the red dais on the lawn in front of Government House looked impressive. A very smart guard appeared, with the band of the King's African Rifles. We sat in chairs behind the dais; on one side of me was the Ambassador from Tunis. After a while Lady Mary emerged with her party, which included the Aga Khan, and took her seat. Finally, the Governor walked across the parade ground in full dress with his plumed hat, wearing his Orders, and preceded by his ADCs. Behind him came his General, his senior RAF officer and other senior members of the Forces. Having arrived on the dais, Sir Evelyn took the salute and then inspected the guard. More saluting, and the guard moved off. The band beat the Retreat and he descended from the dais into a motor car in which he drove slowly round the crowd. (Light relief was provided when the plumes fell off his hat.)

After this a large company swarmed into Government House to have a drink, and the Barings joined them after they had changed. Some of us left early because we had special passes for the railway station. In due course the Barings arrived there, and the inevitable presentation of a bouquet by the station-master's daughter, and more goodbyes, took place. At last they walked up onto the platform of their special coach, three cheers were given, the whistle sounded, and they were off.

There has been great interest in a paper tabled by the Government in which it is proposed to open up the White Highlands so that land can be owned by a person regardless of race. The emphasis is to be on better land utilisation rather than the colour of the skin. To my mind it is statesmanlike to take this step, inevitable in the end, before the pressure of African nationalism makes us yield under duress. It removes one of the principal points of discrimination between races. In practice the new proposals will have little effect for many years, because there are virtually no Africans who have the money and the know-how to farm on a European scale. The Asians have the money but are not usually interested in mixed farming; they may come into coffee, sisal and tea, and if they do it will probably put up the value of land. So, on the whole, I take a philosophical view of this revolutionary change in the basis of our land tenure.

16

There was for a time no proper government in Kenya, and the economy suffered as a result. A rare glimmer of positive action in the depths of the recession was the launch of the Daily Nation *with the Aga Khan's backing. Tony was asked to be on its Board of Directors. For our part, we knew we had to leave, and we were even willing to sell off the coffee land separately from the farm. Tony was closer than ever before to the seats of power, but rejected formal political involvement. He was deeply suspicious of Jomo Kenyatta at this time. A tendency to vilify this man, who later turned out to have statesmanlike qualities, is perhaps understandable in view of the Mau Mau atrocities which had taken place, and contemporary events in the former Belgian Congo, which dominated the news on our return from a spell in England.*

17th July, 1960

A lot of people are helping with the streams of Belgian refugees who are pouring into this country. The Nairobi schools have closed ten days early, so that accommodation can be found for them. They arrive without anything, desperate and dazed, and they say they will never go back, even if they are asked. A thousand Africans gathered at Nairobi station to meet the trains, shouting,

'Go back! We don't want you. The same will happen to the Europeans here when *Uhuru* (Independence) comes.'

They had to close Nakuru station because of the Africans waiting to greet the trains. There is growing evidence of communism at work in the Congo and in this country and, as we have said all along, if the Belgians scuttle out and the British

294

follow suit, will not Russia fill the void? That is the most serious implication of all the muddle-headed thinking of people in Europe. Kipsang and our close personal boys, such as the *syces* and the houseboys (with the exception of the Kikuyu cooks) will openly say how mad it is to talk of *Uhuru*. They seem to understand the position and, though naturally they wish for better living, they say they could not get that if we all leave the country. Amongst the Europeans we have met there is much more anxiety than when we left, and an even deeper distrust of the British Government. Quite apart from the political out-look, the economic prospect for the country is very poor.

24th July, 1960

On Monday the Solai Association met and elected a Com-mittee under the chairmanship of a retired airman, Sir Francis Fressanges, to prepare a plan for the district in the event of law and order breaking down as in the Congo. What people forget is that just after Independence the Congolese disarmed the European population, and it is not easy to make a good plan unless we can be sure that we will retain our arms.

Out of the blue last week the telephone rang, and we were asked to ring Pat Flatt, who is a partner in a large estate agents' in Nairobi. He has two buyers for the coffee on our farm, and we are prepared to make a sub-division, for the price is good and we could liquidate this company and send the money back to England – plus what we get from the sale of the grade herd, which we are planning to auction in the autumn. We would be left with two houses, the buildings, and the bulk of the arable land, which would greatly simplify our position here.

We have also planned to send back the best furniture, pictures, some china and silver and a little linen. We can do this without making the house too empty. It will take a bit of rearrangement, but it is quite easy. We shall start packing in November and it will be shipped to arrive in February, when we are back to sort it all out.

Do not imagine that the papers have been exaggerating the

stories from the Congo. Not at all. Kenya has now taken in some 2,500 refugees, and wonderful voluntary work has been done by many of our friends. Tales of rape, murder, of people being separated from their families and, of course, of the majority losing everything they possess, are the usual thing. The effect on the children is especially depressing. However, on the other side, you will be glad to hear that the refugees passing through Tanganyika have been well received by the Africans; and at our Coffee Conference, we voted £1,000 to the Mayor's Relief Fund, on the proposal and seconding of two Africans.

During the past week I have been somewhat tied up with coffee matters – a meeting of the Marketing Board, a Planters' Day, and the Coffee Conference – while Rosemary has been spending a lot of time with the horses, for there are numerous shows in the near future. I have been offered a number of jobs since I have been back, and I may take on a few, because I want to be right in on everything that is going on at this vital juncture in the history of Kenya. We feel that if only we can make these sales of the coffee land and the stock, and can get the furniture safely back, we shall be able to remit back to England as much as we ever brought out here (quite apart from what has already gone back) and then we can stay here with less anxiety, and move at a moment's notice if necessary.

7th August, 1960

On Monday evening a friend from far-back Young Conservative Union days came to see me. He is running a mail-order business for Africans. Out in the Reserves countless thousands have little chance of seeing the shops. Their wants are usually served by one wretched *duka* (shop) in the district, run by an Asian. However their income, though still pitifully low, is slowly increasing, and they have more purchasing power. This friend of mine, Donald Hamilton-Hill, has produced an illustrated catalogue and compiled a sort of African *Who's Who*, comprising some 15,000 names to whom he has circulated it. He sells anything from one-man tractors to brassières and life insurance! The response is steadily growing, and he may have the basis of a big business.

21st August, 1960

The Minister of Agriculture has appointed me Chairman of the Board of Governors of Egerton Agricultural College, the only Diploma Course college in Kenya. It was established many years ago, by the generosity of Lord Egerton, as a college for European students. Owing to the political difficulties which now face this country, insufficient pupils are coming forward (the full complement is eighty) and the highly qualified academic staff is restless. The last Chairman was Sir Ferdinand Cavendish-Bentinck, but his ten-year term ended at the end of July. He was opposed to opening the College to all races on account of the wishes of its original benefactor (who is now dead). The Kenya Government has spent some £200,000 on capital improvements and provides about £40,000 annually for the running of the place. It has decided that it can only continue on an inter-racial basis, and I agree. It is now my task to put this radical change in policy across to the Board and to the European community here.

Our efforts to sell Rhodora have not yet met with success. We are told by the agents that the interested parties have not turned us down, but their interest is dormant for at least two more weeks, because they are preoccupied with other investment activities.

Whatever you may think about the idealism of our keeping this farm, and however much the seriousness of what is happening out here is minimised in England, we ourselves have only one idea, and that is to sell if possible, and save at least something of the very large amount of capital which is sunk in the property. We have decided to devote the rest of this letter to a review of the political situation, so that you will see more clearly the great dangers which threaten us.

The British Government long ago, in our view, made up its mind that it cannot resist the march of African nationalism. Its

297

efforts are now directed to retaining some influence in the future African State. To this end, it cynically aims to divide the Africans amongst themselves, so that some of them may conclude that they cannot get along without European help. Similarly, it keeps the Europeans divided, lest they should cause trouble by uniting, and delaying or opposing the aspirations of the Africans. It selects quislings whom it boosts in every possible way in their support for an inter-racial approach, and it pours scorn on anyone who tries to stand up for European rights as a minority race – let alone anyone who has the temerity to suggest that Europeans know how to run the country and Africans, so far, do not.

The effect of this policy is to split the Europeans hopelessly, into three groups:

1) the stooges of the British Government, i.e. the New Kenya Group, led by Blundell;
2) the right wing party, i.e. the United Party, led by Briggs; and
3) a middle group, the Kenya Coalition, led by Cavendish-Bentinck.

Thus, whilst it pays lip service to the idea of partnership, the British Government in reality seeks to keep everyone at sixes and sevens, and in this way – by some curious feat of reasoning – it expects to be able to retain a finger in the pie after Independence.

I have a great deal of confidential information at my disposal, and I am convinced that this is a true picture of British policy in Kenya. Sir Evelyn Baring played a big part in building up the so-called 'political leadership' at present exercised by Europeans who are not elected, but who hold their positions in Government under a special formula introduced by the British Government to ensure that the leading political positions would be held by those complacent to British policy.

There are strong indications of an overwhelming accession of strength to the African Nationalist Party (KANU) led by Tom Mboya. Unless the other African party (KADU) can be built up (and plans are afoot for this), KANU will sweep the polls at the elections in February. If it does it will throw aside the Lancaster House agreements and demand immediate 'Responsible Government' (a majority in the Council of Ministers). Now this will be awkward for the British Government, because McLeod has stated that the Constitution agreed at Lancaster House must work smoothly before he will consider a further advance. (It is generally assumed – though McLeod has never said so – that it must be seen to work for at least three years after the elections.) However, plans are afoot to meet any possible demand for immediate self-government; McLeod may, therefore, be able to say, when the time comes, that the Europeans themselves agree to a further constitutional advance.

Of course the vast majority of Europeans would never agree. But I have already explained how their leaders are selected.

The outlook for any European owning land is very poor if KANU takes power. They have repeatedly said that they will not recognise land titles, and that Europeans have no right of any kind to own land in Kenya, because all land in Africa belongs to Africans and always has done. At the same time we expect that managing the farm will get more difficult. In order to reward their followers, KANU will probably force through very large wage increases, regardless of whether the country can afford it. Trades Unions will be more thoroughly organised, with an anti-European bias. There may be breakdowns in administration, because many European civil servants will want to leave, being fed up with the depression and unhappiness in the colony. Schools and hospitals may become inter-racial. The currency may be affected. There could be a ban on sending out capital.

However, the one thing we do not expect on a wide scale is a breakdown in law and order, owing to the presence of four British regiments in the colony.

The price of coffee is still falling (unconnected with events here), and the market is still in great danger.

28th August, 1960

From Nairobi I went on to Ndola and thence to Kitwe, spending three days in the Copper Belt. The mining companies are doing better and better, yet the shares are very low. This is because there is a general feeling that the British Government will hand the territory over to an irresponsible African government as soon as it can, and that even if the mines are not nationalised, there will be much interference with management.

In spite of this underlying uneasiness people are fairly calm, and there is industrial peace. Plans are constantly made for further African advance in the industry. A new law has just been passed which names many places or occasions where a colour bar would be illegal. People are anxiously awaiting the report of the Monckton Commission, and especially its recommendations about the future of the Federation.

On my way home I had to return via Salisbury, and found the same sense of insecurity. There is a feeling that Southern Rhodesia cannot stand on its own feet if the Federation breaks up; and if, as expected, the Monckton Commission recommends that Northern Rhodesia and Nyasaland be given the option to secede in five years, this will prolong the uncertainty. These territories cannot go on unless capital flows in again, and at the moment there is no possibility of getting capital from outside for anything.

To the north there was very little news from the Congo. The Copper Belt offered hospitality to 10,000 refugees but now they have all gone: the women and children to Belgium, and most of the men back to the mines in Katanga. After a ten-day interruption these mines are now working at 95% of normal output. Over in Kasai the industrial diamond mines were said to be up to 85% of normal output. The frontier post with Katanga is manned as usual, and very few people go across. The post and telephone to Elisabethville is working. There is little news about Lumumba's Congo, but it is known that he has two communists in his Cabinet and a communist mistress. He does not make a move without first getting his orders from the Russian 'Ambassador'.

To the south the Union is beginning to feel the impact of the boycott of South African goods and things are slowing down. Anglo-American has met with blank refusal and polite indifference in several capitals of Europe when trying to raise capital for what would formerly have constituted perfectly ordinary projects.

On Tuesday we went to lunch with Air Marshal Sir Francis and Lady Fressanges, and there we met Sir Robert Scott, the Commandant of the Imperial Defence College. He was a charming man, and whilst wishing to find out about conditions in this country, was not unwilling himself to answer questions. I asked him the usual one about the relationship between the Polaris missile and the base at Nairobi; and then about the importance of a settled hinterland to the base; and finally, about the importance of Northern Rhodesian copper to the British armaments industry. At the end he spoke roughly as follows:

'Most of your questions have an economic basis to them, but you must realise that the overriding factors in Britain tend to be moral, human and emotional. It is the voter who counts, and therefore political considerations will tend to outweigh all others.'

I replied,

'That is exactly what we all feared.'

On the subject of the Base, we think that the Prime Minister is sending Lord Louis Mountbatten out here at the end of the month, to report to him just how vital it is to British world strategy. If, after his visit, he reports that it is indispensable to Britain, there might be a new thinking about the role of white settlers in the hinterland, and that may mean a change of attitude towards the African politicians who have been saying that after Independence they will no longer tolerate a British base in their midst. Cyprus all over again! Perhaps all this is wishful thinking but when you come to think of it, now that the Suez Canal is lost, where else can Britain maintain her fire brigade in the event of a conflagration in the Far East?

The great event here in Kenya is a speech by the Governor, Sir Patrick Renison, last night. He stated that there would be no short cut to Independence, and that he was determined that the Lancaster House constitution should be made to work 'if Independence is to be linked with prosperity and not with misery'. His speech has been described to me, by a very old and brilliant settler, as the best speech by any Governor in the thirty-six years this man has spent in this country. What is really interesting about it is that, according to my information, it was made without prior clearance with the Colonial Secretary, and throughout it he never refers to McLeod, but he does refer to himself as the 'Queen's representative'.

It was a very firm declaration of policy and I hope you have all read it. We may have got a real Governor who can make up his own mind, and not just take his orders from the Colonial Office.

Reactions are very favourable so far, except from African nationalist politicians, who describe it as a threat to African advancement and an indication that the British intend to keep the Africans down by force!

17th September, 1960

Last Sunday Steve and Margaret Stephen brought a Mr Elwyn-Jones to see us. He is Recorder of Cardiff, and being a QC, was out here on a law case. He was also a supporter of the Labour Party and obviously thought we were rather reaction-ary in our views about Kenya's problems.

Another day we had up here a representative of the firm which packs and ships furniture, and we took him round the house, showing him the pieces we want to send back to England. Rosemary is now busy sorting out what she will put in the gaps.

Politically, the country has been fairly quiet since we last wrote, except that Tom Mboya has made one or two defiant speeches in reply to the Governor's statement, and all the workers in the tea industry are on strike. Yesterday, for the first time, we had an accredited collector of Union dues for the Agricultural Workers' Union on the farm.

The Kenya Coalition and the United Party held a joint meeting, at which I was present, and they decided to unite against the New Kenya Party for the coming election. The disadvantage of this marriage is that it makes the Coalition appear more racial than it is.

It has been suggested that I might stand in February for this constituency against Michael Blundell, but there is no future for the European in politics in this country now. In the next Parliament (Legco) there will be only ten European Elected Members out of a total of fifty-six, and although there will still be two or three elected Europeans in the Cabinet (Council of Ministers), it is not expected that this state of affairs will continue for more than a year or two. The next step forward in constitutional advance will probably be the elimination of elected Europeans, both from Legco and the Council of Ministers, and the Chief Secretary (an official) will be replaced by an African Chief Minister.

Another suggestion is that I should allow my name to go forward for election to the post of Vice-President of the Kenya National Farmers' Union. The present President wants to stand in the elections and his place will probably be taken by Lord Delamere, the present Vice-President.

The second of these suggestions attracts me most, but Rosemary and I are uncertain whether it is wise to become further involved in this country which will shortly have an African-dominated Government. It is very difficult to foresee what the future of the European settler is going to be.

3rd October, 1960

A Mr Gerald Sayers came to stay with us. He lives at Guildford, and is adviser on Colonial Affairs to the Conservative party, and a close friend of McLeod. We worked on him as hard as we could, but made no great impression. He left us feeling that while the communist intrusion in the Congo is making the British Government pause and think, yet the European settlers are expendable once they have served their purpose. However, he did write afterwards a particularly charming bread-and-butter letter and said he wanted us to know that he really understood our problems.

One evening we were invited to dine with General Sir Nigel Tapp, the GOC. Principal among the twelve guests were Lord Louis Mountbatten and Lady Brabourne. They were easy to get on with. He said he had got rid of his Guernsey herd at Broadlands in favour of Friesians. He seemed to bring the talk round to the Navy whenever he could. Rosemary was seated next to Sir Richard Turnbull, the Governor of Tanganyika, and she found him most entertaining. He pointed out that the sun would not suddenly turn round the other way, and neither would Britain hand this colony over to Independence overnight.

The following day there was a garden party at Government House for Lord Louis and Lady Brabourne. Monsieur Français, the new Consul General of France, was wearing a most splendid uniform. For that matter, so was Lord Louis – very good-looking in a beautiful white uniform with rows of medals. One lady wanted to tell him that she had danced with him in 1924, and another that she had served under his command in Burma . . . poor man!

The Royal Show had come round again:

It was not until the last day that we got our greatest thrill. This was the day for the children's ponies, and we did not expect to win, partly because of the two splints on Porcelain's forelegs (a legacy from the time she spent with the Leavers whilst we were in England). David did an excellent show and was pulled in first. Then came the great moment in the Championship class, before the President's box again.

Six ponies, first and second prize winners, all ridden by boys, came into the huge arena. David was riding really well and looked very smart in his brown Weatherall jacket, brown velvet cap, beige jodhpurs and brown jodhpur boots. The judges

304

lined them up and then made them each in turn leave the line, and go right down to the end of the arena to do a show. Not one pony appreciated this exercise except Porcelain. David walked her away from them and, having reached the place indicated, he did the usual figure of eight at trot and canter, changing leg successfully. Not content with that, he put Porcelain first into an extended trot and then into an extended canter along the edge beside the crowd, then pulled her up smoothly and quietly. Finally, he trotted back to the judges, stopped before them, reined back, and dropped the reins on her neck, whilst she stood stock still.

Someone behind said, 'That is Richmond standard' and I personally felt it was the best show I have ever seen, even by a grown-up rider in a Hack class. After a while the judges made him gallop out fast, and again he pulled up the pony gently and stood still. Eventually they pulled Porcelain out as Champion child's pony and by that win David won for Rhodora the Gold Cup for the most points in the show.

We left late that night for home. We had all Sunday to sort things out, whilst lorry loads of animals and equipment returned. David spent a quiet day – a game of canasta was fitted in, and a rest in the afternoon – then we left again for Nairobi airport after a late tea. We dined on the apron and said good-bye, sadly, to him at the entrance of the transit lounge. Then we went off to see the first issue of the *Daily Nation*, a copy of which I am sending to some of you. The new rotary press was most interesting and the 7,000 copies of the first edition were produced in ten minutes.

This is only a sketch of many crowded activities in our present life. Whilst writing this letter to you we have had a visit from the General Secretary and the Local Secretary of the Agricultural Workers' Union, both black but they sat down in the drawing-room and talked quite a lot of sense, and we agreed on many points. A useful meeting, I feel.

23rd October, 1960

For the benefit of those of you to whom we have not written for some time, we go back to October 7th, when we were in Nairobi for Lord and Lady Delamere's dance. It was held in the ballroom at Muthaiga Club, which was decorated with fifty dozen dark red roses, some on the tables and some hanging in Constance Spry festoons from the wall lights. The lighting was subdued and there were candles on the tables, and as there were only 200 guests, everyone was able to sit in parties around the dance floor. Champagne *ad lib*. contributed to the general sense of well-being. We dined beforehand with Sir Charles and Lady Markham and the Robin Longs. Rosemary and I felt it was the nicest party we have been to in Kenya. We left at three and motored back to Rhodora: into bed at five fifteen, which is quite late for us . . .

The Prime Minister's speech at the Conservative Party Conference illustrated the considerable change of view on colonial affairs which has taken place since the Congo disaster. He used such phrases as 'obligations of honour' and 'duties to those of our own blood'. Any reference to such trivial matters a few months ago would have been laughed to scorn in London.

Unfortunately, this welcome change may be too late, for much fundamental damage has been done. Business in Nairobi in the past month has taken a marked turn for the worse. The building industry is at a standstill, and so much money is leaving the country that the banks are pressed to retain liquidity. Lombank has ceased hire purchase business and the building societies are very rocky. The British Government, instead of frightening the European away, may have to take some positive action to persuade him to stay, or they will find themselves handing over a bankrupt country to our black brothers on Independence Day. The same sort of trend is apparent in Central Africa.

Last Thursday, after a Board meeting of East African Newspapers, we had lunch with Charles Hayes, in charge of the African newspaper side. He is a brilliant and (Rosemary says) very attractive if somewhat scruffy journalist. His other guest was Arwings Kodek, a prominent African nationalist with communist leanings. This latter character has a great sense of humour, a white wife and two coffee-coloured offspring. We all got on well over an excellent lunch at the Lobster Pot, and no political tensions appeared to mar the occasion.

Last night we were invited to the Fifth Kenyan African Rifle Regimental Ball at Nakuru. They had cleverly converted the Mess into Trafalgar Square Underground Station, with all the posters you would expect to see, newspaper placards and so on – the detail was perfect, and the background painted by a local artist. One really felt one was back home. It was a very pleasant party, as we were in the CO's group which included the new GOC, General Goodwin, and his wife. She used to show hacks and he also loves horses, so there was plenty to talk about.

27th December, 1960

Margaret Stephen came up here with Rosemary from Nairobi last Wednesday, and on Thursday we started getting ready for our party. She decorated the verandah too beautifully for words: lovely soft white nylon, with gold spots on it, on each window, and pelmets with bunches of gold and silver balls, like bunches of grapes, in the middle. She had painted false holly leaves gold and made them up into sprays. . . . We bought three white Chinese lantern shades for the main lights out there, and she put silvery stuff on them, so that they shivered in the breeze and looked most attractive. The whole effect was very airy-fairy with silver and gold. The finishing touch was the two Christmas trees from Harrods with their miniature coloured electric candles.

The drawing room Rosemary left more or less as it is, just taking away the carpets. There was a huge vase of false flowers and others of yellow arums and pink arums and those green-brown, waxy leaves we have here.

Down on the sunken lawn by the pond we put the dance floor, with coloured lights all round. The pond and the surrounding trees were lit with spotlights with plain and coloured screens. It looked most romantic; and we had a perfect balmy night with a clear velvet sky and a half moon.

The band from Nairobi was mediocre, I thought.

The buffet was round by my bedroom and was completely eaten – people piled their plates. By the pond there was a barbecue for the children presided over by Tudor Ace, and we had a Master of Ceremonies, called Hooky May, who roped in the very shyest of the kids. Having started at seven we closed the entertainment at eleven, because most of the parents were thinking of Christmas next day and did not want a lot of tired children on their hands. Some came long distances – even one family from Nairobi.

22nd January, 1961

Sir Ferdinand Cavendish-Bentinck, as you may have seen in the press, is contesting this constituency against Michael Blundell. Because I am Vice-President of the Kenya National Farmers' Union I cannot take any part in politics; but this does not mean we cannot have our friends to stay, so the Cavendish-Bentincks have made their Headquarters here during the election and we are right in the middle of the fun.

Voting in the primary election will take place tomorrow. It is in this election that only the European voters will vote (and only in the ten reserved European seats, of which this is one); so it is vital that C-B should get a good majority over Michael, so that we can say he truly represents the Europeans, while Michael does not. Ideally, we want C-B to get 76% of the votes or better, so that Michael does not go forward to the second election. (Every candidate who gets 25% or more of the votes in the primaries goes forward to the second election.) In the second election all the Africans in the constituency will vote as well as Europeans, and of course Michael is their preferred candidate. I do not really think we can keep him out, but at least if C-B gets a substantial majority over him in the primaries we will have proved our point: that the Europeans were virtually disenfranchised by the Lancaster House agreement. Is it not wonderful that the Europeans, who contribute 90% of the country's exports, will have no effective say in the country's government? A curious conception of democracy!

Tomorrow the packers arrive, and we are sending some of the furniture – including the Van Goyen picture – back to England.

We return to England on 14th February and will stay until the end of March. We have finally decided that the outlook in this country is so bad that we must rearrange our lives and build up something in England: so during our visit we will concentrate on how we can expand our farming there.

15th April, 1961

Kenya has undergone its worst drought for over sixty years, and its effects can be seen on the farm. The fields are bare, and in every group of trees some have died and stand out brown amongst the others. Our stocks of hay, silage and roots have been adequate, so that the cattle are well, though a little thin, but the coffee has suffered severely in parts; some coffee trees have turned brown and there has been considerable defoliation owing to high winds. We shall not get the large crop we expected. Of course our troubles are nothing compared with those of some other farmers.

Famine relief has been in full swing in parts of the Reserves. Some 100,000 bags of maize have been given to us by the Americans. The Masai have been losing 5,000 cattle a week, and game of all kinds has been dying by the hundreds and thousands.

However, on April 7th the rains broke and the whole country feels happier. We had heavy rain for five consecutive days, nearly four and a half inches, and the farm is already turning green. We are planting maize and oats from early morning until late at night.

The Governor of Kenya has still not been able to form a government, and the African leaders continue to make speeches which offer no comfort to the immigrant races either now or in the future. The result has been a marked deterioration in the morale of European farmers during our stay in England. Jomo Kenyatta's press conference has not helped. The impasse remains: the Africans refuse to enter the Government until he is released.

It is now said that 90% of the farmers would leave this country immediately if they could get something for their land, and I am starting a proposal for a referendum to find out whether this is true. It is said that if we go on much longer without a stable government there will be some kind of economic collapse, but I do not think so, for the prices which farmers are getting for their produce are mostly quite good. Of course the colony would collapse if they left in large numbers. The British government speaks of a multi-racial or non-racial state for Kenya in the future, but everything that it does is leading to a totally African constitution, and the Africans are showing only too plainly that they are not sufficiently well educated or sufficiently responsible-minded to run a modern civilised country.

17

The Mau Mau were active again in Kenya and it seemed increasingly likely that Southern Rhodesia would somehow secede from Whitehall's control. All over Central and East Africa, settlers felt as embittered and confused as we did. We were not quite sure whether to be mollified by conciliatory overtures from African leaders, or not. On balance, we decided not.

23rd April, 1961

Rosemary and David and a visiting girl-friend, Anita Fielding, have all gone for a drive in the pony trap with Prydus providing the horse-power, and I am taking advantage of a quiet moment to draft this letter. It is a typical Sunday morning at Rhodora. Rosemary and I got up rather late, whilst David and Anita (guarded by a *syce*) went for a long early-morning ride right into the crater. The sun is shining brightly and the birds are busy building their nests; the farm is green again.

Last night we had a small teenage dinner party with David, Edmund Hempstead (seventeen), Richard Chaundy (sixteen), Anita (fourteen) and Linda Ace (fourteen). The Hempstead parents came too, so we had a cosy corner of our own whilst roulette went on to the backgrounds of *'Baby-sitting Boogy'* and *'Walk Right Back'*.

Anita Fielding is the star-turn child rider out here. Aged fourteen, she looks twenty-one, stands five feet ten, and behaves alternately like a responsible grown-up and an irresponsible ten-year-old; you never can tell. On a horse or pony, anything goes for her, and she does not know the meaning of fear. She eggs David on to do things he never thought he was capable of doing. Very good for him in many ways – although there are times when we have to put our foot down firmly or things would get quite out of hand.

She has been staying in the room next to David's. One night last week Rosemary and I came back in the dark from our last walk with the dogs and saw that his light was on, so we peeped in from the verandah. Whom should we see but Anita, sitting on David's bed and talking to him. I walked in immediately and told David to get up and go to sleep in my dressing-room; he was far too old for this sort of thing, I said. And I meant it! Her parents would have been horrified.

The next morning Rosemary confronted Anita, who sat on the bed in her own room and stared at her fingernails. Apparently the conversation went as follows:

'What were you doing?'

No reply.

'Anita, what were you doing?'

Still no response, not so much as an upward glance. Anita simply hung her head.

'Look at me when I'm speaking to you, Anita.'

She looked up at last and Rosemary asked again:

'What *ever* did you think you were doing?'

'We were planning a midnight ride down to the crater,' muttered Anita.

I couldn't make up my mind which had been worse: my unfounded suspicion of high jinks in the nursery wing, or my fears for their safety in the crater in the middle of the night.

There has been quite a good flowering in the coffee this last week, better than our expectation. The maize planting has gone well and with our own planter and a borrowed one we have completed nearly 400 acres. A bit of coffee has also been planted right down in Stroat, marking the beginning of a policy which is going to revolutionise Rhodora. If we stay here long enough, coffee will stretch on all sides almost as far as the eye can see; the cowsheds will have become a huge factory capable of processing perhaps 400 tons in a season. In pursuance of this policy we are going to follow up the sale of grade milking stock

312

which we held last year with a sale of fifty in-calf heifers in June (after the Nakuru County Show).

We have had more rain, but not enough. In some districts, having survived the drought, the poor farmers now have an invasion of Army worm. This is a tiny worm which advances in millions, in a line, eating everything in its path.

The more moderate Africans (KADU) have now decided that they are willing to take part in the government, and the Governor is busy trying to find some ministers and make sure he has a majority in Legco. The news has reduced tension. We must see, now, what sort of government emerges.

It is an indication of the way the wind is blowing that I am going this week to the first meeting of a newly formed high-level committee to consider ways of restoring the value of European land. If something workable can be agreed it may help not only those who want to leave, but also those who have not quite enough confidence to stay.

By the way, the new name for Legco is 'Afrigas'. . . .

9th May, 1961

Almost as we were putting the stamps on our last letter to you, the Army worm arrived. Black caterpillars in their millions invaded every corner of the farm. They start as tiny wriggly objects, and in full enjoyment of our greensward, rapidly grow to about an inch. Every four days or so a new wave appears. We rushed to our sprayer (spraying is very effective), and first tried to protect the maize, but soon discovered that while this kills those caught in the act of eating, it does not prevent others from coming in afterwards from the verges. It is surprising how quickly they move. So we turned our attention to the grassland.

The battle has now been going on for a fortnight, and they are still with us. We think we have saved the maize, except for about twenty-five acres, but all the grazing has been eaten out and looks brown and bare. The cattle are in the yard day and night, feeding on such small stocks of silage and hay as we have left after a long dry season. The cost of the spray is heavy, and is

313

running into £30 or £40 a day, but we are luckier than many other farmers who have no reserves of keep and are forced to sell their animals. In some parts of the country a virus is now attacking the worms, and they are dying out. We hope it will reach us soon.

Rosemary has been active in the fight and can be seen at almost any time round the house and buildings, pointing out heavy caterpillar concentrations to her garden boys, who are armed with a stirrup pump. One of the best sights is to see her riding off with Arap Genich armed with a Flit gun.

On Saturday we attended a dinner in Nairobi given by the *Daily Nation* for the Sportsman of the Year. Both the Governor and the Aga Khan were there. Speeches were interminable and my neighbours (Lady Philippa Wallop and her mother – the former known to Barbara and Sue) got into a frightful dither because they had to catch a plane. In the end they rushed out between speeches, but I doubt whether they had time to change out of their evening gowns before take-off. Rosemary was terribly bored with the two people next to her, who were monosyllabic. On my other side I had an Asian who was champion ping-pong and badminton player of Tanganyika. The Sportsman chosen turned out to be a black distance runner who represented Kenya at the Olympic Games. Judging by the rain which drenched us as we came in, we had expected it to be awarded to a swimmer.

Next morning, Sunday, we had to visit some people who live an hour down the Mombasa road. We were somewhat reluctant to go because of the worry back here at Rhodora but in the event really enjoyed it. It is a huge property of 23,000 acres, owned by a very old settler called Sir Frank Wilson, and managed by his two sons. They have 1,000 Ayrshires, of which 750 were in milk, and the principal income derives from the sale of milk to Mombasa. The dairy is quite a big affair. The milk is pasteurised and some of it is tinned, and some is sealed in cellophane packs.

They also have an income from a flock of Karakul sheep. The lambs are not aborted but are killed immediately on birth, and the Persian lamb skins go to the Hudsons Bay Company in London.

In addition there is a herd of 500 beef cattle, but the farm has been decimated by Army worm and they are thinking of sending all of them to the meat factory. Many ranches in this district have no grass at all, and the owners face bankruptcy.

Lady Wilson has quite a mob of Arab horses, including two stallions. They were nice and Rosemary was most interested to see them; the foundation stock came from Lady Wentworth.

I have been to Salisbury for a few days, and went to tea alone with Sir Roy Welensky. He was in fighting mood. If the British Government force through a constitution in Northern Rhodesia which results in a break-up of the Federation, I am sure Southern Rhodesia will go it alone. The Rowlandsons, with whom I stayed, told me that one has to be quite careful what one says when going out, as so many people are now vehemently anti-British.

Here in Kenya, the murder of Mrs Osborne has aroused everyone to the growing threat of Mau Mau. He is recovering in hospital, and is left with five young children. He was a screener in the Emergency and a part-time member of the CID; he was also a member of C-B's delegation to London last August. It is obvious to us that it was a Mau Mau revenge murder.

And we now have Michael Blundell as our Minister of Agriculture!

We have been thinking a lot about David beginning his first term at Harrow. It must be a great adventure, and we hope to get a letter from him soon.

23rd May, 1961

The battle against the Army worm continues. Having sprayed the crops and verges, we then found we had to spray all the grassland, or they would have reduced it to dust and desert; then it was necessary to go round the crops each day and check for a break-in and divert the sprayer to it. Bit by bit, we got the better of them, and helped by a little rain, the maize started growing nicely again and a green tinge came over the brown fields. A few days ago ominous reports arrived from various parts of the country that there was a re-infestation.

Yesterday here at Rhodora we found them again! There are tiny little pin-point size caterpillars all over the maize, and certainly all over the farm. They will grow and grow, eat and eat, and slowly reach maturity. Once again the sprayer has swung into action and we have ordered another new one. This time, too, we are obtaining a small quantity of virus and will experiment to see whether it will infect this new attack.

The political and economic situation here has now become so serious that Hugh Fraser, Parliamentary Under-Secretary of State for the Colonies, has come out to see it for himself. In a nutshell, if the British Government persists in handing the country over to the Africans too quickly, it looks as though there will be both an economic and a physical Congo.

I am closely concerned with the discussions with Fraser and that is why this letter has been delayed; it has meant a lot of work.

Yesterday afternoon there was a meeting with him and Galsworthy (Economic Adviser to the Colonial Secretary) in Nakuru, at which all the local leaders from town and countryside were present. It really would have brought tears to your eyes if you had heard them: one after another they said that they wanted to stay but saw no future here and felt they might have to abandon it all to start a new life somewhere where there was some sort of stability. Fraser had come from a similar meeting at Molo and we (the KNFU) entertained him to lunch at the Rift Valley Club. I spoke a lot (much too much!) but we shall see if it had any effect.

One day last week a very sad thing happened at Rhodora: the vet came up and shot the old bull, Valentine of Fernhill Park. Ace recorded the entry on the daily sheet:

'Valentine of Fernhill Park Put to Rest.'

We brought him out here at the age of two, when we ourselves first came and he, more than any other single animal, contributed most to making the name of the Rhodora herd.

On Sunday night we had a scene in the kitchen. The cherub-faced kitchen boy Odhiambo, having come back late for work, was reported to us by Ahamed. After a little while he threatened to knife him for telling tales. Unfortunately for him he made the mistake of saying it in front of witnesses, so there followed a long session with the police whilst charges and counter-charges were made. We are now without Odhiambo.

3rd June, 1961

The Army worm is passing away from the land, though it has left a trail of devastation and many farmers are in a critical financial situation. There is now a new anxiety, because the main rains seem to have failed.

On Saturday last week I shot my first big game since I came to Africa. Amdurhaman, the baboon guard, was down in the crater when he heard a noise on the rocks and saw a leopard, always a menace to stock. He opened up with his Mannlicher .256 rifle at a range of 250 yards. The leopard retreated to the very top of one of the high cliffs. With his twelfth and last shot he hit it, and it rolled right down the cliff – about 200 feet – to the bottom and disappeared into the undergrowth.

We were therefore faced with an unpleasant situation: a wounded leopard on the farm. Armed with my 16 bore shotgun and SSG shot, which is all I seem to have here, I went with Amdurhaman to the spot, and we saw by the blood-marks where the animal had rolled down and where it had rested up. The trail took us right into the dense bush, in the corner of the old lucerne field where the crater stream disappears. We dared not go any further, so we left a man watching the place, and sought out a neighbouring farmer's guard who had a pack of four dogs and a 12 bore shotgun. We then crept into the undergrowth again.

The dogs soon showed their fear, and we realised that we were very close. Suddenly there was that paralysing sound that you hear when the big game are being fed at the zoo. The dogs danced around while the leopard reared up snarling, uncertain

317

where to spring. There was a crash of musketry, and a short silence. We advanced a few steps and again he reared, with that frightening snarl . . . but this was the last time. We struggled to keep the dogs off the skin.

Although the leopard was only three-quarters grown it took five of us to carry it to the car. The final scene will stay in my mind for a long time, for it was exactly like one of those pictures in *Jock of the Bushveldt*.

Reading through our air mail *Times* on Wednesday night we found that Kipsang had won his race at Newbury. For those of you who do not know who Kipsang is, he is Bar's first race-horse, and this was his first outing as a two-year-old. Great excitement when we found the news. Kipsang, after whom it was named, was also delighted when we told him next morning.

26th July, 1961

Rosemary arrived safely home, but we find that we still cannot take an optimistic view about the long-term prospects in Kenya. There may be some sort of a lull, a small recovery of confidence during the time that Independence is actually achieved, but we do not think it will last. We think that tribalism is still so strong that the country will gradually disintegrate and we may well end up with civil war. At the same time the standards of administration will decline, so that for this reason alone the country will be unattractive as a place in which to reside. As for the date of Independence, we expect it to be some time in 1962. The British Government has, in our opinion, lost control here, and the Africans have only to agree on a course of action (which they are finding it difficult to do) and their demands will be met. The safety of the immigrant races or the sanctity of treaties made with various tribes will be overlooked with facile abandon.

Accordingly, we have taken certain steps which will make it possible for us to come back to Hardwick Farm for a longer stay than usual next spring: on Saturday we sold off sixty-three

318

more Guernseys at a somewhat lower price than at our sale of 147 head last October; there are seventy-eight Guernseys still here, the cream of the herd, and we will decide later whether to keep them all or reduce the numbers still further.

Plans at the moment are that Varley Everett and Mumford will hold the fort here in our absence, and gradually the place will be turned over to a vast coffee farm; Tudor Ace and his family will come back to Hardwick.

8th August, 1961

You will not be surprised to hear that I have not been asked to sit on the Reception Committee for the return of Jomo Kenyatta. We are wondering how long it will be before he dances with a member of the Royal Family at a ball at Government House or is invited to stay at Buckingham Palace. How humiliating can appeasement be? Here is an extract from the Government White Paper on the Origin and Growth of Mau Mau (p. 170):

> *The positive killing oath which bound its adherents to kill all and sundry emerged about May, 1952. This signalised the final ostracism of the oath-takers from their tribal affinities, and can only have been instituted by Jomo Kenyatta, their known and accepted leader.*

Tony, David and I wrote separate accounts of the show held by the Show Jumping Association of Kenya. First, David (who was on his strawberry roan with Anita on a palamino):

21st August, 1961

Another exciting event was the fancy dress for juveniles, in which Porcelain appeared as Strawberries, with me riding, whilst Caramel appeared as the Cream, with a friend of mine

319

riding her. Daddy was on the touch line in front of the stands. He kept running up and down giving good advice but unfortunately someone had left a pole on the ground and every time he ran up and down he tripped over it, which was a source of amusement to the crowd. It took three *syces* and Jane to cajole Caramel to join up the Cream with the Strawberries, but in the end we managed to get Second prize. The winner was a sweet little Shetland pony with a golden horn on its head (Unicorn) and a tiny child dressed up as a lion on its back. Just as they were going to give the rosette to this pony the child quietly fell off without telling anybody, and had to be picked up and put back again by the judges.

In the Driving class the only one to survive was Prydus. He charged around with Jane, who looked very pretty in a grey dress with a large black hat and gloves. I sat beside her looking pompous in her bowler hat and a dark suit, and holding on for dear life. My job was to act as lackey, and jump out when the cart was stationary in the ring. The other carts in the class suffered a series of disasters: a governess cart was gradually broken up in front of the crowd under a hail of kicks from its pony, another one refused to move even when pushed by four men, and a third went backwards faster than it went forwards. A fourth pony behaved perfectly until the judge got in, when it too broke up its cart as rapidly as possible. I think the judge was very lucky to get away with his life.

Now my account:

Hampers, cases, tinned food for *syces*, food for us, tents, tent equipment, bridles, saddles, horse food . . . to my astonishment I found camp life very pleasant, in spite of the long trek across the whole camping area to the rather primitive Ladies accommodation which the Royal Agricultural Society of Kenya seemed to think adequate for fifty or sixty camp sites.

The comfort of having taken sisal rugs and chests of drawers for each tent, and the joy of having our house boys with us, the cook well organised by Tony, Ochieng with his iron and the pantry boy to be a skivvy to all, the cosiness of one's camp bed at night with two hot-water bottles – all these things offset the squalor of camping. I enjoyed hearing the barking of the baboons outside, the shrieking of the bush-babies in the trees, the whistle of a train at the nearby siding and the muffled, soft, whinnying noises from the stables behind the tents.

And now, Tony's mock-pathetic contribution:

I am just a maid of all work, useful on account of my tremendous weight for exercising difficult horses, useful as a pourer-out of drinks for the endless stream of visitors to our tent, and as Mess Officer in charge of rations at the cook house. Between whiles I can be found sitting on a bench round a ring, watching the horses misbehaving, with my mind firmly set on the implications of Jomo Kenyatta's release. Nobody takes much notice of me but Rosemary and David kindly say that I am quite indispensable. Anyway, it was a very pleasant show, and I enjoyed it as much as anyone.

Tony and I made a memorable trip to Murchison Falls, in Uganda, with the Everetts.

11th September, 1961

We found our motor launch, *ML Murchison* waiting alongside so we got our luggage on board, parked the cars and pushed off at 5 pm. There was a crew of six, including a Captain and a Chief Engineer. Downstairs, or below decks or whatever you call it, there were four double cabins, a shower, a w.c. with a very complicated hand pumping arrangement, and a small saloon – all a little airless. On deck, open-sided but roofed-in, was a large table and some nice chairs and we had our meals there. There was an open upper deck with a table, two raft benches and a perfect view all round.

We proceeded northwards down Lake Albert (a small sea). At the north end is the Albert Nile, which drains it. The Albert Nile becomes the White Nile, and is joined by the Blue Nile at Khartoum, and eventually runs into the Mediterranean.

It was dark by seven when we had dinner on deck. There was no moon and no shore lights. The only light was an occasional fire in the Congo mountains, and we imagined cannibals dancing around some cooking pot. . . .

The Captain had steered a compass course down the lake, but he told us he had no chart, and we were very intrigued to know how he discovered his position. He had a searchlight on the front of the ship, and this picked out innumerable cabbage-like plants, small gardens a few feet across and larger islands which floated on the surface. Suddenly, for no apparent reason, he turned the ship towards the eastern shore, found an unlighted buoy, and headed into a gap in the papyrus which turned out to be the mouth of the Victoria Nile, up which we steamed. It was an amazing piece of pilotage. Smell, instinct or what?

We drifted off to bed one by one, but it was difficult to sleep until we anchored and the engines stopped at about eleven.

The next morning we got under way at first light, about 6 am, and most of us were up soon after. The river is about as broad as the Thames, and is packed with humps and bumps which, on closer acquaintance, turn out to be hippopotami. They honk and snort or silently dive under water; one can see them on the bank, or partially submerged in the mud. . . . In fact one knows one's hippo pretty well, after a few miles up that river. Similarly with crocodiles. They lie on the bank, grinning and showing their huge teeth, enough to make one's blood turn cold. When one approaches, they will sometimes open their mouths wide and leave them open. When they want to move, it is surprising how quickly they get into the water. Altogether, they are quite revolting.

At 8.15 we secured to a jetty on the south bank just below the rapids. Leaving Rosemary and Joyce (the grandmothers!)

322

behind, we proceeded on foot, with a man with a gun in front, for some two miles to the top of the Falls. It took us nearly an hour, more or less along the river's edge, and quite close to some hippos at one point. There was a climb including 200 man-made steps. The Falls are stupendous. The whole river, a vast mass of water, narrows to pass through a gap of only eighteen feet between the rocks. It then tumbles 400 feet to the rapids below. In the good old days, when men were men, it is said that the youths of the local tribe had to prove their manhood by leaping the gap. Now, I am glad to say, the march of progress has made things easier and we could stand on a bridge over the gap itself and marvel at the ferocity of the turbulent water. Not only that, but to lighten the burden of the journey a thoughtful sailor from our ship had brought some Coca-Cola for us.

14th November, 1961

It is an extraordinary year: first the drought, then the Army worm, and now the drought has been broken by torrential rain. Never before have communications been so interrupted, and many areas of the country are flooded.

In the country of the Masai and the Kamba both the drought and the floods are at their worst. We have all been horrified by the photograph of an emaciated little Masai girl which was printed in the paper. There are now 400,000 people in need of famine relief, but the problem is to get the food to them in their isolated huts across the sodden plains. The Masai are said to have lost half their cattle.

We heard on the news last night that *The Sunday Times* had featured the disaster and this is no doubt because Roy Thomson has just been visiting Nairobi. The *Nation* newspaper, in which he has an interest, gave a luncheon for him. I sat next to him and discovered that he was Chancellor of the University of Newfoundland and gave the degree of Honorary Doctor of Law to Eddy a few weeks ago. He was surprisingly easy to talk to and I enjoyed meeting him. He now has an interest in papers in West Africa (Nigeria), East Africa, Ethiopia, and Somaliland and he is trying to penetrate into Central Africa.

The political situation continues to drift towards chaos. Ten per cent of the farmers have now left and many businesses have closed down. Africans on every hand are showing that they are incapable of running anything, let alone the country; nonetheless, the British Government is pressing on with its plans to grant Independence as soon as possible. The national economy, which two years ago was fairly buoyant, is now bankrupt, and it is estimated that the British taxpayer will have to find about £10 million by next June if this country is to be kept afloat. Maudling is coming out here shortly and I hope I shall see him.

We in the KNFU, of course, are still waiting for firm undertakings (given in public) from the African political leaders that they will respect land title and property rights after Independence. I am fairly certain that we shall get those assurances, and I only hope they will be worth something. Kenyatta is meeting Lord Delamere and me on November 22nd, and we meet Ngala on November 24th. (Needless to say these two will not come into the same room together so we have to see them separately.)

Obviously there is no point in spending any money here until we see which way things will go; nonetheless Rosemary has found it imperative to redecorate the sitting room. When I remonstrate, she says it is all because Leo is coming out in December, and then adds that morale must be kept up – to which I can find no adequate answer. Her latest plan is to repaint the office.

However, she is seriously preparing herself for our return by taking cooking lessons twice a week. When she gets back from her class she tries out the recipe on me. The rest of the time our old cook, Chege, carries on quietly. As I was writing this he sent me in his requirements for the next few days, which the lorry will fetch from Nakuru when it takes the cream down. *Mafuta taa* means lamp oil, which we use in our fridge.

Caster sugar
Vim
Mafuta taa
3 brown breads
1 whit bread
1 pockt fish
2 lbs peas
1 dozen eggs.
Sir here is 2 chiken only what? fillet of beef.

3rd December, 1961

The visit of the Secretary of State for the Colonies coincided with the conference. I went twice to Government House to see him on behalf of the farming industry. When I was introduced to him, he said at once 'Have you got a son at Harrow?' and when the interview was over we had a short chat about Elmfield and its Housemaster. Evidently David had been talking over his Kenya problems with Maudling's son, who, I gather, is a senior boy in the same house.

Maudling only came to hear about our difficulties, but he was a good listener. We felt he cared about Kenya, whereas McLeod gave the impression that he wanted to hand the country over to African government as quickly as possible, regardless of the consequences.

Two other interesting meetings we had last week were with Jomo Kenyatta, the leader of KANU, and Ronald Ngala, who leads KADU. They came separately, to address the Executive of the Farmers' Union, and they stayed to answer a lot of questions. We received assurances from both on land title and the rights of private property, and we also spoke of such matters as the future structure of the agricultural industry, citizenship, education and many other points. Jomo gave the impression of ability, but seemed lacking in sincerity; Ngala did not seem to be so able, but did seem more sincere.

Our farm school is making progress. There are now 120 pupils, who are taught by two unqualified teachers. There are two classrooms, and we are adding a third, and the number of pupils will go up to 180 next term, with the addition of one more teacher. Recently, our school won the singing event at the regional rally in Nakuru, competing against twenty others, some of which were Intermediate schools – ours is Primary. Last Sunday was Parents Day, which I did not attend, but I heard it was well organised by the teachers, assisted by the school committee. And on Thursday there was a mass (we sent down a trestle table and a tarpaulin for the altar), said by the Holy Fathers who superintend the education and appoint the teachers. On Friday I went down to give away the prizes at the end of term, and I first had to hear the songs which won the prize for them at the regional rally. These were in English and two or three native languages, without the assistance of any music, and they were really very well done. The best boy got a torch for his prize, and the best girl a small handbag. Other form prizes ranged from a biro pen to a couple of pencils and a rubber. All the children were delighted, and so am I, for the effect of the school – which is excellently run – is to occupy the children, and to instil in them discipline and manners.

27th December, 1961

It is really too long ago, now, to tell you in detail of our trip to Rhodesia and South Africa with Leo. Suffice to mention the fabulous house of the Oppenheimers with its many French Impressionist pictures and the Epstein bronze. Descending in terraces below it is the most enchanting garden, which when lit up at night looked like the backdrop for *Swan Lake*. To say that we were comfortable there is a vast understatement, and we enjoyed every moment, right up to the last, when we left the racecourse to go to the airport to the ringing cheers of the crowd as the Oppenheimers' horse won the big race of the day at 10–1 – and we had £50 each in our pockets.

27th February, 1962

On one of the evenings when we were in Nairobi we went to see the film *Spartacus*. This is a four-hour epic mainly devoted to scenes of gladiators fighting to the death, or great armies locked in bloody combat. We had given a ticket to our driver, Kiberengi, but I was a little nervous, for I knew he had never heard of the Romans and would not understand much of what it was all about. When we were driving back to the Club, Rosemary was saying that she thought it was a horrible film – and we discovered that Kiberengi was completely shattered. He had never seen anything like it in his life and all he could say was,

'That is exactly what it is going to be like in Kenya after Independence.'

We stayed up late listening to the wonderful radio broadcast on the Voice of America, when Colonel Glenn was orbiting the earth. It was very thrilling. Rosemary, of course, kept saying,

'What could poor Mrs Glenn be feeling?'

– and I kept assuring her that Mrs Glenn was really rather unimportant compared with her husband, just at that time. When it was over, and we were talking about the great achievement, she said,

'Now don't you start going up in one of those things – I won't allow it!'

We send our fond love to all of you.

Rosemary and Tony

FINALE

We left Kenya for good at the end of 1962. We were desperately sad to leave the country, our dear friends, our way of life and the African staff we had come to like and respect.

In 1963 Kenya achieved *Uhuru*. Tony and I returned on several occasions.

In 1973 I had been invited to judge Guernseys at the Royal Show. We paid many social calls, of course. Some of the people we knew who had stayed were suffering from the difficulties of the transition, yet managed to keep their land and homes in excellent order. There was no dramatic external appearance of change.

On Judging Day at the show, Jomo Kenyatta asked if there could be a mini-parade for him, and all the judges from England were asked to comment on why they had put up the Best Male and Best Female of their breed. When it came to my turn, I was standing behind him, leaning over and explaining to him the points of the Guernseys I had selected. I was conscious of the two very large bodyguards with guns bulging inside their uniforms who stood alongside him.

Our last visit to Kenya together was in 1983. Here are some notes I made at the time:

> *We landed on time. Nairobi Airport seemed a strange place, much built on and enlarged. We were met by a Mr Dean, a well-spoken nice-looking African from Abercrombie and Kent. He whisked us through everything. . . . I asked him how long it had taken to make the airport as it is now.*
>
> *'About three years,' he said, and then added proudly 'and it is called Jomo Kenyatta Airport.'*

The mini-bus sent for us was loaded up and off we bumped to the Muthaiga Club. It was an overcast morning with a breeze, quite unexpectedly cool for January. Muthaiga seemed different, less pretty in this dull light, and we were shocked at the deterioration of the place: paintwork which needed seeing to, parts of the ceiling plaster crumbling – but the flower arrangements were lovely and, as time went on, one got over the first impression and it all became more familiar. Our room, no. 12, an end one on the ground floor West Wing, was very full of memories: in fact I am pretty certain it was in that same room that we made the decision to turn down an offer of £115,000 for Rhodora.

We visited Michael and Gerry Blundell in their home near Muthaiga, where everything was perfect. Gerry had not been well, although she was still beautiful, and Michael was as exuberant as ever amid the profusion of flowers, shrubs and trees which were his passion. We undertook a couple of delightful tours and in between whiles, met a lot of old friends; the younger European community, at least, seemed to be thriving. Facilities for tourists were, on the whole, good. Some roads were poorly maintained, however, and behind the scenes farmers found life difficult without imported fertilisers, implements and sprays.

Nakuru in our time had presented a fresh, white-painted aspect; now it was a shanty-town.

At last we drove up to Rhodora: a visit of no little poignancy.

The house, standing in what used to be a tidy, cared-for garden, was almost in a field – tattered curtains draped across the windows. The large main verandah had been shut in with stone walls. The house was no longer black and white; its walls were dun-coloured and the tin roof was painted red. . . . Mbuni *drying in the yard, families living in the bull pens and calving boxes; and in the office, doors swinging loose, the iron-work pulled apart, families were squatting everywhere.*

The manager, a Mr Williams, was not around.

Ahamed was found and came to the cowshed neatly dressed,

older of course, but a sad person. Times were hard, he said, introducing his English-speaking son; he wanted us to find work for the son. We gave him some money but. . . . the whole thing needs sorting out.

We returned to Rhodora at the end of the month to try and 'sort something out' for Ahamed, who had served us with such loyalty for so many years.

Mr Williams, the manager, and his Kipsigis wife gave us tea and coffee in the house. It was an eerie feeling, sitting in the familiar sitting room. The verandah has been incorporated into the room with French windows into the so-called garden. The wooden floor gleamed with polish, but the curtains hung in tatters at the windows.

Mr Williams took us into his bedroom – my lovely big roomy dressing-table was still there, and also our bed. The bedroom is now very dark, because the verandah has been blocked in.

I looked at the alcoves in the dining room and thought of the Dresden swans and other ornaments we used to have there.

The Ahamed problem seems to be insoluble. He had had a very bad cough, which led him to be made redundant, and now he lives on one acre and a house down by the coffee factory. His son works in the office but is said to be useless. We talked to them both in the office but got nowhere. Really all very unsatisfactory.

In the office one wall was covered with the rosettes we had won all those years ago, now brown with dust. On a post was tacked a list, in my own handwriting. It was a reminder of the shoe sizes and worming doses of Star Sight, Prydus, May Queen and Cellarette.

Seeing the desolation and disintegration of all we had achieved on our farm and others, and the difficulties now experienced by the Africans on the land, I wonder if those constructive years we spent there could have continued, and the partnership one always hoped for could have come to pass to the benefit of this beautiful and charismatic country, Kenya.

330